LOVE
THE DRIVING FORCE

MARY WARD'S SPIRITUALITY:
ITS SIGNIFICANCE FOR MORAL THEOLOGY

JEANNE COVER, IBVM

MARQUETTE
UNIVERSITY

PRESS

MARQUETTE STUDIES IN THEOLOGY
No. 9

ANDREW TALLON, SERIES EDITOR

Library of Congress Cataloging-in-Publication Data

Cover, Jeanne.
    Love—the driving force : Mary Ward's spirituality : its
significance for moral theology / Jeanne Cover.
        p. cm. — (Marquette studies in theology ; no. 9)
    Includes bibliographical references.
    ISBN 0-87462-637-4
    1. Ward, Mary, 1586-1646. 2. Christian ethics—History—16th
century. 3. Christian ethics—History—17th century. 4. Institute
of the Blessed Virgin Mary. I. Title. II. Series: Marquette studies
in theology ; # 9.
    BX4705.W29C68 1997
    282' .092—dc21   96-51198

Printed in the United States of America

MARQUETTE UNIVERSITY PRESS
MILWAUKEE

The Association of Jesuit University Presses

Mary Ward (1585-1645)
Foundress of the Institute of the Blessed Viegin Mary
(Original in the Institute of Mary Ward Sisters ([Augsburg])

Table of Contents

Abbreviations

AB: Autobiographical Fragments covering the period of Mary Ward's life up to 1595 written from 1617; and fragments from a fuller autobiography covering the years, 1600-1609, written between 1624 and 1626.

CRC: Catholic Recusant Catalogue—facsimiles of recusant works made under the direction of D. M. Rogers, and published in the series: *English Recusant Literature* 1558-1640 by The Scolar Press, London, England.

CRS: Publications of the Catholic Record Society.

MonPaed: Monumenta Paedagogica Societatis Jesu. Containing the Ratio Studiorum of 1586-1599 and correspondence relevant to these plans of studies. Published in the series *Monumentum Historica Societatis Jesu.*

Introduction

In 1951, at the First World Congress of the Lay Apostolate, Pope Pius XII extolled Mary Ward, Foundress of the Institute of the Blessed Virgin Mary, as "that incomparable woman given by Catholic England to the Church in the darkest and most blood-stained of periods."[1] Three hundred-twenty years earlier, this same woman had been imprisoned as a "heretic, schismatic, and rebel to holy Church." Although this charge was later rescinded by the then reigning Pope, Urban VIII, it was not until 1909 that her members were permitted to acknowledge her as their Foundress. While appraisals of Mary Ward both by her contemporaries and by subsequent historical commentators have varied, they leave no doubt as to the original contribution she made and continues to make to the Church.

This study examines this original contribution in an area that to date has not been the subject of systematic research, namely, the theology and anthropology underlying Mary Ward's spirituality and its significance for today, specifically for moral theology. This study presupposes that any divorce of moral theology from spirituality results in their mutual impoverishment. Moral theology not only bears the marks of its contemporary situation but must also critically judge this situation. At the same time, developments do not emerge in a vacuum but are influenced by and reflect this tradition. Mary Ward's lifetime (1585-1645) coincides with a significant period in this tradition. The decrees of the Council of Trent, which concluded in 1564, barely two decades prior to her birth, decisively affected how moral theology emerged as an independent discipline and was systematically separated from other branches of theology. Divorced from dogmatic and spiritual theology and having as its central aim the training of confessors, it became virtually identified with the resolution of cases of conscience.

Four centuries later, the second Vatican Council called for the renewal of church and society and demanded that special attention be given to moral theology. The Council delineated the task of moral theology as the communication of the nobility of the Christian vocation and directed that its scientific exposition be more thoroughly nourished by Scriptural teaching.[2] Reiterating the Council's concern, John Paul II, in his encyclical letter, *Veritatis Splendor*, emphasized the enrichment brought to moral theology through a closer relationship with Christian ascetical and mystical theology.[3]

Mary Ward was not only aware of the dichotomy which existed in her era between moral theology and spirituality but experienced its effects in the ill-considered spiritual guidance which a professor of moral theology gave her. Her understanding of how spirituality enriches both personal moral formation and the principles for determining morally significant actions was reflected in her concept of morality and her approach to moral guidance. Her insights enrich both moral and spiritual theology and provide a means of bringing them into harmonious conversation.

Mary Ward's spirituality and theological insights are important for a number of reasons. First, following Vatican II's call for renewal, moral theology today is not only experiencing the tensions which accompany significant changes in content and methodology but is seeking a closer interaction with spiritual theology. Second, despite increasing recognition that Mary Ward's creative vision of the role of women in the service of church and society was significant for counter-Reformation spirituality, there is a parvity of research into the anthropology and theology underlying her spirituality. Third, while there is greater recognition that the recusant women in England and foundresses of religious congregations in Europe during the period of the counter-Reformation played significant roles, scholarly studies in this area have been relatively few. This work hopes to redress these inadequacies.

Mary Ward

Mary Ward's life (1585-1645) spans a period of religious, political and economic conflict and its consequent social upheaval. Her life coincides with the final years of the Protestant Reformation and post-Tridentine period of the counter-Reformation. The much interrupted Council of Trent ended in 1564. Cardinal William Allen's founding of Douay College in 1568 for educating English priests and the work of the English Jesuits brought about a new mental climate for English Catholics. Entwined with a genuine love for the faith and a desire to protect and purify it were confusion and political manoeuvering, such as the rivalry between many of the secular clergy and the Jesuits. This had serious repercussions on Mary Ward's plans for her Institute.

On the one hand, the Catholic Church's desire for genuine renewal and the spirituality and concern for reform of such princely rulers as Maximilian of Bavaria and the Archduke Albert and his wife

Isabella of Brussels, whom Mary Ward numbered among her bene-
factors, strengthened the Catholic cause. On the other hand, the
political, economic and imperialistic motivation of the monarchs of
Spain, France and England produced conflicts of interest. Spain, which
promoted the Catholic cause and facilitated the establishment of seminaries and colleges for the English clergy roused the hostility of the
mercantile societies because it supported princely states. During the
1620s, a decade when Mary Ward was formulating her plans for her
Institute and of necessity was seeking the support of friendly princes
and bishops, hostility to the Renaissance courts and their whole culture and morality flourished. The Thirty Years War (1618-1648),
which brought political and social disruption to Europe, coincided
with the last twenty-seven years of her life.

At the same time, the sixteenth and seventeenth centuries marked
a watershed in the development of human knowledge and consciousness; great achievements took place in art, literature, political theory,
economics, and natural philosophy. Machiavelli had died only sixty
years prior to Mary Ward's birth, while Galileo faced his second trial
in 1633, two years after the suppression of her Institute. Conscious
of the changing political, social and economic climate, Mary Ward
aimed to establish a religious Congregation of women, unenclosed and
governed by women, which would meet the needs of church and society.

The history of her struggle to accomplish this task can be divided
into three periods. The first, 1600-1615, is characterized by her attentiveness to the insights she received from God about the nature of
her vocation. The second, 1615-1631, contains the story of her attempts to gain approval for her Institute, and of the opposition which
culminated in its suppression and her imprisonment by the Inquisition. The third period, 1631-1645 sees her personal vindication by
the Pope, and her continued fidelity both to her vocation and to the
church which rejected her work.

Mary Ward was born in 1585 at Mulwith near Ripon in Yorkshire, England. Of a strong Catholic recusant family, she numbered
among her relatives and acquaintances many who suffered prison or
death for their faith. She also came into close contact with many of
the courageous English clergy whose missionary activities had to be
conducted in secrecy and in fear of imprisonment or death. At the
age of fifteen she became aware that she was called to enter Religious
Life. In order to follow this vocation, she had to leave England where

religious houses were forbidden. In 1605, at the age of twenty, she set out for St. Omer in the Spanish Netherlands, where many of the English who had left their homeland for religious reasons had found a safe haven. Here also were Religious Orders for women following the Benedictine, Augustinian, and Franciscan Rules.

Upon her arrival Mary Ward went to the Seminary of the English Jesuits in St. Omer to present her letters of introduction to the rector, Father William Flack. Her first meeting, however, was with Father George Keynes, Professor of Moral Theology at the seminary, who assured her, contrary to her inclinations, that it was God's will for her to enter the Poor Clares, who urgently needed an out-sister at this time. Two months later, August 1606, he just as assuredly informed her that the role of a lay-sister was not God's plan for her. Some months later the Franciscan General Visitor affirmed this.

Between March 1607, when she left the Flemish Poor Clares, and 1615 Mary Ward received the key experiences which held definitive significance for her understanding of God's will and for the foundation of her Institute. The first of these experiences occurred in 1607 on March 12, the Feast of St. Gregory, Patron of England, and, significantly, while she was praying for the people of her own homeland. Realizing the difficulties experienced by English women because they lacked English Religious Orders, she was filled with a great desire to found a convent for the English Poor Clares.

In November 1608 this desire came to fruition and she was admitted as a novice into her new foundation at Gravelines. In the same month, at her instigation, she and the other members of this convent made the Spiritual Exercises of St. Ignatius with Father Roger Lee, who became her confessor. On May 3, 1609, however, she became certain that she was not to remain in this foundation. In September 1609, therefore, she returned to England where she spent her time in catechetical works, particularly among the poor, strengthening those suffering for their faith and visiting prisons.

While engaged in this apostolate towards the end of 1609 Mary Ward came to understand that monastic life was not her vocation, but that she was called to "some other thing" which, for her, was incomparably more to God's greater glory.[4] In 1610 joined by her first companions, she returned to St. Omer and opened a school for the daughters of English refugees and local children. In 1611 she received final clarification of the "mode of life" to which she was called and understood that God was directing her to model her Institute on the Society of Jesus, both as to "matter and manner."[5] How this directive was to be carried out was revealed to her in October 1615. In what she termed "the estate of justice," the well-ordered personal disposition, characterized by freedom, justice and sincerity/ verity, she found both the essence of and the means towards the following of Christ in a new form of religious life for women where contemplation and apostolic activity are in harmony.

In a letter of 1621 to the Papal Nuntio, Antonio Albergati, at Cologne, Mary Ward described the inner conflict over her vocation which she had experienced in the years 1607-1611. This conflict was between the value of the contemplative life which existing religious orders provided and doing good to others, which she valued above all and which, given current views of religious life for women, she had not thought possible.

Mary Ward's sufferings were not confined to her early search for the knowledge of God's will. From 1611 she faced resistance to the new kind of religious life for women which she envisaged. This opposition came initially from the Society of Jesus, although many individual Jesuits strongly endorsed her work. In addition, because of the similarity of her aims to those of the Jesuits, she was faced with attacks from their opponents among the English clergy who resented the Society's influence through its seminaries, colleges, and missions.

In 1615 Mary Ward presented the "Ratio Instituti," a plan for the Institute, to Pope Paul V for approval. Receiving a favorable but not definitive response, she opened houses in Liège (1616, 1618), Cologne and Trier (1620/1621). Her companions also worked in London (from 1618) and in Suffolk (from 1621). With the death of Paul V in 1621, she presented to the new Pope, Gregory XV, a revised plan based more exactly on the "Formula Instituti" of the Society of Jesus which had already received Papal approbation. The primary apostolic purpose of her Institute was a "striving for the defence and propagation of the faith and the progress of souls in Christian life and doctrine," first with reference to England but now also having a world wide reference.[6] Mary Ward envisaged the means to this end as the establishment of a different type of women's religious order, unenclosed and engaged in education and other works "congruous to the times." Moreover, in England, where religious houses were banned, enclosure would have been impossible.

While the Congregation of Bishops and Regulars was dealing with Mary Ward's petition for approval, she was permitted to open a day school in Rome in 1622, and two years later in Naples and Perugia. During this period, however, opposition to the Institute increased. In the eyes of the Papal advisors lack of enclosure was the greatest obstacle to receiving official approval. In addition, members of the English clergy, who by this time had their own agent in Rome, also bitterly opposed approval of the Institute. In their criticism they cited the "boldness" of women who seek to instruct others in the catechism and "bring them to acts of contrition and meditation," whose lives resemble "those of the laity," and who cause scandal by their lack of enclosure.[7] In 1622 Mutius Vitelleschi, General Superior of the Society of Jesus, while publicly affirming Mary Ward's and her companions' goodness of life, prohibited the Jesuits from giving her any special assistance.

In 1624, with the election of Urban VIII as Pope (1623) after Gregory XV's death, Mary Ward again sought papal approval. In 1625, as a result of the Cardinals' and Bishops' Regular deliberations, Urban VIII ordered the suppression of Mary Ward's foundation in Italy, although she and her companions were permitted to continue living in Rome and Naples. At the same time the Institute's educational work continued to be valued. Two years later (1627), with recommendations from Vitelleschi and the personal help of individual Jesuits, Mary Ward was favorably received in Munich and opened a house there followed by schools in Vienna and Pressburg.

In March 1628, the Congregation of Propaganda set up a special body to examine the question of the English sisters. Its secretary was Francesco Ingoli, a strong opponent of Mary Ward's aims. A month later, this body declared that absence of enclosure was contrary to Canon Law and that the "Jesuitesses" should be suppressed. Mary Ward again went to Rome and was granted an audience with Urban VIII (May 1629). She agreed to give up her cause if the Pope and Cardinals so ordered, but, in conscience, could not alter it. Not having received a definite answer from the Pope, in April 1630 she wrote to the members of the northern houses urging them to remain loyal to the Institute. Extracts were taken from this letter by her opponents and used to her disadvantage.

In November 1630 Mary Ward sent a Memorial to Urban VIII attesting both to her conviction that her vocation had been "ordained and commended" by God and her willingness to desist if the Pope gave her the least intimation of his wishes.[8] This memorial was not answered and the Bull, *Pastoralis Romani Pontificis*, suppressing the Institute, was signed on January 13, 1631. In February 1631 Mary Ward was imprisoned for two months in the Poor Clare Convent in Anger, Munich.

In its condemnation of the Institute the Bull of Suppression was governed by established canonical decrees and by traditional concepts regarding women's capabilities. Describing unenclosed religious communities as "pernicious growths" which had to be eradicated from the Church, it went on to criticize Mary Ward and her members for undertaking tasks that were not suitable for their sex, or to their weak intellect, their womanly modesty, or most of all to their moral life as virgins.[9] The Bull declared their vows dissolved and forbad them to recruit new members. They were given the alternatives of joining existing Orders, living together under vows to local bishops, or marrying. The Bull was published in Rome in May 1631, and two months later in Bavaria, Vienna and Belgium.

Following the suppression of the Institute there was no legal security for its members, now greatly reduced in number. They were allowed to live in Rome by personal permission of the Pope, a concession that did not mitigate the Bull of 1631. Two years later the Holy Office issued a vindication of Mary Ward stating that "the English Ladies who have lived under the Institute of Donna Maria della Guardia, are not found nor ever have been found guilty of any failure which regards the holy and orthodox Catholic Faith."[10] It appealed to the Nuntio in Cologne to give them material assistance in view of the unjust occupation of their properties by others.

During the last fourteen years of her life Mary Ward, whose educational works had not been included in the Bull, remained true to her vocation and faithfully obedient to the Church. Between 1632 and 1634 she lived in Rome under Urban VIII's protection. In 1639, having gained his permission to go to England, she and her companions worked in London until the political and religious repercussions of the English Civil War in 1642 forced them to move to Yorkshire. It was here that Mary Ward died in 1645. As at that time Catholics were forbidden to have their own cemeteries, her burial took place in the Anglican cemetery at Osbaldwick, where today her name is held in honor.

Although Mary Ward was acquitted of charges of heresy and schism by Urban VIII, the Bull of Suppression destroyed what was known as the "first" Institute. Nevertheless, under the protection of local bishops her early companions and later members maintained the essentials of the Institute and refused to compromise with respect to enclosure. In 1703, Pope Clement XI approved the Institute's Rules and in 1749 the office of General Superior received approbation from Benedict XIV who, however, made it clear that he was not rescinding the Bull of 1631. In 1877 Pius IX granted final approbation to the Institute and by the twentieth century foundations had been established on every continent.

Mary Ward's innovative vision of service to the Church which could be made by an apostolic congregation of religious women reflects her awareness of the importance of the intellectual ministry of the church. As Ignatius of Loyola had recognized a century earlier, the Church was in danger of losing its cultural initiative in intellectual as well as in political, social and economic affairs. Mary Ward valued the acquisition of knowledge and sought a sound theological basis for her spirituality. She tried to provide the intellectual and moral formation which would enable women to contribute to the church and the society of their time in either the "secular" state or in religious life. In a period characterized by religious strife and social inequality she sought to aid the renewal of the clergy's lives, to reconcile those estranged from the church and to meet the needs of the oppressed, particularly of women and of the poor.

The type of religious congregation she envisaged raised significant questions for the moral theologians and canonists of her time, questions which largely remain unanswered today. They concern the matter of God's unique commands to individuals, the Church's relationship with those who receive such commands, and the recognition that God's individual invitations may anticipate what is currently positively approved and laid down by the official church authority. The later approval of the Institute and its enriched development during subsequent centuries indicate that ecclesiastical laws can be adapted, and point to the need for the recognition of the historical nature of such laws.

Today, Mary Ward's name is found in both *The New Dictionary of Theology* and *The Oxford History of the Christian Church*. The former describes her as a "remarkable lay apostle" with "practicality, zeal and charm" as well as Foundress of a Religious Order. It notes that her wish to adopt the rules of the Society of Jesus and her desire for a group of uncloistered nuns, without any distinctive habit, bound together by their vows and their rule, and under a superior general with authority to transfer the sisters, were regarded in her own era as "dangerously novel" ideas. The latter work, likewise, notes the non-traditional lines upon which her project was conceived, and the resultant suppression of her Institute.

Mary Ward's contemporaries provide mixed reactions, both as to her personal qualities and her apostolic work. A contemporary obituary for Mrs Anne Petre states that until about the age of fourteen she had been brought up in great piety by "the virtuous gentlewoman Mrs. Mary Ward and her companions."[11] The Chronicles of the English Canonesses of St Monica's in Louvain (1548-1625) contain a reference to "the saintly Mary Ward."[12] In his report of 1622, Dr. Kellison, President of Douay College, and no proponent of the Institute, refers to Mary Ward as "a lady of striking talent and eloquence."[13]

Mutio Vitelleschi, Superior General of the Society of Jesus from 1615-1645, while opposed to Mary Ward's plan to model her Institute after the Jesuits, nevertheless praised her integrity. John Gerard S.J., Mary Ward's Retreat Director from 1618 until 1620, pointed to her "readiness in doing good to all, and her great love for friends and enemies."[14] In 1621, Andrew White, S.J., a professor of divinity in Liège and later one of the first missionaries to North America, called attention to the value of the Institute's involvement in bringing others to conversion and teaching higher learning, "moral and divine."[15]

In contrast, Francesco Ingoli, Secretary of the Congregation of Propaganda and writing in 1628, attributed the Institute's foundation to a Jesuit of little education (Roger Lee) and to a former Poor Clare nun (Mary Ward) "of a masculine cast of mind." Drawing upon the criticisms of Mary Ward's opponents among the English clergy, he described her and her companions as "proud, with a mania for liberty, and garrulous."[16] In similar vein he condemned their rejection of enclosure, stating that it mattered "little" what the times required.[17]

Historical accounts likewise vary in their portrait of Mary Ward and their assessment of her work. *Dodd's Church History of England* describes her as a lady of "good address" and of "singular zeal and qualifications."[18] Walter Walsh, no friend of the Jesuits, considers

her "no ordinary woman" in that "she possessed more than a woman's
average share of courage and perseverance." He adds that these qualities were assisted by her having at hand "the crafty advice of the ablest
heads of the Jesuit Order." He goes on to accuse the Jesuits of having
an "intimate relationship" with her Institute and of using these "female Jesuits" as "instruments" for "the carrying out of their policy
and work throughout the world."[19]

Ludwig Freiherr von Pastor in his monumental history of the Popes,
refers to Mary Ward's Institute as "an original foundation" in the
sphere of female associations, one which was "destined to have considerable bearing on the future of these communities."[20] Other authors comment more specifically on the contribution her Institute
offered to the preservation of Catholicism in England. Leo Hicks,
for instance, points to her "admirable apostolic work, acutely demanded by the circumstances of the time" and attributes its condemnation to the "hide-bound conservatism - to put it at its best - of
a few ecclesiastics."[21]

Basil Fitzgibbon describes Mary Ward as a "woman of genius who
had the clear vision of the immense field which lay open to dedicated
women if the forms of religious life were adapted to the urgent needs
of changing modern conditions." He points to her as a leader of out-
standing capacity, who showed every promise of being able to contribute strong support to the recusant women and through them to
the Church not only in England but further afield.[22]

John Bossy goes further, stating emphatically: "if I were asked to
choose a single incident to illustrate the turn of the tide [against Catholicism in England] I would suggest the rejection of the ideal and
practice embodied in Mary Ward's Institute of Mary which became
final in 1631." He believes that her Institute offered the English
Catholic community "the opportunity of a second wind which could
have carried its phases of primitive expansion on through the seventeenth century", and that "in rejecting it, it registered its determination to play safe, and missed the boat for a couple of generations."[23]

Joseph Grisar, S.J, onetime professor of Church History at the
Gregorian University in Rome and student of Mary Ward's history
provides one of the best researched assessments of Mary Ward's character and work. He places particular emphasis on her courage, understanding of her vocation, willingness to serve the Church and love
of the truth. Grisar regards the large-scale work Mary Ward envis-

aged as not merely beneficial to the Church, but necessary for it. In the history of its destruction by ecclesiastical authorities he finds a struggle between progressivism and conservatism, between inspiration and rigid observance of Canon Law.[24]

In similar vein, James Cain, in his historical study of the canonical laws dealing with the question of cloister, points to Mary Ward's insights into woman's role in the Church during a period "when the role of woman was shrouded in the darkness of danger and suspicion."[25] Today, when the church and society in general are still coming to terms with this role, Mary Ward's vision appears prophetic: "And I hope in God it will be seen in time that women in time will do much."[26]

Sources

Given the political instability of Europe during the period in which Mary Ward's foundations were made, many documents relevant to a study of her lived and formulated spirituality no longer exist. Nevertheless, a considerable number of valuable documents have survived. These include Mary Ward's autobiographical notes covering her life up to 1595, written between 1617 and 1619 at the direction of Roger Lee, S.J., her spiritual director for almost eight years. From 1624 to 1626 she dictated a fuller autobiography in Italian covering the years 1599 to 1609. We have her spiritual reflections and retreat notes from the years 1612 to 1620, 1624, 1628 and 1636, and many of her letters to Roger Lee, John Gerard, and to her companions, including those written from prison in 1631. Copies of the Institute's Plans presented to Popes Paul V, Gregory XV and Urban VIII and of some of Mary Ward's communications to church officials are also in existence. The bulk of this material has been collated by Immolata Wetter, I.B.V.M. and duplicated in her *Letters of Instruction*.

The earliest biographical work of substance consists of manuscript lives written by two of her companions between 1647 and 1657, one in English the other in Italian. Other unpublished biographical sketches include one written in Italian in 1662 by Vincentio Pageti, Secretary of Cardinal Borghese and Apostolic Notary, and presented to the Electress of Bavaria. A second sketch was produced in Latin in 1674 by Dominic Bissel, Canon Regular of the Holy Cross in Augsburg. A third, written in German in 1689 by Tobias Lohner, S.J. includes Mary Ward's addresses to her companions, the originals of which have not survived. In addition, fifty large oil paintings depicting aspects of Mary Ward's life and spirituality are at the convent of the Institute in Augsburg, founded by Mary Poyntz, one of Mary Ward's first companions. The eighteenth century saw two published works, those of Corbinian Khamm, O.S.B. (1717) and of Marco Fridl (1732).

Since 1882 three authoritative historical studies have been published. The first, in two volumes, was published between 1882 and 1885 and written by Mary Catherine Elizabeth Chambers. Chambers made careful use of relevant documents from archives and libraries in Europe and records held by the Institute of the Blessed Virgin Mary in England, Germany and Rome. This work also provides excerpts from Mary Ward's letters and reflections.

Joseph Grisar, S.J. examined intensively the history of Mary Ward's Institute and the reasons for its suppression. He located nearly 1169 handwritten documents ranging from a few lines to more than fifty pages. These are held in libraries and archives in Belgium, Germany, England, France, Italy, Austria, Switzerland, Czecho-Slovakia and Hungary. They are written in English, Italian, Latin, French, German and Spanish. In addition he had access to a considerable amount of material held in the Vatican archives. The fruits of his investigation, covering the period up to 1631, are contained in his book *Mary Wards Institut vor Römischen Kongregationen 1616-1630*.

Henrietta Peters' biography, published in German (1991) and English (1994) includes data from newly discovered documents held in libraries and archives at Liège. With access to the resources of archives of the Vatican and of the Society of Jesus in Rome and to the source material amassed by Joseph Grisar and Immolata Wetter, Peters has been able to go beyond the limitations of the earlier biographies. While she provides many insights into Mary Ward's spirituality, it is not her purpose to examine its underlying theology and anthropology. Rather, the scope of her work, as she writes, has been restricted to a study of Mary Ward's personality and her Institute. Peters focuses first on Mary Ward's background and youth in England as the basis of her maturing personality. Second, she demonstrates Mary Ward's utterly loyal consistency in carrying out the commission which God had entrusted to her: to found a congregation for women on the model of the Society of Jesus. Her work is an invaluable resource for a study of the history of the Institute and its Suppression.

Barbara Hallensleben's study, *Theologie der Sendung: Die Ursprünge bei Ignatius von Loyola und Mary Ward*, is helpful in suggesting Ignatian influences on the theology and anthropology underlying Mary Ward's spirituality. This work was published in 1994 and is not yet available in English. In addition, many journal articles exist which examine at depth various aspects of her life and thought. In particular, those of Immolata Wetter, Barbara Olga Warnke, Leo Hicks and Walter Principe are most valuable to this study.

Collations of records held at the seminaries and colleges during Mary Ward's era provide a resource for identifying the courses given in moral theology and the background of influential English priests who were involved in Mary Ward's life. In addition, historians and scholars have collated a vast array of contemporary material from the Recusant period in England. Their work and the new climate of ecumenism fostered by Vatican II enables a more objective examination of the religious and political conflicts of Mary Ward's era.

Outline

A comprehensive study of Mary Ward's spirituality requires not only examination of her practice and teaching, but also of the extent to which she was influenced by and is reflective of her religious, theological and historical context. This study, therefore, is divided into two parts. The first three chapters examine the spirituality and moral theology of the late sixteenth and first half of the seventeenth centuries. Here the focus is, for the most part, on those aspects of spirituality and moral theology which most affected the English Catholics and the priests who ministered to them. This material reveals formative influences on Mary Ward's spirituality and provides the basis for consideration of the extent to which her insights are both reflective of and go beyond those of her era.

In these chapters consideration of the period's spirituality and moral theology relies heavily on the use of selected primary sources. These comprise mainly the literature used by English recusants, formulations of Jesuit spirituality and moral theology such as the *Spiritual Exercises* and the *Ratio Studiorum*, and the *Manuals* and *Handbooks for Confessors* used in the seminaries in which priests were trained for the English mission. Since many of these priests had a significant influence on Mary Ward and on the development of the Institute, considerable attention is given to the training they received and to the dilemmas they faced in their apostolate. The positive attempts made by the clergy to deal with the problems of their times provide practical instances of the strengths and limitations of casuistry.

The second part of this study opens with chapter 4 which examines Mary Ward's spirituality and its underlying theology and anthropology through a close analysis of her writings and practice. The focus is on her exposition of what she termed "the estate of justice". Here is found the definitive formulation of her own spirituality and that which she envisaged as the means by which her members could live the manner of life of the Institute. While the immediate context of her insights relevant to spirituality and moral theology was her attunement to the Holy Spirit in prayer, other probable sources for her theology and anthropology are suggested. Readers who have a particular interest in this area may prefer to read it in advance of the preceding chapter.

Within the context of the moral theology of Mary Ward's era and recent developments in its content and orientation, chapters 5 and 6 consider the significance of the theology and anthropology underlying her spirituality. Her concepts of the human person as a moral subject, freedom, moral rectitude, sin, morality, conscience and discernment bear similarities to and, in many cases, enrich the views of theologians today. In pointing to these similarities the aim is not thereby to provide justification for her understanding of morality. Rather, comparison of her insights with both her era's moral theology and recent approaches provides a richer understanding of the central concepts of moral theology.

Mary Ward was a woman ahead of her time. In her communication of a new creative spirit she was representative of the potential dynamism of the intellectual, cultural and religious achievements of her era. Of greater significance, however, is the anthropology which inspired her creativity. Her conviction of the role which can be played by women in the church stands in strong contrast to the prevailing anthropology of her era which, with its inadequate and, more often, negative view of the capabilities of women, rigidly distinguished between the manner in which men and women can seek to serve God in religious life. Mary Ward made no such dichotomy. Rather, in her exposition of the "estate of justice" which unites contemplation and apostolic activity she formulated the disposition and virtues which should be characteristic not only of women but of all Christians. Her uncompromising fidelity to her vocation and her loyalty to the Church is a significant instance of the well-ordered relationship with God, oneself and others which constitutes moral goodness, the essential source of morally right actions.

Notes

[1] From Pope Pius XII's address at the first World Congress of the Lay Apostolate, 1951, cited by Emmanuel Orchard, I.B.V.M. ed., *Till God Will: Mary Ward Through Her Writings* (London: Darton, Longman & Todd, 1985), foreword.

[2] *Documents of Vatican II*, "Decree on Priestly Formation," #16.

[3] Sacred Congregation for Catholic Education, "The Theological Formation of Future Priests" (22 February, 1976), no. 100, cited in *Veritatis Splendor, Encyclical Letter of John Paul II, On Certain Fundamental Questions of the Church's Moral Teaching*, #29,#111).

[4] Letter from Mary Ward to the Papal Nuntio, Antonio Albergati, Liège, 1621; cited by Mary Catherine Elizabeth Chambers, *The Life of Mary Ward*, ed. Henry James Coleridge, 2 volumes, (London: Burns and Oates, 1882, 1885), vol. I, 227; Orchard, 27; Henrietta Peters, *Mary Ward: A World in Contemplation*, trans. Helen Butterworth, (Leominster, Herefordshire: Gracewing, Fowler Wright Books, 1994), 108, note 5.

[5] Ibid., cited by Chambers, vol. I, 283; Peters, 115.

[6] *The Third Plan of the Institute*, given in full in *Letters of Instruction*, (IV), edited by Immolata Wetter. Henceforth references to the *Letters of Instruction* will be in the following form: Wetter (relevant letter number): page number.

[7] E.H. Burton and T.L. Williams, eds., *The Douay College Diaries: Third, Fourth and Fifth, 1598-1654 with the Rheims Report 1579-80*, two Volumes, (*CRS*, vols. X & XI, London, 1911, 1912), vol.I, 397, 398; Peters, 338-344.

[8] "Memorial to Pope Urban VIII," November 28, 1630, cited in full by Chambers, vol.II, 330-331. See also: Peters, 563, 564.

[9] For a more detailed account of the Bull of Suppression see Peters, 565-567; Ludwig Freiherr von Pastor, *The History of the Popes*, trans. Dom Ernest Graf, OSB, volumes XXIV-XXIX, (London: Routledge & Kegan Paul; St. Louis, Mo.: Herder Book Co., 1938-1952), vol. XXIX, 31.

[10] "Letter from the Secretary of the Congregation of the Holy Office to the Nuncio at Cologne," from a copy in the archives of the Institute of the Blessed Virgin Mary at Munich, undated but considered to have been written in 1633, quoted in full by Chambers, vol.II, 410-411. See also: Ludwig Freiherr von Pastor, vol. XXXIX, 32; Peters, 597, note 5.

[11] *Westminster Archives: XXIX (1637-1640)*, 425.

[12]Dom Adam Hamilton, ed., *The Chronicle of the English Canonesses Regular of the Lateran, at St Monica's in Louvain*, vol. I. *1548 to 1625*, vol. II, *1625-1644*, (London and Edinburgh: Sands & Co. 1904, 1906), vol. I, 185.

[13]Burton and Williams, *The Douay College Diaries*, vol. I, 397.

[14]John Gerard's letter to Father Henry Lee, March 8, 1637, excerpts cited by Chambers, vol. II, 227-229.

[15]Excerpts from Andrew White's document of February 4, 1621 cited by Chambers, vol.II, 53-57.

[16]Peters, 468.

[17]From the Vatican Archives, cited by Peter Guilday, *The English Catholic Refugees on the Continent 1558-1795* (New York: Longmans, Green, and Co., 1914) 199.

[18]Rev. M.A. Tierney, *Dodd's Church History of England: from the Commencement of the Sixteenth Century to the Revolution in 1688 with Notes, Additions and a Continuation* (London: Charles Dolman, 1841 -1843), vol. IV, 108, 109. Also cited by Henry Foley S.J., ed., *Records of the English Province of the Society of Jesus*, seven volumes (London: Burns and Oates: 1877-1883; vol II, The Manresa Press, 1875), vol. II, 341.

[19]Walter Walsh, *The Jesuits in Great Britain: An Historical Inquiry into Their Political Influence*, (London: George Routledge & Sons, Ltd., New York: E.P. Dutton & Co. 1903) 334, 336.

[20]*Pastor*, vol. XXVI, 205; vol. XXIX, 33.

[21]Leo Hicks, S.J., "Mary Ward's Great Enterprise," *The Month*, Volume CLI (March 1929): 236.

[22]Basil Fitzgibbon, "Mary Ward," *The Month* no. VIII (1952): 356-357.

[23]John Bossy, *The English Catholic Community, 1570-1850* (London: Darton, Longman & Todd, 1975), 282.

[24]Joseph Grisar, S.J., *Mary Wards Institut vor Römischen Kongregationen 1616-1630*. Miscellanea Historiae Pontificiae, vol. 37, (Rome: Pontifical Gregorian University, 1966), 2, 6, 157, 621, 626, 635.

[25]James R. Cain, "Cloister and the Apostolates of Religious Women," *Review for Religious*, 27, no. 4 (July 1968): 668.

[26]From Mary Ward's addresses to her companions at St. Omer, December 1617 to January 1618, contained with two other addresses, possibly in an abridged version, in the "*Liber Ruber*", manuscript held in the archives of the Institute of the Blessed Virgin Mary at Munich, excerpt cited by Chambers, vol. I, 410; Orchard, 57.

Chapter 1

Formative Influences on Mary Ward's Spirituality
1585-1607

I was commanded three or four years since by my confessor, Father
Roger Lee of the holy Society of Jesus, unto whom I vowed obedience,
to set down in writing all that I could remember to call to mind of my
life past ... before going to England or any place where my life or
liberty might be endangered.

My parents ... suffered much for the Catholic cause ... My grandmother had ... suffered imprisonment for the space of fourteen years
together. When by occasion we were living for any little time with
such of our kindred as were schismatics I shall never forget the exhortations [my father] would give us ... and his burning desires... that all
should live and die children of God's church. I had during those years
burning desires to be a martyr, ... delighted in reading spiritual books
... and had little other instruction at that time than what I got by
reading.[1]

Mary Ward's autobiographical fragments, written between 1617
and 1627, record the significant events of her life up to the end of
1609. They also reveal those features of the spirituality of her era that
influenced her own spirituality and theology, namely: the Catholic
recusants' fortitude, the inspiration of martyrs, and the religious practices and devotional literature of the English recusant Catholics.

The term "spirituality" as used here implies life in union with and
in response to God, in Christ Jesus, and empowered by the Holy
Spirit. The devotional literature from Mary Ward's era retained the
distinction between "Spirit" (*Pneuma*) and "Flesh" (*Sarx*), which is
found in Paul's letters. In general "spirit" comprises all in the human
person that is ordered by the Spirit of God, and "flesh" refers to that
which is opposed to this influence of the Spirit of God. The opposition is between two ways of life. During the same period *spirituality*
was frequently used also in its religious sense of the devout life.[2]

1.1 The Fortitude of Catholic Recusants
The early formation of Mary Ward's spirituality, up to 1606, took
place in Yorkshire. Contemporary writers record that Yorkshire was

one of the strongest areas of Catholic resistance to attempts to enforce religious conformity with the state Church.[3] Although the deep
religious conviction of English Christians was far more significant
than that which separated them, in the time of Mary Tudor (1553-
1558) almost 300 English Protestants were executed, and of the 314
Catholic martyrs 189 were put to death between 1570 and 1603.[4]
The most severe reprisals against Catholics came after the publication of the Papal Bull *Regnans in Excelsis* (1570) which excommunicated Elizabeth. Reprisals included measures taken to counter
recusancy, that is, refusal to attend Protestant Church services.

Records indicate that penalties increased in severity after 1559.
That year English law required people to attend Anglican Church
services on Sundays and holidays. In 1564 attendance was required
from 70 to 77 days each year and absentees were fined twelve pence
per day's absence. By 1581 the fine had increased to twenty pounds a
month or 260 pounds a year. When the recusants' subterfuges ham-
pered the collection of fines, a Statute was enacted in 1586 enabling
courts to seize their property in lieu of unpaid fines.[5] The effectiveness and severity of these laws depended on the zeal of those who
enforced them. One of the most zealous was the Earl of Huntingdon,
President of the Commission of the North, from 1572 to 1599.

Many of Mary Ward's relatives and friends suffered for their faith.
In 1586 Christopher Ward of Newby, Mary Ward's uncle, was declared a recusant. Mary Ward's parents, Marmaduke and Ursula Ward,
were listed as recusants in 1590. Ursula Ward's first husband, John
Constable, had been imprisoned in York for recusancy in 1580 and
died there in 1582. The recusant rolls of 1591-1592 list Ursula as
indicted on four counts of recusancy and fined a total of eighty
pounds.[6] Mrs Ursula Wright, Mary Ward's grandmother, with whom
she lived from 1590 to 1595, remained a staunch recusant. Despite
being in prison for a total of fourteen years' before 1590, she was
again cited as "a popishe recusante" in 1595.[7]

In 1597/1598 after continued persecution forced her father to
break up his household, Mary Ward was sent to live with Catherine
Ardington, daughter of Sir William Ingleby of Ripley, and two years
later, to the household of Grace and Ralph Babthorpe.[8] Despite Sir
William's Protestant conformity, Huntingdon counted the family
among the strongest supporters of Catholicism in Yorkshire. Catherine
Ardington was listed as a recusant in the Pipe rolls of 1585-1587 and

in 1591-1592 was imprisoned in York Castle with Isabella White-
head, a religious who lived with the family. One year later, Ladies
Ingleby and Grace Babthorpe were imprisoned for periods of up to
two years. Grace Babthorpe in her "Recollections" referred to Catholics as being imprisoned because they refused to hear "Protestant sermons." She also noted that the poor suffered as they "could not keep
any goods."[9]

Among those who could afford the recusancy fines were members
of the Rookwood family, according to the 1593-1595 recusancy rolls
for Suffolk. Mary Ward was distantly related to them through the
Babthorpes and had lived with them briefly upon her return from St.
Omer in 1609. Ambrose Rookwood was hanged for his part in the
Gunpowder Plot in 1605, together with Mary Ward's maternal uncles,
Christopher and John Wright.[10] Henry Garnet, S.J. described the
period of 1590-1592 as a "stormy one" for Jesuits as for all Catholics."[11] In 1592 Mary Ward's confessors, Richard Holtby, S.J. and
John Mush were named by the Earl of Huntingdon as "principal"
recusants.[12] Holtby had established permanently the Jesuits in the
north east the previous year.[13] John Gerard, S.J. later to become Mary
Ward's Retreat Director, friend and supporter, suffered imprisonment
in 1583 and 1593.[14]

Holtby noted that some husbands, who dutifully attended Protestant services, resented their wives' imprisonments and accused them
of "having hard hearts for being recusants." The authorities, however, were not overly sympathetic to these men. They considered them
to be "dissembling schismatics and secret favorites of their wives' religion."[15] In an attempt to counter the women's resistance, officials
amended the Act of 1581 so that two thirds of a widow's dower could
be seized; dissenting women had no income.

Bossy claims that "on few points in the early history of English
Catholicism is there such a unanimous convergence of evidence as
on the importance of the part played in it by women."[16] His claim,
however, that their resistance was due to gentry women's social dis-
satisfaction is not supported sufficiently. It is difficult to believe that
these women were willing to suffer the distasteful and painful conditions at Yorkshire prisons[17] for other than strong religious commitment. Moreover, Margaret Clitherow, who was not from the same
social class as the Inglebys and Babthorpes, was willing to endure
martyrdom in 1586.

In 1619-1620 Mary Ward recalled the apostolic spirit of the strong
recusant women who suffered for their dissent from the state church.[18]
She was influenced by their courage and was herself representative of
the dissenting women. In London in 1609 Mary Ward worked under threat of the established penal Laws, and in 1618 she and her companions were forced to move from house to house to escape capture.

1.2 The Inspiration of Martyrs

In his study of English Benedictines (contemporaneous with Mary
Ward) David Lunn finds one of the strongest spiritual influences on
these nuns in the martyrs' heroism, many of whom were relatives.[19]
Among those martyred between 1586 and 1601 and connected with
Mary Ward were Francis Ingleby, Ralph Grimston, Edward Thwing
and Robert Middleton.[20] Thomas Worthington describes the martyrdom of Christopher Wharton captured on the Ingleby property
in 1585, a year after his ordination.[21] According to one list, fourteen
were martyred at York in 1582, including John Constable and William Wright, and forty seven were martyred between 1583 and 1589.
While the accuracy of this list may be questioned, John Hungerford
Pollen's research indicates that at least twenty were martyred at this time.[22]

In 1585, one year after the assassination of the Prince of Orange,
an Act was passed against Jesuits and Seminary priests and "such like
disobedient persons."[23] This Act forbad their return to England, and
declared it felony for any person to shelter or assist priests. Although
this act applied to priests not ordained in England, the imprisonment and exile of Catholic bishops had stopped ordinations after 1558.
The Act was retroactive and declared all non-Marian priests traitors.

Accounts of martyrs' sufferings proliferated during this period.
These works had a dual purpose. They not only provided inspiration
and consolation to suffering recusants but were used politically to
illustrate how Catholics suffered for their religious beliefs. Robert
Persons' *De Persecutione Anglicana* and William Allen's *A Briefe history of the glorious martyrdom of xii reverend priests* were translated
into French, German and Italian. A manuscript detailing the life of
Margaret Clitherow, martyred for sheltering Francis Ingleby, was
written by John Mush. In 1593 both Holtby's account of the Yorkshire martyrs and Garnet's *Treatise of Renunciation* appeared.[24]

In an age of suffering and martyrdom imitation of Christ was expressed mainly in terms of the crucified Christ. The aim was to mol-

lify suffering by transforming it. Robert Southwell, martyred in 1595, portrayed affliction in terms of the Beatitudes. Both he and Allen stressed the relationship between the sufferings of the Head of the Mystical Body and its members.[25]

At the same time anger was expressed at the injustice which was the immediate cause of suffering. Worthington's work was intended as a reply to adversaries while Allen contrasted "Apostats and Heretikes" unfavorably with "heathens" through the ages beginning with the Arians and Vandals. Since the discovery of the Catacombs in 1578, martyrdom had been linked to the mystique of Catholic heritage and presented as the reward of Catholicism, a chance to achieve salvation.[26]

Mary Ward was acquainted with the martyrs' lives and records the desires for martyrdom that she experienced in her youth and retained twenty-five years later. According to one of her contemporaries, Adam Contzen, S.J., Rector at Munich, she was imprisoned in London in 1618 and a "sentence of death was passed upon her for religion, but there was no execution for fear of odium."[27] At the same time, she was aware that the martyrs' strength and courage flowed from their interior disposition and inner freedom. She had read Robert Southwell's *Short Rule of Good Life* which states graphically that disciples need "first to have killed their passions before they be killed by their persecutors." [28] In 1618 and 1619 she recorded her insights that discipleship is first evinced by interior asceticism and can take a variety of external manifestations. The *Painted Life* records Mary Ward's realization that to help others to salvation was, for her, a far more excellent gift.[29]

1.3 The Religious Practices of English Recusant Catholics

The recusants' constancy was due in large part to their life of prayer and religious practices. Mary Ward's autobiography and her contemporaries' records provide valuable testimony of this spirituality. Mary Ward recalls her father's exhortations, especially when the family were forced to live with relatives who were schismatics, and his desire that his children live and die members of the Catholic Church. She also records having by the age of ten, "great confidence in the power and help of our Blessed Lady."[30] Mary Ward's biographers describe her as sufficiently proficient in Latin as to be well read in the writings of the Fathers. Her frequent citations from the Vulgate edition of the Scrip-

tures provide additional evidence of her grasp of Latin and its influence on her thought and expression.[31]

The religious practices of the gentry households indicate the importance they attributed to the Mass and the Eucharist, to Marian
devotions, and to religious instruction. Significantly, with their husbands in many cases resorting to full or partial conformity to the
established Church, women were largely responsible for the role these
establishments played in enabling Catholics to practise their religion.
These households contained large numbers of young people, provided shelter for priests, and exerted a powerful influence on spiritual life through their intense devotion to the Sacraments and to the
hours and methods of prayer.

Father James Sharp (alias Pollard), writing in 1610, described the
religious life of the Babthorpes with whom Mary Ward lived for seven
years. Each day had begun with two Masses. Evensong at 4 p.m. was
followed by Matins, with the Litanies at 9 p.m. Sermons, catechism
and spiritual lessons were given every Sunday and holy day. Most of
the household also attended meditation and mental prayer and all
would confess and receive the Eucharist at least every fourteen days.[32]
Mary Ward recorded the influence of this household in which she
lived for seven years, and it was here, through the conversation of one of
the servants, that she first experienced a desire to become a Religious.

The Chronicle of St. Monica's Convent in Louvain provides evidence of a similar regime in the household of Dorothy Lawson, who
had four granddaughters later enter Mary Ward's Institute. Elaborate
Christmas and Holy Week ceremonies continued for nine years. Jesuits took their Retreats at her home where Mrs. Lawson was also
given the Spiritual Exercises. William Palmer, her confessor, described
her method of prayer as that "usually observed in the Society," and
its matter as consisting of "the life of our Saviour taken from points"
which he read to her each night. Mrs Lawson "made her prayer soli-
tary in her closet, with all the preparatives and preambles prescribed
in the Introduction or Instruction to Meditation."[33] The devotion to
the *Primer* of Dorothy Vavasour who died in prison in 1587 and
Anne Stonehouse's custom of fasting each Saturday in "honour of
our Lady" are recorded.[34] These emphases were not confined to the
gentry. Margaret Clitherow read the *New Testament*, the *Imitation*,
and learned the Latin *Primer* by heart.[35] The recusants' lived spirituality
reflects many of the themes formulated in the devotional literature.

1.4 The Devotional Literature of the Recusants

The years 1585-1645 saw an abundance of devotional works, and in particular the proliferation of these works among the recusant Catholics of England. This literature was intended for the laity and laymen played a significant role in its production. Although the influence of medieval spirituality can be detected, in general the literature reflects the need for works which countered religious dissension and philosophical scepticism to strengthen intellectual conviction and present Catholic life as logical and reasonable. In addition, because the laws restricted the free movement of priests, these works were intended to act as "dumb preachers" to recusants and those committed to Catholic beliefs who attended the Protestant Church. Even while living with the Babthorpes, Mary Ward recalled her dependency on reading for her instruction.

The amount of recusant literature published is significant given the current legislation. In England after 1524 the book trade was subject to restrictions. From that year onwards it was prohibited to sell imported books or print new books in England without permission from ecclesiastical authorities. Further legislation in 1558-9, 1566, 1601, 1637 and 1643 meant that Catholic books had to be secretly printed or smuggled in from abroad. Adrian Morey cites evidence that the literary output of the exiled writers at Louvain, Douay and Rheims had a marked effect on the educated Catholics' morale. Bishop Pilkington of Durham believed that circulation of these books "did much to keep Catholicism alive in the North."[36]

The most successful period for recusant publications opened in 1580 with the arrival in England of the Jesuits Robert Persons and Edmund Campion.[37] George Birkhead, Head of the Secular Clergy in England, attested to Jesuits' influence in a letter in 1584 to the English College Rector in Rome.[38] Persons' printing press produced a large number of works. Many translators and writers, including Thomas Worthington and Stephen Brinkley, were closely associated with the Jesuits.

Ironically, knowledge of recusant works was in many cases spread by the practices of Protestant controversialists. The latter frequently printed texts of the works they were challenging or provided lists of Catholic books to be avoided.[39] In the 1580s books confiscated by the Master of the Stationers' Company included 430 copies of six printed books and 700 loose sheets. That eight printers of the Stationers' Company stocked Catholic books suggests a great demand for them.

Recusant literature included both controversial and devotional works, the former decreasing after the defeat of Mary Queen of Scots in 1587 and of the Spanish Armada in 1588. In 1582 Robert Persons expressed concern that works dealing with controversies might hinder devotion. Both he and Birkhead, however, considered it necessary to meet "the adversary at every moment with strong and learned writings."[40]

Hopkins, a layman responsible for many devotional works, also seems to have kept two strings to his bow. In his introduction to Luis de Granada's *Memoriall of a Christian Life*, he emphasised that in order to reform Christendom bishops and pastors must not only preach penance, contempt of the world and mortification but give good example thereof to the common people. Hopkins' words are somewhat undermined, however, by his insertion of "divers additions" with regard to "the present generall infection of our Countrey with manie pestilent Heresies." Nor are his concluding remarks any more conciliatory. Expressing hope that his readers may enjoy the "felicity" of Eternal Life, he denies this happiness to any of the Lutheran, Zwinglian, Calvinian, Puritan or "other damnable Hereticall Sectes, that have died unrepentant therein."[41] In a similar vein, another work compared the fall of heretics and schismatics to "The Pigeons Flight from out of Noes Arke." The Rheims New Testament, first published in 1582, was unsparing in its efforts to point out the errors of heretics and schismatics.

Controversial literature seems to have been entered into with zest on all sides, particularly from 1569 to 1573 and 1584 to 1590 when English Catholic refugees and recusant writers urged a policy of political resistance. Not all such literature was polemical, however. George Tavard notes the positive nature of works treating of Scripture and Tradition. He sees their attempt to deal responsibly with the development of doctrine as anticipating the later work of Vatican II.[42] Without ignoring these positive aspects, it is suggested here that to a large extent controversial literature characterizes the defensive or "counter" aspects of the counter-Reformation, while devotional literature reflects its thrust as "first and foremost a powerful religious movement."[43] Characteristics of contemporary devotional literature, and its underlying theology and anthropology, can be ascertained from the types of works published between 1558 and 1603. Their concerns covered: Christian living, instruction in prayer and meditation, the importance of the sacraments, and the transformation of popular medieval practices and devotions. In addition to original publications, one finds translations of Latin, Italian and Spanish works.

Close examination of individual works reveals the innovative characteristics of the period's spirituality together with its underlying theology and anthropology. Two opposing emphases are apparent. On one hand, in tune with Renaissance humanism, human nature is seen as basically good and the potential of human reason is acknowledged. On the other hand, human nature is portrayed as being in a state of warfare between reason and unruly passions. In tune with the Council of Trent's doctrinal decrees the literature treating of the moral life strongly endorses the necessity of grace. At the same time, in an attempt to combat protestant teaching, it also emphazises the importance of good works and moral responsibility.

The following works are adequately representative of the devotional literature of the period: Robert Southwell's *A Short Rule of Good Life* (1596-1597); Lorenzo Scupoli's *The Spiritual Conflict* (1598); Gaspar Loarte's *The Exercise of a Christian Life* (1579); Lawrence Vaux's *Catechism* (first issued 1568); Robert Persons's *The First Book of the Christian Exercise* (1582);[44] Luis de Granada's *A Memoriall of a Christian Life* (1586); and *The Imitation of Christ*, *Treatises on the Rosary*, *Manuals* and *Primers*.

Mary Ward's spirituality suggests that ascetical and devotional literature had a greater influence on her early formation than did the controversial writing described earlier. Although she argued persuasively in defence of her faith, her aim was to reconcile rather than condemn those "estranged" from the Church. Moreover, her writings reveal none of the acrimony which so often characterized the controversial literature.

Mary Ward refers specifically to two devotional works which played a significant formative role on her spirituality, namely, *The Rules of a Christian Life* and *The Spiritual Conflict*. While she does not name the author of the former there is evidence that it is Robert Southwell's *A Short Rule of Good Life*. When visiting England several years later, Mary Ward recalled her early practice of "distributing the days of the week for the exercise of divers virtues, and of dedicating the rooms of the house to various saints."[45] Southwell recommended this practice. Printed secretly in London in 1596-1597, the work would have been available to recusant households by the period to which Mary Ward refers (1599-1600). Moreover, the Institute's library at the Bar Convent at York, founded in 1686 by Frances Bedingfield, one of Mary Ward's early companions, contains a copy of the earliest edition of this work.

The popularity of *A Short Rule of Good Life* is evident by the fact that it went through eight publications between 1588 and 1622. The work is generally attributed to Robert Southwell;[46] the editor of the preface indicated that the author was a martyred priest and well known to the English. In 1593 Southwell was a member of the English mission in London. That same year he was listed by Lord Huntingdon as among the Jesuits, seminarists and priests currently in England. The inclusion of advice about the proper care of servants and children validates Christopher Devlin's claim that the work was written for Anne, Countess Arundell and her children. The editor of the Protestant version produced in 1620 advertised the work as providing "method and order" in the art of becoming virtuous.[47]

Although Mary Ward's formal experience of the *Spiritual Exercises* came after 1608, *A Short Rule of Good Life* was one of the first literary sources from which she received some knowledge of their themes. Southwell closely follows the plan of the Exercises adapting their spirit and practice to the needs of lay people. He grounds the good life on the "First Principle and Foundation," moving from there to an elaboration of human beings' duties towards God, Superiors, neighbors and oneself, and the impediments to these. Southwell relates religious obedience to obedience to one's confessor or "ghostly father."[48] This emphasis is characteristic of the literature of the period and influenced Mary Ward's obedience to her confessors Richard Holtby and Roger Lee.

As with other authors, Southwell views human nature as changeable and corrupt. He advises "continuall warfare" against the world, the flesh and the devil. At the same time Southwell believes human beings are capable of co-operating with God's grace and puts before them the ideals of Christian perfection. The desire to suffer with Christ is the motive for choosing the more perfect, that is, what is more conducive for God's glory. His description of perfect resignation as being equally ready to serve God "in misery, need and affliction as in prosperity and pleasure," one's "chiefest delighte" being to be used as God wills[49] comes from Loyola's explanation of the "third degree of humility." "Indifference", defined in the Ignatian sense as an attitude of mind that enables one to choose what is more conducive for the end for which one is created, is the means for attaining "resignation," the acceptance of what God wills.

Southwell recommends daily examination of conscience to avoid even venial sin.[50] He focuses first on active love and service of God and neighbor and leaves specific consideration of mortal sin until his final chapter. His appreciation of the positive role in moral decision making which can be played by the affections reflects a more positive approach than other works dealing with the christian life. Southwell's statement, "Passions I allow, and loves I approve, onely I woulde wishe that men would alter their object and better their intent"[51] is echoed almost verbatim by Mary Ward in her comments of 1624-1626 on moral and spiritual guidance.

Similarly, Southwell treats the affections of indifference and gratitude towards God within the context of Loyola's Contemplation to Attain God's Love: "All creatures must be as it were bookes to me to reade therein the love, presence, providence and fatherly care that God hath over me."[52] Faithful to Loyola's stress on equilibrium in the practice of virtue, however, he emphasizes that exercises to maintain an awareness of God's constant presence must be a "spiritual recreation", not a toil.[53]

A Short Rule of Good Life is one of the few original recusant works that examines doctrine without using polemics. Consonant with the Council of Trent's decree on Justification in 1547, Southwell seeks a sound theological basis for spirituality. He parallels in diagrammatic form the relationship of God's grace and human co-operation: justification as the action of God and its effects in human beings. Shown is the action of grace, with each of the theological virtues bringing about a human response. This response begins with the intellect's consideration of God's justice and mercy and the merits of Christ and culminates in the will's desire to avoid all sin.[54] The theology underlying Mary Ward's later description of the "estate of justice" (1615) suggests the influence of Southwell's exposition.

While Southwell dedicates his work to a laywoman, Scupoli dedicates his to women religious. Cognet notes that the origins of *The Spiritual Conflict* are still in many ways a mystery and he suspects a number of authors. Signs of Ignatian influence have led some scholars to propose the Jesuit Achille Gagliardi (1537-1603) as one of its authors. Since the seventeenth century the work has generally been attributed to the Theatine Lorenzo Scupoli (1530-1618). The first edition (1589) contained twenty - four chapters; with revisions the number of chapters increased to sixty six.[55] The edition cited here

(1603-1610) contains thirty-three chapters. [56] In 1624-1626, when recording for her companions the significant events leading up to the founding of the Institute, Mary Ward described *The Spiritual Conflict* as her "best master and instructor" in spiritual exercises. According to her companions she based her early spiritual life on the book and was able to "tell without looking on the book the substance of every chapter." [57] It was recommended to her in 1601-1602 by a Jesuit supplying at the Babthorpes' household while John Mush was in Rome because of "controversies between the secular clergy and certain religious in England." [58]

Chambers suggests that Mary Ward may have read the work in the original Latin or Italian or in manuscript form. In 1598 an English translation had been made by John Gerard, S.J. He had worked at the English mission at the time and later became an influential friend of Mary Ward. A second edition of *The Spiritual Conflict* was issued between 1603 and 1610. Interestingly, the facsimile of the 1610 edition reproduced by David Rogers contains a handwritten inscription indicating that it had belonged to the English convent of Poor Clares at Gravelines which had been founded in 1608 by Mary Ward. It seems somewhat prophetic that both Scupoli and Mary Ward were destined to receive calumnious denunciations. In the year of Mary Ward's birth Scupoli submitted to disciplinary action, laicization, by his Order and spent the remaining twenty - five years of his life in retirement and prayer.

Cognet describes the *Spiritual Conflict* as "the most representative work of the Italian ascetic school." [59] The book reflects a dominant theme of Italian spiritual authors: asceticism and the notion of self-conquest. [60] Scupoli describes "spiritual conflict" as an interior struggle. Human beings are endowed with reason and freedom but moved by two opposed forces, the spiritual and the sensual, the ideals one consciously desires and "foeful" nature which "doth kicke and resist." [61] Reason is in a state of tension, drawn to the divine will on the one hand, and to the will of sense on the other. Scupoli's anthropology is evident in his contrast of "the good estate of grace" and "nature, despoiled of God's divine help" and thus powerless to do any good. [62]

Scupoli intended to set down precisely "wherein constitutes the truth and perfection of spirituall life." [63] In contrast to the prevailing disbelief in the capabilities of women, he urges his readers "unto the height and top of perfection." [64] Scupoli stresses the positive role of the affections in discernment and prayer, and allows for a more mystical form of prayer than other ascetical writers.[65]

While the method and tone characterising Scupoli's description of God's presence in all creatures are reminiscent of the Ignatian "Contemplation to Attain Divine Love," there are significant differences. Ignatius counterbalances contempt for the world with the notion of the world as the place of God's presence and labor. Scupoli, however, while not ignoring creation's wonders, points to the "infernall serpent" underlying them.[66] Outram-Evennett points to the severe ascetic spirit in *The Spiritual Conflict* which he sees as "in full accord with the new tide" of Counter Reformation spirituality.[67] In spite of his endorsement of the importance of human striving, Scupoli seems more concerned with establishing that perfection does not lie in the rigor and austerity of life but in the interior self and the building up of the habit of virtue. While he views distrust, even hatred of self, as essential, Scupoli stresses that the focus in prayer and practice is God who deserves to be loved and pleased. Trust in God's goodness and liberality must be the source of resignation to God's will and love for all creatures solely for love of God.[68]

Mary Ward's later writings illustrate the debt her spirituality owes to Scupoli and also how she surpassed him. In 1615 Mary Ward described the disposition of those who seek to follow Christ, as one in which "sense obeys reason and reason the divine will."[69] Both Scupoli and Mary Ward relate knowledge and love. Scupoli advises his readers to base their affections on a sound knowledge of "things as they are and not as they appear."[70] Mary Ward saw a quality of just persons that "we be such as we appear and appear such as we are."[71]

Both Scupoli and Mary Ward describe freedom of will as freedom from all love which does not bring one toward God. While Scupoli stresses separation from human affections, Mary Ward stresses that the state of freedom is such that "one is free from all, desiring only to love God," but, at the same time, is "present to all" in being able "to refer all to God."[72] Both emphasize seeking God's glory and having an "indifferent" attitude, expressed in the determination "not to worke or refuse any thing till … moved and drawn unto it by the onely and pure will of God."[73]

Mary Ward's experience after reading the above works brought initial insights into the nature of inner freedom, which was to become a central component of her spirituality. She writes that she tried to practise the exercises recommended in *Rules of a Christian Life*. Her zeal, after reading *The Spiritual Conflict*, however, was such "that what at first was easy and pleasing became on a sudden difficult and wearisome." Mary Ward came to understand that, with respect to matters not of obligation but of devotion, God was "not pleased with certain acts made thus by constraint and to acquire one's own quiet," and that she would "do these things with love and freedom, or leave them alone."[74]

Mary Ward's reading of *The Spiritual Conflict* coincided with her discernment that she was called to religious life. Writing of this period (1600-1605) she tells of the inner conflict she experienced because of opposition from her family and confessor. She found peace in the words *Quaerite primum Regnum Dei*, realising that if she preferred before all God's honor and service, God's Goodness would supply for her every deficiency.[75]

Mary Ward's mature spirituality and practice reflected her early realization that one's interior disposition gives validity to external performance. In general, devotional literature in its focus on the exercises necessary for the acquisition of perfection reveals a strong preoccupation with human performance.

The focus on asceticism and a general suspicion of mysticism resulted in the relative absence of mystical works during this period. Given the trust that Mary Ward was later to place in John Gerard, it is interesting that the works he made available to the English recusants are more mystical in content. In 1595, three years prior to translating Scupoli's work, Gerard cooperated with Philip Howard to produce Lanspergius' *Epistle in the Person of Christ to the Faithfull Soule*.[76] This work, first published in 1572, stressed the importance of the interior disposition as giving validity to human performance. Its intensely personal and mystical tone is apparent in the dialogue where the soul is addressed variously as "daughter", "sister" and "spouse." It is not known if Mary Ward was given this work. The existence of a 1595 edition at the convent of the Institute at York suggests that early members of her Institute were familiar with it.

The Institute's library at York also holds a first edition copy of Gaspare Loarte's *The Exercise of a Christian Life*. This was translated from Spanish in 1579 by Stephen Brinkley who was imprisoned from 1581 to 1583 and his printing press seized. By 1634 six more editions had been published, including a Protestant one in 1594. Loarte's intention was the provision of exercises to enable those engaged in "temporall businesse" to live uprightly and deal justly. The priority given to considerations of mortal sin seems to have appealed to the editor of Southwell's book. This editor recommends Loarte's work or others with a similar approach as providing the "middle steppes" which first need to be taken in the pursuit of perfection.[77] The influence of the *Spiritual Exercises* is noticeable in Loarte's emphasis on "referring all things to God's service," a theme later taken up by Mary Ward.[78]

Mary Ward's life attests to the value she placed on the acquisition of human knowledge. In contrast to Scupoli,[79] but in common with most English recusant authors and in the wake of Renaissance humanism, Mary Ward recognised the integral relationship of the mind and heart and the intellect and will. She was described as "a great ennemy of ignorance" and was "wont to say that she could not find a reason why knowledge should be damageable but many that it might be advantageous."[80]

A similar recognition of the inter-relationship of understanding and will is reflected in Vaux's *Catechism* that was later supplanted by an "amplified and Englished" edition of Peter Canisius' work.[81] Vaux's *Catechism*, one of the most popular of recusant works, encompassed nine editions. Addressing his reader as "a reasonable creature of God" Vaux sought to explain how one ought to believe and live. He draws from the Scripture, the Church Councils, and from works of the early Church Fathers, St. Bernard and Peter Canisius.[82]

In a similar vein, Robert Persons' *The First Book of the Christian Exercise* conveys an intellectual understanding of the importance of devotion to God. Persons focuses on those affected by indifference, schism and atheism. Seeking to move the will by providing a rational basis for desiring conversion, Persons appeals to both Scripture and human experience. He presents consideration of God's deeds as well as one's duties towards God as a means towards amendment of life and a main "gate to salvation." "Consideration" is portrayed as a work of the understanding and reason, a search for the "truth of matters." It moves the will to "true devotion," that is, "a prompt will towardes all things that concern God's glory."[83] For Persons, the manifestation of this promptness is a "continual" warfare and resistance to all sin, and the "incessant" exercise of piety and good works.[84]

Joseph de Guibert does not consider the *Christian Directory* a "book of spirituality." Rather, he calls it a work of higher catechetical instruction. He includes it in his discussion of Jesuit spiritual writings because of its influence in urging human beings to a fully Christian life.[85] Birkhead comments on the number of people converted as a result of the book.[86] Those converted include Benet of Canfield, Thomas Nashe, Richard Baxter, Edmund Gibbon and Ralph Babthorpe. The book was popular among Protestants; Bunny's 1594 adaptation ran twenty editions.

Persons' work reveals the emphasis on asceticism as a means for the attainment of virtue, which Mary Ward experienced in 1600 after reading Scupoli. This emphasis also characterises the writings of Louis de Granada.

Luis de Granada's *Memoriall of a Christian Life* addresses both the spiritual and moral life. Although he does not decry the role of reason in guiding human action, de Granada believes that practice is more important than speculation. In keeping with the Council of Trent's recognition of the need for reform he stresses the priestly role of teaching Doctrine and Truth. He offers his work as a preacher and laments the lack of preaching which makes such works so necessary. De Granada's work reflects the strong emphasis placed on the role of grace in salvation, the effect of the Protestant challenge. He equates being "spiritual" with living a "divine life" through the grace won for humanity by Christ. Concurrently, however, he stresses that perfection does not exclude human industry and provides exhaustive (and exhausting) exercises to attain perfection.[87]

De Granada's purpose was "to forme a perfecte Christian." He offers two separate rules of good life, one for beginners, the other for those seeking a more perfect way of following Christ. The first four treatises deal with moral obligations and the last three with the exercise of prayer and love of God.[88]

In general, de Granada's anthropology borrows from St. Thomas and St. Augustine. On the one hand, as with recusant literature, he endorses the goodness in human nature and of God's benefits in creation. Refreshingly, he likens purity of intention with the faithfulness of an honest woman. In addition, his recommendations for the reception of the Eucharist do not rigidly differentiate between religious and laity. On the other hand, de Granada does show a pessimistic view when he calls the human being a "miserable" sinner. Seeing fear as the most effective motive for conversion, he begins his exposition of the first rule (for beginners) with a lengthy consideration of God's punishments of those who live a sinful life.[89]

De Granada, a Spanish Dominican, admitted his debt to the *Spiritual Exercises*. Its influence can be seen in his emphasis on true liberty of mind, the imitation of Christ, "the exemplar cause" of all our perfection, the necessity for guidance from a "good Ghostlie father," the application of the senses and imagination in prayer, and the apostolic thrust of love of neighbor.[90]

Recusant literature centers on discipleship as the essence of Christian life. Devotions surrounding the Imitation of Christ were more fully developed in the Middle Ages by St. Bernard, with whose writings Mary Ward was familiar.[91] Other promoters of these devotions were Francis of Assisi, whose Rule Mary ward followed from 1606-1609, Ludolph the Carthusian, Thomas a Kempis and Ignatius of Loyola. The most popular work treating of discipleship was *The Imitation of Christ* by a Kempis.

Anthony Hoskins by dedicating his translation of *The Imitation of Christ* (1613) to Elizabeth Vaux - whose devotion is described by John Gerard - indicates the book's importance to the recusant community.[92] Prior to this translation, recusant Catholics used Whitford's and Rogers' Protestant translations that were published before the end of the sixteenth century. Whitford's 1585 version includes St. Bernard's *Golden Epistle*.

The popularity of the *Imitation* is indicated by the numerous Catholic and Protestant versions.[93] Its dominant themes of self-conquest, abnegation, contempt of the world, docility to the movement of grace and familiarity with God are common features of recusant devotional literature. Jean Delumeau suggests that the *Imitation* was responsible for introducing the philosophy of "contempt of the world" to a large reading public.[94] In contrast to the retirement from the world emphasised by a Kempis, however, some Protestant modifications reveal the apostolic thrust common to the recusants. For Rogers, the imitator of Christ is "godly and zealous," rather than "godly and devout" as in the original book.[95]

The tendency to promote works of medieval spirituality, giving them new structures and making a more explicit appeal to the understanding, can be seen in the treatment of Marian devotions. The Rosary became the lay person's Bible; the average Catholic could not turn to an English translation of the Bible despite the production of the Douai New Testament in 1582. Loarte and another author known only as "I. M." provide meditations on the mysteries.[96] John Bucke states explicitly that his 1589 compilation is addressed to lay persons to assist them in the practice of mental prayer.[97] Henry Garnet's *The Society of the Rosary* is an adaptation for English Catholics in penal times of the rules and statutes of the Jesuit sodality.[98] There is reason to believe that the copy of this work which is held in the library of the Bar Convent at York once belonged to Mary Ward.[99]

The popularity of the *Primer* (Little Office of the Blessed Virgin Mary) also evinces the importance of Marian devotion. The *Primer* and the *Manual* differ in that the latter is post-Reformation. The *Primer*, however, was reformed by the Council of Trent and translated into English in 1599. Its popularity suggests the laity's tendency to seek a form of devotion comparable to the clergy's Divine Office. The *Primer* was reprinted fifteen times between 1604 and 1632. Twenty-seven editions of the *Manual* were made after 1583 in spite of the 1605 Act that forbade the importation of such literature.[100] J.M. Blom claims that for a book of this size each edition could run from 2500 to 3000 copies. Using conservative population figures, he estimates that not only literate but semi-literate and even most illiterate Catholics were familiar with a primer or manual.[101]

An original prayer book of the period which has been preserved is the Sydenham Prayer Book used by the Bedingfield family. This book, an adjunct to the *Primer*, contains many prayers from the *Manual*, some unedited Catholic verse from the Elizabethan period and a prayer of Mary Tudor.[102] The *Manual* was first published in 1583.[103] Eleven editions were printed secretly in England between 1575 and 1624. George Flinton and John Heigham, both laymen, were instrumental in its production. The copy in the Institute's Library at the Bar Convent at York is thought to have reached Mary Ward through Bishop Blaise who supported her work in St. Omer.

Within the manuals one finds prayers to cover almost every eventuality. This reflects a trust in the Providence of God. Interestingly, there are also prayers by Thomas Aquinas and Thomas More, an indication of the respect each held at the time. Prayers stressing forgiveness of enemies and a concern for creation are also included. J.D. Crichton's comment that the Manual's stress on the "awesomeness" of the Eucharist would have caused its readers to receive communion only rarely[104] is not borne out in the case of either Mary Ward or the Babthorpes.

Recusant devotional literature generally provided methods of prayer for the lay person, thus reflecting a desire in its readers for such instruction. John O'Malley notes the period's fascination with "method."[105] Louis Martz attributes the remarkable similarity in fundamental procedure in the important treatises about meditation to the influence of the *Spiritual Exercises*.[106] This is especially true for the Manuall or *Meditation* which uses Peter Canisius's meditations. Incidentally, this is one of the first books published by the Greenstreet Press.

Loarte's *Exercise of a Christian Life* (1579) and Granada's *Of Prayer and Meditation* (1586) extol the value of mental prayer. The identity of their fourteen meditations: the Life, Passion and Resurrection of Christ for morning prayer, and consideration of personal sin, the vanity of this world, death, judgement, heaven and hell for the evenings, suggests that this was a traditional pattern.[107] Early editions of Granada's and Loarte's works can be found in the Institute's convent in York, together with Richard Gibbon's 1599 translation of Vincenzo Bruno's meditations on the passion.

John Roberts suggests that since recusant literature was addressed to the laity it had to provide more direction about methods of prayer than is found in the *Spiritual Exercises*.[108] This suggestion needs some qualification. Contemporaries of the period provide ample evidence of the Exercises being given to the laity. As a layman Roger Lee (Mary Ward's confessor for eight years) was given the Exercises by John Gerard and Ralph Babthorpe made them shortly before his death. Dorothy Lawson's method of prayer, as has been noted, followed that of the Jesuits. Richard Holtby pairs the *Spiritual Exercises* with the reading of devotional literature to show how recusants were able to remain steadfast in their faith.[109]

Noticeably absent in recusant literature at this time are the works of the famous thirteenth and fourteenth-century English mystics. Rolle's works and *The Cloud of Unknowing* had been popular among Carthusians including those of the London Charterhouses. During the repression of the Charterhouses in 1535, their books were confiscated. An anonymous collection published in 1603 does include one meditation on contrition ascribed to Richard Rolle.[110] A.F. Allison identifies Garnet as the editor of Luca Pinelli's *Meditations on the*

Eucharist (15971600). Adjoined to this work is a translation of St. Teresa's *Avisos* first published in Spanish in 1583.[111] Southern suggests that the strong resemblance in style and tone of *The First Book of the Christian Exercise* (1582) to Hilton's *Scale of Perfection* (1494) indicates Persons' familiarity with Hilton's work.[112]

In addition, many Spanish writers were attempting to curb the rise of Illuminati groups' false mysticism. Knowles and Roberts suggest that the need for a more explicit grasp of doctrine and a desire to renew the spiritual life of the laity resulted in most books having an ascetical rather than mystical orientation.[113] Notable exceptions were William Howard and Robert Cotton whose collections included medieval mystical treatises.[114]

Many aspects of recusant spirituality in this period reflect national characteristics. Anglican spirituality, for instance, is described by Gordon Wakefield as a spirituality for the laity. James Devereux points out that 66 of the 101 "collects" in the Book of Common Prayer are based on Latin originals found in the service books of pre-reformation England.[115] Similar continuity can be detected in the popularity of works such as the *Imitation of Christ*, the *Jesus Psalter*, primers and manuals among all Catholics.

In the above discussion of the spirituality (lived and formulated) of the period 1585-1607, attention has been confined to England and specifically to the recusants. It must be noted that this group was a minority living in political and religious conflict. Original works and those selected for translation, while representing many of the characteristics of counterreformation spirituality, were intended to meet the particular situation in which English Catholics found themselves. Features of post-Tridentine spirituality cannot be disassociated from the effects of disestablishment of the Catholic church in England. The fact that large households generally had resident priests smoothed the path for the enforced movement of sacramental practice from the parish to the household. Elsewhere the Council of Trent had banned Masses in private houses.

Moreover, while the gentry household was not necessarily typical of English Catholicism, contemporary records provide less information with regard to the spirituality of other than the recusants among the gentry. This is due in part to the obstinacy of sections of the nobility and gentry in adhering to Catholicism, which was of considerable concern to the authorities. David Matthew sees a strong link between the survival of Catholicism and the Catholics' economic situation.[116] The poor in the Midlands and south along with the London artisans had little chance to practise their religion. The agricultural laborers in the south relied entirely on the presence of missionary priests which was contingent on the hospitality of landowners or substantial farmers. Significantly, it was in London that Mary Ward directed her first efforts. One of her members also worked in Suffolk.

On May 14, 1606 Mary Ward left England for St. Omer. Her subsequent writings and practice indicate that between 1607 and 1615 the definitive characteristics of her spirituality emerged. During these years her insights regarding God's will were primarily received through prayer. Nevertheless, the immediate circumstances in which she received these insights reveal the significance of the formative influences of the spirituality, lived and formulated, of the period before 1607.

Notes

[1] *AB*, cited by Chambers, vol. I, 10-13,49,50; Orchard, 5,6; Peters, 18,35,47.

[2] This definition is a broad one and follows in general the understanding given to it by Joseph de Guibert, S.J., *The Jesuits: Their Spiritual Doctrine and Practice* (St. Louis: The Institute of Jesuit Sources, 1986), 2, and Walter Principe, "Defining Spirituality," *Sciences Religieuses/Studies in Religion*, 12/2 (Spring 1983): 135, 136.

[3] John Morris, ed., "Father Pollard's Recollections of the Yorkshire Mission" and "Father Richard Holtby on Persecution in the North," in *The Troubles of our Catholic Forefathers–Related by Themselves*, third series, (London: Burns and Oates, 1877), 170, 171, 467.

[4] David L. Edwards, *Christian England: From the Reformation to the 18th Century* (Grand Rapids: William B. Eerdmans Publishing Company, 1983), 28; Martin J. Havran, "The British Isles," in *Catholicism in Early Modern History: A Guide to Research*, ed., John O'Malley, S.J. vol. 2, *Reformation Guides to Research* (St. Louis, Missouri: Center for Reformation Research, 1988), 71.

[5] Clare Talbot, ed., "Documents relating to the Northern Commissions for Compounding with Recusants 1627-1642," *Miscellanea: Recusant Records* (*CRS*, LIII, London, 1961), 291-306.

[6] UYBI York, Diocesan Registry York, Archiepiscopal Visitation Book, 1590-1591, CB 1, f. 56r, 64r, (University of York, Borthwick Institute for Historical Research): M.M.C. Calthrop, ed., *Recusant Roll No. 1 Michaelmas 1592-1593, Exchequer Lord Treasurer's Remembrancer Pipe Officer Series* (*CRS*, XVIII, London, 1916), 61,65,98,103,108,125; cited by

Peters, 33,37. John Hungerford Pollen, S.J., ed., *Unpublished Documents Relating to the English Martyrs,* vol. I, *1584-1603,* (*CRS,* V, London, 1908), 19).

[7]Talbot, "A Book of Recusants; Recusants in the Province of York, 1595," *(CRS,* LIII, London, 1961), 23.

[8]Peters, 41,45; Adrian Morey, *The Catholic Subjects of Elizabeth I* (London: George Allen & Unwin Ltd., 1978), 213. Morey states that one method of evading penalties for recusancy was to move from the house of one relative to another over a period of years. He cites the practice of Thomas Meynell of Kilvington in Yorkshire, a contemporary of Marmaduke Ward. (Morey, 141).

[9]Timothy McCann, ed., *Recusants in the Exchequer Pipe Rolls, 1581-1592* (*CRS,* VII, London, 1986), 11, 13: John Morris, S.J., ed., *The Troubles of Our Catholic Fore-fathers,* first series (London: Burns and Oates, 1872), 229, 230; third series, 214, 240-247, 314, 328, 462. See also: Peters, 41, 45, and note 52.

[10]Dom Hugh Bowler, ed., *Recusant Rolls, Nos.2 (1593-1594),3 (1594-1595) and 4 (1595-1596):* Abstracts in English with an Explanatory Introduction, (*CRS,* Record series, London, 1970), vol. 57, 88-90, 94, 166; vol.61, 225-227; John Morris, ed., *The Condition of Catholics Under James I: Father Gerard's Narrative of the Gunpowder Plot* (London: Longmans, Green, & Co.,1981), 111.

[11]Morris, *Troubles,* first series, 149-150.

[12]John Hungerford Pollen, S.J. ed., *Unpublished Documents Relating to the English Martyrs* vol. I, *1584-1603* (*CRS,* V, London, 1908), 213; McCann, 67.

[13]J.C.H. Aveling, *Northern Catholics: The Catholic Recusants of North Riding of Yorkshire 1558-1790* (London: Geoffrey Chapman, 1966), 159.

[14]From the Official Lists of Catholic Prisoners during the Reign of Queen Elizabeth, 1581-1602, given in *Miscellanea II* (*CRS,* II, London, 1906), 233, 235, 286.

[15]Morris, *Troubles,* third series, 219.

[16]Bossy, *The English Catholic Community 1570-1850,* 153,158.

[17]These conditions are described by Father Pollard in his Recollections of the Yorkshire Mission, and cited by Morris, *Troubles,* third series, 463.

[18]From the Latin manuscript: *Rationes de subordinatione* preserved in the Archives at Brussels, cited by Immolata Wetter in "Mary Ward's Apostolic Vocation," reprinted from *The Way,* supplement 17 (Autumn 1972): 81.

[19]David Lunn, *The English Benedictines 1540-1688: From Reformation to Revolution* (London: Burns & Oates and New York: Barnes and Noble, 1980), 198-199.

[20]Aveling, *Northern Catholics,* 179; McCann, 73. Chambers, vol. I, 5, 58.

[21]Thomas Worthington, *A Relation of Sixtene Martyrs: Glorified in England in Twelve Monethes* (Doway: widow of James Boscard, 1601); Godfrey Anstruther, O.P. *The Seminary Priests: A Dictionary of the Secular Clergy of England and Wales 1558-1850*, vol.I, *Elizabethan 1558-1603*, (Gateshead, England: Northumberland Press, Ltd., 1968), 377.

[22]Pollen, *Unpublished Documents Relating to the English Martyrs*, 191.

[23]Edmund H. Burton and J.H. Pollen, eds., *Lives of the English Martyrs: Second Series, The Martyrs Declared Venerable*, vol. I, *1584-1588*, (New York: Longmans, Green & Co. 1914), xii, xiii.

[24]Peter J. Holmes, *Resistance and Compromise: The Political Thought of Elizabethan Catholics* (New York: Cambridge University Press, 1982). 65,66; Morris, *Troubles*, third Series, 221-230, 331-440; A.F. Allison, "The Writings of Henry Garnet, S.J. (1555-1606)," *Recusant History*, I no.1 (1951): 11.

[25]Josephine Evetts Secker, "The Consolatory Literature of the English Recusants," *Renaissance and Reformation*, n.s., 6, o.s., 18, (1982): 124-130. Robert Southwell's *Epistle of Comfort* was printed secretly in England, 1578-1588. It is listed by A.F. Allison and D.F. Rogers in *A Catalogue of Catholic Books in English Printed Abroad or Secretly in England 1558-1640* (London: Wm. Dawson & Sons Ltd., 1964), 278.

[26]Cardinal William Allen, *A Briefe historie of the glorious martyrdom of xii reverend priests, 1582* (Rheims, Jean Foigny), 1; Thomas H. Clancy, S.J., *Papist Pamphleteers: The Allen-Persons Party and the Political Thought of the Counter-Reformation in England 1572-1615* (Chicago: University of Loyola Press, 1964), 126; Holmes, *Resistance and Compromise*, 48-53.

[27]Chambers, vol.1, 335, 436.

[28]R.S. Southwell, *A Short Rule of Good Life. To Direct the Devout Christian in a Reguler and Orderly course* (printed secretly in England, 1596-97).

[29]Interestingly, Margaret King confines herself to areas other than England for examples of the fanatical self-denial which she considers to have been characteristic of many Renaissance women. Margaret L. King, *Women of the Renaissance* (Chicago: University of Chicago Press, 1991).

[30]*AB*, cited by Orchard, 5,7.

[31]Chambers, vol. I, 22; James Walsh, Introduction to Orchard's work: *Till God Will*, xvii. Contemporary documents attest to the knowledge of Latin of young women with a background similar to that of Mary Ward. Accounts of Margaret Clement and Mary Wiseman, members of the convent of St. Ursula's at Louvain, indicate that in the households of such Englishmen as Thomas More, Dr. Clement, and the Wisemans, young women were offered the opportunity to learn Latin and in many cases Greek also. (C.S. Durrant, *A Link Between Flemish Mystics and English Martyrs*, (London: Burns, Oates and Washbourne, Ltd., 1925), 420-422).

[32]"Father Pollard's Recollections of the Yorkshire Mission," in Morris, *Troubles*, third series, 468.

[33]William Palmer, "Life of Dorothy Lawson," in Philip Caraman, ed., *The Years of Siege: Catholic Life from James 1 to Cromwell* (London: Longmans, Green & Co. Ltd., 1966), 39-40; Hamilton, vol. I, 177, 178.

[34]Morris, *Troubles*, first series, 223.

[35]Aveling, *Northern Catholics*, 191.

[36]Morey, 103-104.

[37]Southern, *Elizabethan Recusant Prose 1559-1582: A Historical and Critical Account of the Books of the Catholic Refugees Printed and Published Abroad and at Secret Presses in England together with an Annotated Bibliography of the Same* (London: Sands & Co., Ltd., 1950), 31; Holmes, *Resistance and Compromise*, 31,35,36. Southern calculates that between 1559 and 1595 over two hundred English books, including fifty eight pamphlets, were published.

[38]John Hungerford Pollen, S.J., ed., *Memoirs of Father Robert Persons (continued)* (Miscellanea IV, *CRS*, IV, London, 1907), 153.

[39]One such instance is John Gee's catalogue of English books known to have been reprinted or dispersed by priests published in 1624. This is given in full by Henry Foley, S.J. ed., *Records of the English Province of the Society of Jesus*, VI, supplemental volume, *The Diary of the English College, Rome, from 1579 to 1773* (London: Burns and Oates, 1880), 671-675.

[40]Robert Persons, *The Christian Directory, Guiding Men to Eternal Salvation*, (S. Omer, François Bellet, 1607), third part of the preface, par.46; Pollen, *Memoirs of Father Robert Persons Continued*, 153 - 155.

[41]Luis De Granada, *A Memoriall of a Christian Life*, trans., Richard Hopkins, (Rouen: George L'Oyselet, 1586), translator's preface.

[42]George H. Tavard, *The Seventeenth - Century Tradition: A Study in Recusant Thought* (Leiden: E.J. Brill, 1978), 246 -266.

[43]H. Outram Evennett, *The Spirit of the Counter-Reformation*, John Bossy, ed., (Cambridge at the University Press, 1968), 24.

[44]In editions from 1585 this work was known as *The Christian Directory*.

[45]*AB*, cited by Chambers, vol. I, 50; Peters, 47,53, n.87. Such practices are not mentioned in the following works which are suggested by Henrietta Peters: St. Bernard's *Golden Epistle*, Picus the Elder's *Rules of a Christian Life*, (both included in Whitford's edition of *The Imitation of Christ*), and Gaspar Loarte's *The Exercise of a Christian Life*. Mary Ward may have been familiar with Loarte's work which is recommended by the editor of Southwell's work. In addition, Mary Ward's apparent lack of accuracy in the title by which she refers to the work is not significant. First, she was referring to it after a number of years. Second, individual

pages of the work are headed *The Rules of Good Life*, similar to the title used by Mary Ward. Third, William Barrett' entitles his Protestant version of 1620 *Short Rules of Good Life*.

[46]Allison, and Rogers, *A Catalogue of Catholic Books in English Printed Abroad or Secretly in England 1558-1640*; Christopher Devlin, *The Life of Robert Southwell, Poet and Martyr* (London: Sidgwick & Jackson, 1967):198; Foley, *Records*, II, 386, (see also: VII, lxvii).

[47]Richard Loomis, "The Barrett Version of Robert Southwell's Short Rule of Good Life," *Recusant History*, 7 no.5 (April 1964): 245.

[48]Southwell, 28.

[49]Ibid., 22, 23.

[50]Ibid., 5, 6, 41, 42, 46, 144.

[51]Robert Southwell, "Mary Magdalen's Funeral Teares," (London: 1591) excerpt cited by Helen C. White, *Tudor Books of Saints and Martyrs* (Wisconsin: University of Wisconsin Press, 1963), 262. Compare: Chambers, vol. I, 166.

[52]Southwell, 20, 22. These sentiments are similar to those expressed in a later work by Robert Bellarmine, Southwell's teacher at the Roman College. See *A Most Learned and Pious Treatise, full of Divine and Humane Philosophy, framing a Ladder, wherby our Mindes may ascend to God by the Steppes of his Creatures*, trans. T.B. Gent/Francis Young, (printed secretly in England, 1615).

[53]Southwell, 45,47, 133, ch.6.

[54]Ibid., 122-123.

[55]Louis Cognet, *Post-Reformation Spirituality*, trans., P. Hepburne Scott, (New York: Hawthorn Books, 1959), 53.

[56]Lorenzo Scupoli, *The Spiritual Conflict. Written in Italian by a devout servant of God: and lately translated into English* (Douai, Charles Boscard, 1603-1610).

[57]*AB*, cited by Chambers, vol. I, 53,54.

[58]Ibid.

[59]Cognet, 53.

[60]Thomas H. Clancy, S.J., *An Introduction to Jesuit Life: The Constitutions and History through 435 Years* (St. Louis: The Institute of Jesuit Sources, 1976), 43.

[61]Scupoli, ch. 8, c. 6r.

[62]Ibid., ch. 19.

[63]Ibid., A 4, l.

[64]Ibid., A 3 r.

[65]Ibid., ch. 22, F; ch. 4, B 6; ch. 11, D 4.

[66]Ibid., ch. 13.

[67]Evennett, 41.

[68]Scupoli, chapters 1-3, 14, 15.

[69]Retreat Notes," April, 1619, Wetter (VIII): 7; Orchard, 41.

[70]Scupoli, ch. 4.

[71]Letter to Roger Lee, November 1, 1615, see Appendix A.

[72]Reflection, Spa, Liège, 1616, Wetter (VI): 8, cited in part by Chambers, vol.I, 396.

[73]Scupoli, ch.5. This theme permeates Mary Ward's writings.

[74]*AB*, cited by Chambers, vol. I, 55.

[75]*AB*, cited by Chambers, vol. I, 69; Orchard, 12.

[76]Philip Howard, Earl of Arundel, and John Gerard, S.J., trans., *An Epistle in the Person of Christ to the Faithfull soule* (printed secretly in England, 1595).

[77]Southwell, *Shorte Rule of Good Life*, preface: final paragraph.

[78]Gaspare Loarte, S.J. *The Exercise of a Christian Life*, trans. James Sancer (pseudonym of Stephen Brinkley). (London, William Carter), 1579, 16.

[79]See *Spiritual Conflict*, ch.3, B 6.

[80]Mary Poyntz, *A Briefe Relation of the Holy Life and happy Death of our dearest Mother of Blessed Memmory, Mrs Mary Ward* (manuscript, c. 1647-1657).

[81]Peter Canisius, *Certayne necessarie principles of religion, which may be entitled, a catechisme conteyning all the partes of the Christian and Catholicque fayth... amplified and Englished by T.I.* (London: William Carter, 1578-1579).

[82]Lawrence Vaux, *Catechisme, or a Christian doctrine, necessarie for children and the ignorant people... Whereunto is adjoined a briefe forme of Confession* (printed secretly in England, 1599), author's preface and ch.1.

[83]Robert Persons, *First Book of the Christian Exercise*, (1607), preface; part 1, ch.1, 11-14; part 3, par.39.

[84]Robert Persons, *The Christian Directory* (1607), part 1, ch. 4:33.

[85]de Guibert, *The Jesuits*, 279-280.

[86]Pollen, *Memoirs of Father Robert Persons (continued)*, 153-155.

[87]Ibid., 8, 100, 547, 575.

[88]Luis De Granada. *A Memoriall of a Christian Life.*

[89]Ibid., 2, 5, 21, 22, 488, ch. 3 & 4, treatise 4.

[90]Ibid., 486-540, 554-559, 575, 585. Compare: *Spiritual Exercises*, #23, #165-#167, #326.

[91]In her instructions c. 1613 to one of her companions who was appointed infirmarian Mary Ward cites instances of St. Bernard's care for the sick. (Chambers, vol. I, 301.) An edition of St. Bernard's *Rule of Good Life*, translated by Father Antony Batt and published in 1633 is to be found at the convent of the Institute of the Blessed Virgin Mary in York.

[92]Philip Caraman, trans., *John Gerard: The Autobiography of an Elizabethan* (London, New York, Toronto: Longmans, Greene and Co., 1956), 146-

149. As Vice-Prefect of the mission in Belgium in 1609 Hoskins had care of the spiritual welfare of the recusant exiles there. He had direct access to the Latin manuscript which was in the Jesuit house at Antwerp from 1590. See: David Crane, "English Translations of the *Imitatio Christi* in the Sixteenth and Seventeenth Centuries." *Recusant History* 13 no. 2 (October 1975): 85, 86.

[93]Thirteen translations and three paraphrases of the *Imitation* seem to have been published between 1500 and 1700, nine Catholic and seven Protestant. Nine extant editions between 1613 and 1641 have been located. Worthington's version (1617-1671), connected with Cambridge Platonists became the standard seventeenth Protestant version and was based upon Preston's modification of Hoskins' translation. (Crane, 81, 87, 89, 92, 97n.31).

[94]Jean Delumeau, *Sin and Fear: The Emergence of a Western Guilt Culture 13th-18th Centuries*, trans. Eric Nicholson (New York: St. Martin's Press, 1990), 23.

[95]Crane, 84-86.

[96]Pollen considers that I.M. is John Mitchell of the English Charterhouse at Bruges. (A.C. Southern in *Elizabethan Recusant Prose*, 214).

[97]John Bucke, compiler, *Instructions for the use of the beades, conteining many matters of meditacion or mentall prayer* (Louvain: Jan Maes, 1589), 297-300.

[98]Allison, "The Writings of Father Henry Garnet, S.J. (1551-1606)," 13.

[99]The original end-papers appear to have been forcibly removed at some period, suggesting that the originals bore Mary Ward's signature. In the process the last few leaves have also been removed. When Benedict XIV approved the office of General Superior in 1849 but at the same time forbad the members of the Institute to call Mary Ward their Foundress, Mother Coyney, Superior of the Bar Convent, York, destroyed any material signed by Mary Ward.

[100]This act made it an offence to import, print or buy "any Popish primmers, Ladies Psalters, Manuals, Rosaries, Portals, or lives of the Saints in what language soever they shall be printed or written . . ." (Blom, 35).

[101]J.M. Blom, *The Post-Tridentine English Primer* (London: Publications of the Catholic Record Society, 1982), 13, 46, 47, 113.

[102]John Hungerforde Pollen, S.J., ed., *Bedingfield Papers, &c* (Miscellanea VI, *CRS*, VII, London, 1909), 22, 27, 29.

[103]F.G., compiler and translator, *A Manual of Prayer newly gathered out of many and divers famous authors as well auncient as of the tyme present* (Rouen: Fr. Persons' Press, 1583).

[104]J.D. Crichton, "The Manual of 1614," *Recusant History*, 17 no.2 (October, 1984): 162.

[105]John O'Malley, "Early Jesuit Spirituality: Spain and Italy," in *Christian Spirituality: Post-Reformation and Modern,* eds, Louis Dupré and Don E. Saliers), (New York: Crossroad, 1989), 24-25.

[106]Louis Martz, *The Poetry of Meditation,* cited by John R. Roberts, *A Critical Anthology of English Recusant Devotional Prose, 1558-1603* (Pittsburgh: Duquesne University Press, 1966), 22.

[107]Both may have borrowed from Garcia Ximenes de Cisneros (died 1510). See Pierre Pourrat, *Christian Spirituality,* vol. III, part 1, *From the Renaissance to Jansenism,* trans., W.H. Mitchell, (Westminster, Maryland: The Newman Press, 1953), 19-21.

[108]Roberts, 27.

[109]Foley, *Records,* I, 456; Morris, *Troubles,* first series, 235,982,983.

[110]*A Briefe Collection Concerning the Love of God towards Mankinde. . . . With other vertuous prayers* (Doway: Laurence Kellam, 1603), 47-58.

[111]Allison, "Writings of Henry Garnet," 20.

[112]Southern, 189.

[113]David Knowles, *The English Mystical Tradition* (New York: Harper & Brothers, 1961), 190-191; Roberts, 7.

[114]Morey, 151; Marion Norman, I.B.V.M., *Seventeenth Century Devotional Prose,* paper delivered at Post-Reformation History Conference (St. Anne's College Oxford, 1981), 3, photocopied.

[115]Gordon S Wakefield, "Anglican Spirituality," in *Christian Spirituality: Post-Reformation and Modern,* 261; James A. Devereux, "The Collects of the First Book of Common Prayer as Works of Translation," reprinted from *Studies in Philology,* LXVI 5 (October 1969): 719.

[116]David Matthew, *Catholicism in England 1535-1935: Portrait of a Minority: Its Culture and Tradition* (Toronto: Longmans, Green and Co., 1936), 56-57.

Chapter 2

Mary Ward's Spirituality in the Context of the Period 1607-1645

When I was about fifteen years old I had a religious vocation.... My parents ... would not consent, for I was the eldest child and much loved, especially by my father. I was therefore obliged to remain in England six years and some months longer. During that time God took the matter in hand and freed me by means considered by many, more divine than human." (Autobiography)[1]

It is now ... twenty five years since I left my native country and parents.... Ten years I employed in prayer, fasting and penance, and other things suitable for such a result, to learn in what order of religion or mode of life I was to spend my days. That which unworthily I now profess, and by the mercy of God have for twenty two years practised, was totally and entirely (as far as human judgement can arrive) ordained and commended to me by the express word of Him who will not deceive, nor can be deceived. (Memorial to Pope Urban VIII, November 1630)[2]

On February 7, 1631, nine weeks after writing these words to Pope Urban VIII, Mary Ward, accused of being a "heretic, schismatic and rebel to the Holy Church," was by the order of the Inquisition imprisoned for two months in Munich. In the preceding year her houses in St. Omer, Liège, Cologne, and Trier had been ordered to close. The Bull, *Pastoralis Romani Pontificis*, suppressing her Institute, was signed in January 1631.

The years 1607-1615 were crucial for the emergence of the definitive aspects of Mary Ward's lived and formulated spirituality. The stages in her understanding of the "mode of life" to which she was called comprise her discernment in 1600 that she was called to religious life, her entering the Flemish Poor Clares as a lay-sister in 1606, the foundation of a convent for the English Poor Clares in 1608 and her realization in 1609 that monastic life was not her vocation. In 1611 the nature of her vocation was finally clarified when she understood that she was to model her Institute after the Society of Jesus. This period culminates in the intellectual illumination which in 1615 taught her the nature of the inner freedom which unites apostolic activity with the pursuit of union with God. Through these insights she understood the essential qualities which should characterize not only the members of an apostolic congregation of religious women, but all Christians.

Mary Ward's definitive spirituality arose during the counter-Reformation. Despite national and cultural differences certain common features of the era's spirituality can be discerned. These include: the value attributed to the priesthood and religious life; the renewed interest in mystical works; the role played by female monastic and apostolic communities, and the influence of the Society of Jesus. Mary Ward's endeavor to found a congregation of religious women, unenclosed and governed by women, reflects the spirituality of her age. The failure of her attempts reveals the limitations in its underlying anthropology and in its understanding of how contemplation and apostolic activity can be in harmony.

2.1 The Value Accorded to the Priesthood and Religious Life

Recusant devotional literature stressed that spiritual perfection was not the exclusive property of the clergy or of those in religious orders. In fact, the recusants' lived spirituality endorses the significant role the laity played in the survival of Catholicism at this time. At the same time, the number of priestly and religious vocations and new religious orders in Europe founded during this period reflects the value accorded to the priesthood and religious life.

Statistics for English priests between 1558 and 1800 reveal that in the late sixteenth and early seventeenth centuries the majority came from Yorkshire (388) and Lancashire (394).[3] Of the young Yorkshiremen who either began their studies for the priesthood or joined clerical orders between 1585 and 1606, sixty one had been ordained or professed by 1611.

Many of these came from families either related to or well known by Mary Ward, such as the Babthorpes, Inglebys, Constables, Middletons, Percys, Nevilles, Thwings, and Wrights. In 1618 her brother George was professed as a Jesuit and her cousin William was ordained.[4] Many young men from Yorkshire became priests because the gentry there, including the Wards, sent their sons to the Jesuit College at St. Omer. Six years after its opening in 1593 many of its hundred students became Jesuits, secular clergy, or joined other religious orders.[5]

During the seventeenth century twenty-one religious communities for English women were founded, including twelve between the years 1604 and 1648. While a vocation to religious life is properly seen in the context of God's call to individuals, on the human level, religious literature and historical factors influenced the many religious foundations at this time.

Recusant devotional works not only inspired a desire for more intimate following of Christ but were often written by members of religious Orders and held up the monastic life as a model for the laity. In the late sixteenth century, as Mary Ward's own experience bears out, the dominant belief of English recusants and the clergy who served them was that the interests of Catholicism would be better served by young women remaining in England. Increased religious conflict after the Gunpowder Plot of 1605 and the introduction of the Oath of Allegiance in 1606, however, caused many recusant families, including the Babthorpes, to leave England.

In addition, large households contained young people of related gentry families. The missionary priests to whom they offered shelter not only provided information about religious orders abroad but assisted young women to join these orders. Mary Ward recalled Richard Holtby's accounts of religious life overseas. She was also acquainted with the families of many who entered convents abroad. These included Mary Percy, who founded a Benedictine house at Brussels in 1598, and Margaret Clement, a member of Thomas More's household, who became Abbess of the Flemish Canonesses of St. Ursula's convent in Louvain. Mary Ward prior to leaving England in 1606 stayed with Mrs Bentley, whose mother, Mrs Roper, was related to Thomas More. In 1596 Margaret Clitheroe's daughter had become a member of St. Ursula's.

Assisted by John Gerard, in 1609 Mary Wiseman established the convent of St. Monica's in Louvain for English members of St. Ursula's. Grace Babthorpe joined this Order after her husband's death. One of her daughters and three of her great granddaughters entered Mary Ward's Institute. Mary Ward's sister Barbara became one of her first companions, while another sister, Frances, joined Mary Lovel's Carmelite convent established at Antwerp in 1619.

2.2. The Spirituality Expressed by English Women
in Enclosed Religious Orders

While recusant devotional literature remained popular with women in enclosed religious orders, a growing familiarity with the works of the mystics is evident. The archives of the English Bridgettines of Syon contain lists of works used from the mid-sixteenth century. Included are those of de Granada, Loarte, Scupoli, Lanspergius, Southwell and Persons. In addition one finds Benet of Canfield's *The Rule of Perfection* (1609), Luis de la Puente's *Meditations* (1610), *The Lyf of Mother Teresa of Jesus* (1611), Luca Pinelli's *The Mirror of Religious Perfection* (1618), Alfonso Rodriguez' treatises on mental prayer and perfection (1627-1632) and Francis de Sales' *Treatise of the Love of God* (1630). In Latin are many works by Augustine, Ludolph of Saxony and Tauler.

Religious women played an influential role in renewing interest in both ascetical and mystical works. As early as 1548 Ruysbroeck's writings were being used by the Canonesses of St. Ursula in Louvain. Benet of Canfield (1562-1610) dedicated his *Rule of Perfection* to Agatha Wiseman. Mary Percy collaborated in the translation of the *Breve Compendio* or *Abridgement of Christian Perfection* (1612). In 1617, John Wilson, manager of the Jesuit printing press at St. Omer, dedicated his edition of works by Antonio de Molina and Francisco Arias to Mary Wiseman. Michael Walpole, S.J., confessor to Donna Luisa de Carvajal from 1606 to 1610, produced the first English translation of Teresa of Avila's life in 1611. Two years earlier Mary Ward had received a copy of Teresa of Avila's life and rule from Giles Schoondonck, S.J., rector of the Jesuit College at St. Omer from 1600 to 1617.[6]

In his spiritual instructions to the Benedictine community at Cambrai from 1624, Augustine Baker used *The Cloud of Unknowing* and his own editions of the works of Richard Rolle, Walter Hilton, and Julian of Norwich. A small anthology of Baker's writings contains passages from the works of Tauler, Thomas à Kempis, Teresa of Avila and Henry Suso. Baker's index to the *Sancta Sophia* contains an index of reading for the nuns at Cambrai. Included are the *Breve Compendio*, the works on mysticism by Alvarez de la Paz (in Latin), the *Revelations* of St. Bridget, and Benet of Canfield's *Rule of Perfection*.[7]

At the same time mystical works were held in suspicion. Except for their use by Baker, no works of the English mystics were published in England until Julian of Norwich's *XVI Revelations of Divine Love* appeared in 1670. Fr. Lewis of Lyons in his preface to *The Lyf of the Mother Teresa of Jesus* feels compelled to defend as "signs of grace" the "revelations related and interior matters treated, which pass in prayer and are above ordinary discourse."[8] Associated with the suspicion of mysticism was what later came to be condemned as "Quietism."[9] In 1689 Benet of Canfield's *Rule of Perfection* was placed on the Index. In 1601 the works of Elizabetta Bellinzaga which were submitted to Clement VIII by Claudio Aquaviva, general Superior of the Jesuits, had been condemned as unorthodox. The *Breve Compendio* which she composed under the guidance of the Jesuit Achille Gagliardi was suspected of identifying union with God with deification. From 1585 to 1598 several editions of this work appeared in French, the edition of 1596 including Bérulle's *Bref Discours*. By 1626 fifty translations and editions had been issued. The 1612 edition's warning against misrepresentation was meant to forestall charges against its orthodoxy. The work, however, was placed on the Index in 1703.[10] After the Council of Trent both the active following of Christ in service of one's neighbor and asceticism and union with God in prayer were epitomised in the charism of the Society of Jesus. Many, however, viewed the Society of Jesus as an anomaly because contemplation was still regarded as "more perfect" than the "mixed life" its members exemplified.

Moreover, no religious orders existed in which women could combine religious life and the active apostolate. English women who came to St. Omer, Antwerp, Brussels and Louvain found contemplative orders following the rules of Saints Augustine, Benedict, Francis and Teresa. Until Mary Ward established a foundation for English Poor Clares in 1608 the only specifically English convents for women were Mary Percy's Benedictines (1598) and the exiled Brigettines of Syon.

Contemporary writings reflect the different concepts of religious life for men and women at this time. A Jesuit manuscript of 1604 contains "an instruction and direction for the spiritual help of such English gentlewomen as desire to lead a more retired and recollected life than the ordinary in England doth yield."[11] While young English men were being trained for work on the English mission, religious life for women was envisaged solely in monastic terms.

The condemnation of Mary Ward's plans rested largely on her conviction that enclosure was inconsistent with the apostolic form of religious life she envisaged. Why did the prevailing understanding make enclosure an essential aspect of religious life for women? This understanding identified holiness with "contempt" of and separation from the "world," and included an anthropology which reflected a particular view of the nature of women. Canon law, church practice, and rigid societal requirements and expectations of women, established a tradition regarding suitable apostolates for women religious which succeeding generations accepted in good faith.

Enclosure

Within the lives of all human beings love of God and love of neighbor cannot be divorced. Enclosure, as with all aspects of religious life, must serve these two ends. Monastic spirituality taught that enclosure has a valid place in religious life. Religious life and enclosure, however, are not necessarily synonymous. As Noreen Hunt notes, the study of nuns' enclosure is relatively new but her research suggests that its history is "multifarious and inconsistent." She points out that nuns assisted St. Boniface in his work of evangelization in the year 748, and that while in Anglo-Saxon England enclosure was taken for granted as intrinsic to monasticism, it was not unduly laboured, and nuns enjoyed a freedom later denied.[12]

The standardization of enclosure among the new orders of the late Middle Ages had a pragmatic dimension. James Cain in his study of the canonical regulations regarding enclosure writes that the conciliar legislation of this period understood the juridic status of women as "one of complete subjection to the dominion of man, having no authority of her own."[13] Theologians and canonists generally accepted as a basic reality the idea that woman was a deficient creature. Gratian's legal synthesis *Discordantium Canonum* (the *Decretum*), even denies that woman was made in God's image.[14] Boniface VIII was the first Pope to establish an absolute cloister for all religious women. His decree (*Periculoso*, 1298), made no reference to enclosure being supportive of contemplative life but, as its name suggests was a reforming and punitive measure.

The Council of Trent made enclosure key to reforming convents. In 1563, the Council enjoined all bishops "under the judgement of God" and "pain of eternal malediction" to see that the nuns' enclosure be carefully restored, with the help of secular rulers if necessary. The Council declared that "for no nun, after her profession, shall it be lawful to go out of her convent, even for a brief period, under any pretext whatever, except for some lawful cause which is to be approved of by the bishop."[15] In two further constitutions, *Circa Pastoralis* (1566) and *Lubricum Vitae Genus* (1568), Pius V extended enclosure to women in third orders who had taken solemn vows and lived in community. By the end of the sixteenth century the belief that enclosure was an integral part of religious life for women was firmly entrenched.

Underlying this belief was the concept that "religious perfection," especially in the case of women, lay in separation from activity within the world, a concept far removed from the innovative spirit of the times and its value for human secular life. The dominant role played by the law is also evident. Martin de Azpilcueta, a canonist, was called upon for a decision regarding enclosure in the case of the Roman community of Torre de Specchi, founded in 1433. In Augustus Barbosa's summary of canon law (1620-1621) 106 of the 183 prescriptions referring to Moniales dealt with enclosure. Publication of this summary coincided with Mary Ward's presentation of her proposals to Gregory XIV.[16]

More damaging in the case of religious Orders was the Council of Trent's apparent concentration on the external aspects of reform at the expense of the internal. In 1629 Cardinal Pazmany, Primate of Hungary, defended Mary Ward's work and urged that the danger of the imposition of enclosure would prevent works of education and instruction from continuing. In his view the internal reform resulting from such works far outweighed the possible dangers of non-enclosure. Despite these representations Francesco Ingoli, the secretary of Propaganda and a canonist, stated that it mattered "little" what the times demanded; the Canon Law of the Church would not allow women to live in community unless they became religious and, as this entailed enclosure, all congregations that refused enclosure must be suppressed.[17]

The papal Bull of 1631 that suppressed Mary Ward's Institute reflects the prevailing anthropology regarding the capabilities of women. Condemning Mary Ward's rejection of the main elements of canonical enclosure, the Papal Bull criticized her members' pastoral ministry and catechetical instruction. It declared that ministry in private houses was unsuitable for "ladies and young girls" and that women were incapable of the knowledge necessary for teaching the Scriptures to the laity.[18]

Mary Ward's clerical opponents also attacked her Institute's lack of enclosure and "boldness" in usurping the role of men. In 1615, Bishop Blaise of St. Omer, who had approved Mary Ward's work, found it necessary to defend her and her companions against complaints that they overstepped the "limits of their sex" by rejecting cloister and by teaching.[19] In 1622, Matthew Kellison, President of Douay College reiterated these criticisms. He alleged that there was public criticism of Mary Ward's members because they encouraged others to "acts of contrition and meditation" and because their lives were similar to those of the laity. Robert Sherwood, Procurator of the English Benedictines, accused Mary Ward and her companions of preaching and of causing scandal by their lack of enclosure. William Harrison, Arch-priest of England, who bitterly opposed the Jesuits and saw Mary Ward's Institute as another example of Jesuit influence, regarded women as feeble, erroneous, fickle, soft and garrulous.[20]

In the spiritual literature one also finds similar stereotyped views regarding women, and a sharp distinction between the ways men and women can through religious vows fulfil the twofold command to love God and others. Fr. Lewis, author of the preface to Walpole's edition of the life of St. Teresa of Avila, expresses amazement at Teresa's accomplishments given that she was a woman, and not a "valyaunt man armed with learning." Citing St. Paul, he adds that "it belongeth not to women to teach, but to be taught."[21] The *Directory to the Spiritual Exercises* of 1599 recommends that "the same method should be followed with women as with persons of little education, unless one or other among them should have the capacity for spiritual things" (9:16), advice which is not found in directories prior to 1566.[22]

William Broderick sees Mary Ward as revealing the limitations of the Church in her time and the limitations of her age. John Bossy uses blunter terms referring to "Tridentine rigor and sexual vulgarity" as being "about equally represented" as motives for the suppression of her work.[23] In seeking to adapt the matter and manner of the Society of Jesus to women Mary Ward chose a form of apostolic life which the Church approved. Her problems arose from the fact that she was seeking this for women.

In her initial desire in 1606 for the "most strict and secluded" Religious Order, Mary Ward referred to a "penuriousness" which she "resented even then" which considered that "women did not know how to do good except to themselves."[24] Nevertheless, the influences of her early years spent among the courageous and apostolic lay women of Yorkshire could not be gainsaid. In 1608, through prayer for the people of her own nation she was led to understand that she was to found a convent of Poor Clares for English exiles. Mary Ward's further enlightenment of 1609 and 1611 came while she was engaged in apostolic work, first amid the penal conditions of London, and then while she and her first companions were teaching English refugees and local girls in St. Omer.

The events of 1607-1615 which led to Mary Ward's conviction that it was God's will for her to found an apostolic religious order for women, unenclosed and ruled by women, brought her insights into the particular qualities of women which could enrich the spirituality of all. Referring to the somewhat questionable efforts made in 1608 to convince her to remain with the Poor Clares, she states that "without going against her nature" it would have been impossible for her "to act half - heartedly in things of the soul where all is intended and should be whole and entire." These dispositions were in her view "special gifts of God to any person, but particularly to those of our sex who seek to walk in the way of the spirit."[25]

The interior conflict Mary Ward experienced from 1607 to 1609 arose largely from the prevailing concept of religious life for women and an underlying anthropology that was alien to the harmony her nature sought. Until 1609 she regarded austerity and enclosure as the principle features associated with religious life as it existed in the church of her time. In 1615, through her insights into the interior disposition which she termed "the estate of justice," Mary Ward came to understand how contemplation and action can be in harmony. Both arise from the one source, love of God overflowing into love of neighbor. Mary Ward saw the qualities of this interior state, namely, the "freedom to refer all to God", an "entire application and apt disposition to all good works," and sincerity/verity as "especially requisite," and as the "foundation" of all those other virtues necessary to be exercised by those following the Institute's way of life.[26]

Mary Ward, however, did not regard the virtues of the "estate of justice" as exclusive to women. Rather, she was quick to refute any artificial dichotomy between the spirituality of men and women. Addressing the "fathers of the Society" she emphasized the necessity of these virtues and warned them against relying on their natural

talents and opportunities for learning.[27] Christ is the exemplar of all
virtue and all are called to follow him. Learning that one of these
Fathers had claimed that the fervor of members of her Institute would
soon decline because they were "but women" she replied:

> Fervour is a will to do well, that is, a preventing grace of God and a
> gift given gratis by God, which we could not merit. It is true fervour
> doth many times grow cold but what is the cause? It is because we are
> imperfect women, and love not verity.... It is not *veritas hominum*,
> verity of men, nor verity of women, but *veritas Domini*, and this verity
> women may have as well as men. If we fail, it is for want of this verity
> and not because we are women.[28]

This discernment not only enabled Mary Ward not only to understand how the essentials of the Society of Jesus could be lived by
women, but also broke through the dichotomy accepted in her age
between the spirituality and practice for men and women. Equally
significantly, her insights regarding a spirituality which unites contemplation and action in non-monastic religious life brought her to
a deep understanding of the essential disposition for all. The commonly accepted view, which divorced contemplation from apostolic
activity and regarded contemplative religious life and enclosure as
the more perfect, not only excluded many from joining religious communities but also denigrated the vocation of the laity. Mary Ward
directed her apostolate to the universal good of the Church and the
personal good of individuals, whether their vocation was to a life in
the world or in religion.[29]

André Ravier points out that to "found" a religious order is not
only to provide an original basis but to launch and communicate a
new creative spirit.[30] Joseph Grisar, the historian who devoted many
years to the study of Mary Ward, sees her unique significance
(*einzigartige Bedeutung*) in the fact that she was the first to attempt to
found a strictly-organized order of women who would render to the
Church every kind of service in the apostolate and work for the whole
world, freed from the hindrance formerly imposed upon their mo-
bility of movement.[31] While Mary Ward chose a broader task than
other women founders of her time, she is, nevertheless, representative of the spirituality developing among these women.

All ministry in the Church, as indeed every form of religious life, comes from the Holy Spirit and is the work of the Spirit present in the church and working in individual lives. Evennett notes, however, that every successful movement of general reform within the traditional framework of Catholicism has always been accompanied, if not inspired, by reforms and progress in religious life.[32] Nevertheless, studies of the distinct insights women bring to the carrying out of the universal call to human beings to love God and neighbor have been relatively few. The part played by women to establish new forms of religious life is an important feature of the spirituality of the counter-Reformation period.

2.3 Efforts by Women to Establish Non-Monastic Religious Orders

The women who attempted to establish apostolic forms of religious life without enclosure reflect a realization of the role women could play in meeting the needs of Church and society in the changed situation of their times. It is noteworthy that the most numerous movements of women to apostolic communities were, in the main, in the northern parts of Europe. Here, women generally held a freer and more responsible position in society and accepted enclosure with less docility. It was in northern Europe that the Beguines had made their first establishments. Communities of women in Belgium who took simple vows include the Agnettines, Brigettines, Daughters of Our Lady, and Sisters of St. Catherine.[33] At the same time Rome regarded the "north" with suspicion, associating it with the sources of revolt against the established order in the church.

Robert Bellarmine noted in 1620 that many bishops allowed greater flexibility to communities of women when he remarked to the Bishop of Chur that constitutions regarding enclosure "do not seem to have crossed the Alps."[34] This applied even to such monastic orders as the Flemish female Cistercians who did not observe enclosure. In 1621 Mary Ward, writing to Gregory XV, noted that the absence of enclosure in convents of Flanders caused neither difficulty nor scandal.[35]

Members of Madame Acarie's circle in Paris sought to undertake work appropriate to the needs of the times such as the education of young women and community service. In 1608 Madame de Saint Beuve and Françoise de Bermond established a community similar to the Ursulines. Their members came from those among Madame Acarie's circle who did not feel a vocation to the Carmelites. Despite their reservations, however, they were forced to accept enclosure in 1612 to receive papal approbation.[36]

Jeanne Lestonnac, aided by Père Bordes, S.J., founded the Compagnie de Notre Dame at Bordeaux. Its approval (1617) was conditional upon being subject to the local bishop and associated with the Benedictines. The Visitation Sisters, founded by Francis de Sales and Jane Frances de Chantal in 1618, also had to accept enclosure. Only the Bourgogne Ursulines (founded in 1606 by Anne de Xaintconge) and Louise de Marillac's Daughters of Charity were able to gain approval without enclosure and this only by accepting a status less than that of religious.[37] Marguerite Bourgeois who founded the Congregation of Notre Dame in Quebec declined to join the Ursulines because of their acceptance of enclosure.

The Society of Jesus played a significant role in the spiritual development of many of these religious communities. Individual Jesuits often assisted founders of new Orders, while enclosed Religious, such as Mary Percy's Benedictines and Mary Lovel's Carmelites, favored Ignatian methods of prayer and Jesuit direction. Jesuits also published many of the devotional works these women used.

Ignatian spirituality and the assistance of individual Jesuits were also significant in the development of Mary Ward's spirituality and practice. After establishing a convent for English Poor Clares in 1608 Mary Ward arranged for its members to make the Spiritual Exercises. In 1609 her enlightenment as to God's will was in terms of God's glory, a central tenet of Ignatian spirituality. Realizing the spiritual nature of the directive she received in 1611 to "take the same of the Society" Mary Ward again turned to the Exercises. She based her annual retreats on the Exercises and advised that her novices make them annually under their superior and "not trouble the fathers."[38] In them and in the Formula of the Institute of the Society[39] lies the essential formulation of the spirituality of Ignatius of Loyola.

2.4 The Spirituality of the Society of Jesus

The spirituality of groups and in particular of religious orders is based on the initial experience of the Founder or first members. With the passing of time, however, this spirituality undergoes adaptation and development. In the context of this work, therefore, the phrase "the spirituality of the Jesuits," comprises both its initial formulation and its specific expression within Mary Ward's era. The former flows from the mystical experiences of St.Ignatius of Loyola and receives its most decisive formulation in the Spiritual Exercises and in the Jesuit Constitutions. The latter is manifested in the directives of the Jesuit General Superiors and in the lived and formulated spirituality of its members. The period under discussion here comprises the generalates of Everard Mercurian (1573-1580), Claudio Aquaviva (1581-1615) and Mutio Vitelleschi (1615-1645).

During Mary Ward's era two different, but inter-related tensions can be detected in the spirituality of the Jesuits. First, in their approach to spiritual guidance, some Jesuits stressed asceticism and were suspicious of mysticism in their approach to spiritual direction, while others recognised the validity of affectivity and encouraged contemplation.[40] Second, the Society of Jesus as a whole experienced tension between the demands of the apostolate and certain traditional forms of religious life.

(i) *The Directory to the Spiritual Exercises, 1599*

Heinrich Bacht believes that by using the term "spiritual exercises" Ignatius of Loyola gave a specific emphasis and purpose to the "active-ascetical component developed in monastic spirituality."[41] The Exercises are not primarily an ascetical treatise or instructions on moral living but an experience to be undergone. Loyola was concerned with the dispositions which lead Christians to adopt the values of Christ, and with the freedom that enables them to choose what is for the greater glory of God. Of particular importance is his understanding of discernment and its underlying anthropology. Discernment of the call of Christ and its different implications requires that Christians recognise their own gifts and the action of the Holy Spirit in their life. Drawing from Scripture and the central truths of revelation, Loyola supplied a variety of exercises within a framework which embraces the whole of salvation history.

Loyola writes that the essential purpose of the Exercises is "the conquest of self and the regulation of one's life in such a way that no decision is made under the influence of any inordinate attachment" (#21). He begins by stressing doing God's will. Although his main concern was initially with those who were about to choose a way of life, he recognised the advantages of the Exercises in leading many to reform their lives in the state in which they were already fixed.

Loyola had provided additional directives for those giving the Exercises. Aquaviva formalized and expanded these in a definitive *Directory*, published first in Florence (1599) and subsequently in Antwerp (1600) and Rome (1606,1615).[42] In general, except from 1621 to 1628 when a novitiate existed secretly in London, Jesuits working on the English mission received their initial formation in colleges abroad. In addition, they took their studies for the priesthood in English Colleges in Douay, St. Omer, Rome, or Spain, where students were encouraged to engage in the Exercises. It is reasonable, therefore, to assume that they had access to Aquaviva's Directory or knew its substance.

Historical studies of the Spiritual Exercises indicate the variety of forms in which they were given. According to André Ravier, depending on the situation and the spiritual activity of the retreatant, the simplest form was the exercises of the "first week" with or without the instructions concerning prayer. These lasted eight days. The "Election" (the choice either of a state of life or a re-dedication to the state already chosen) was not necessarily included. In 1588 Peter Canisius introduced the practice of the short retreat which condensed the Exercises to eight or ten days. In 1609, Decree 29 of the sixth General Congregation of 1609 made such retreats an annual obligation for all Jesuits. This decree had wide influence both inside and outside the Society.[43]

Records from Douay college (up to 1616) and the colleges in Rome and Spain indicate that the spiritual formation of seminarians followed closely that laid down by Ignatius for the German College and recommended in the Jesuits' Constitutions.[44] This included a retreat of eight or ten days made shortly after entry to the College. Contemporary accounts also provide evidence that Jesuits saw their role as being to give the Exercises to ordinary Christians and that in doing so they were responding to the demands of the laity.[45] The *Directory* was, therefore, an important vehicle for transmitting Loyola's foundational experience expressed in the Spiritual Exercises.

The strength of the *Directory* lies in its fidelity to Loyola's charism. Expressing Jesuit spirituality as "the glory of God, and the spiritual profit of our Society, and of our neighbors," it sees the Exercises as the most important instrument given to the Society for the carrying out of these aims (Introduction: 1,12). The scope of their concern for reform and renewal is evident in the extensive treatment given to benefits of the Exercises, not only for clergy and those in religious Orders but for all, regardless of their state in life.

The *Directory* endorses Loyola's recognition that the Exercises need to be adapted to the condition of those who are to engage in them.[46] Its instructions regarding these adaptations and of the dispositions necessary before one can engage in the Exercises appear more prescriptive, however, than Loyola's own instructions or those found in the earliest directories. As has been noted, women while not entirely excluded from making at least an abbreviated form of the exercises, are generally considered to be in the same class as the ignorant and unlearned. Loyola, however, had given the full Exercises to some women and had discussed the possibility of one nun giving them to several others.[47]

Given the central place the *Directory* allocates to the making of an election about choosing a state of life or reforming one's life, the instructions regarding married persons are somewhat ambivalent. Generally, Aquaviva recommended that they be given some exercises of the "first week," together with such other exercises as the "three methods of prayer" (I:7). He advised directors to assist parents to rule their children and servants according to the divine precepts (IX:9). At the same time, Aquaviva suggested that many married persons may "in their own way" be called to perfection and that the Society has an obligation to invite them to this perfection (XXXIV:2). In such cases the full Exercises could be given omitting only those aspects of the "election" which were inapplicable.

In contrast to the earliest directories, Aquaviva's Directory recommended specific devotional literature. Mentioned are many works popular with the English recusants such as a *Breviary* or *Primer* and the *Imitation of Christ*. For the "first week" passages from the works of Dionysius the Carthusian on the four last things and St. Augustine's *Confessions* are advised (III:2,4). The Gospels, Lives of the Saints (carefully selected according to the exercitant's state of life), and passages from St. Bernard and Luis de Granada are suggested for subsequent weeks (III:2-4;XXI:2).

The *Directory* reflects the prevailing tension in counter-Reformation spirituality between asceticism and mysticism. By inserting a chapter not found in provisional drafts prior to 1591, Aquaviva linked the four "weeks" of the Exercises to the three ways of the spiritual life, purgative, illuminative, unitive (XXXIX:1-4).[48] In practice, the purgative way seems to have been regarded as the most common. Indeed, the *Directory* warns against rashly seeking the unitive way (XXXIX:7). Although it acknowledges that the advance to the higher way depends on the Holy Spirit's guidance, it stresses the need for the "sure guidance" of the "spiritual father" whose advice must "be followed in all things" (XXXIX:7,8).[49]

Although the value of the "first week" of the Exercises is beyond question, how its content is presented has considerable importance. De Guibert recognises that commentaries produced at this time reflected a "highly unequal degree of fidelity to the letter or even the fundamental thought" of the Exercises.[50] Similar criticism could also be levelled at some aspects of the *Directory*. In 1615, the seventh Jesuit General Congregation stressed the need that "the proportion and method should be preserved which are customary in the integral Exercises."[51]

In presenting sin and examination of conscience, the *Directory* was influenced by the general tenor of the age. An excessive emphasis on fear as the motive for conversion is seen in its specification of "the torments of hell" for additional considerations (XV:4). Again, the *Directory* states that consideration of God's gifts at this stage is not to arouse gratitude to God but, rather, awareness of our deformity through the misuse of creatures (XII:5). This divorce of gratitude to God and of sorrow for sin reinforces the emphasis on human sinfulness. In addition, the *Directory* recommends that "persons of rank and station" prepare for a general confession after the meditations of the "first week" by reading sections on the different states of life from Martin de Azpilcueta's *Enchiridion* (Manual for Confessors) which takes a legal approach and focuses on the negative aspects of morality.

The *Directory* is faithful to the Exercises in highlighting Christ as the model of all holiness. Meditations on Christ's life and Passion and those on the Resurrection were, however, allocated to the "illuminative" and "unitive" ways. Since the *Directory* emphasized the "purgative" way as most common and was restrictive in its choice of those who could make the whole of the Exercises, these meditations were in many cases either curtailed or omitted (XVIII:5,6). In addition, the *Directory's* focus on human sinfulness tends to overshadow consideration of the mercy of Christ which is a key element of the "first week." Many women in Religious Congregations could testify that this tendency persisted until recent years.

As will be developed more fully in Chapter 4, Mary Ward's lived and formulated spirituality shows the influence of the spirituality, anthropology, and theology underlying the Spiritual Exercises. At the same time, the direction she received in 1606-1607, and the matter proposed for her meditations in subsequent retreats reflect the limitations noted above.[52] Her retreat notes and subsequent practice, however, indicate that she was able to go to the heart of Loyola's original inspiration.

Mary Ward's understanding of "the estate of justice" brought insights about how contemplation and apostolic activity can be brought into harmony. Here, it is interesting to note the tensions Jesuits were experiencing between the demands of the apostolate and certain traditional forms of religious life.

The attempts by Mercurian and Aquaviva to clarify the relationship of contemplation and apostolic activity within the Society reflect that tension. Both affirmed the efforts of the Second General Congregation under Francis Borgia to introduce uniform hours of prayer for all Jesuits. In these moves Robert O'Malley finds a drift from that freedom of spirit on which Ignatius' spiritual doctrine rests and an increasing shift toward system, regulation and uniformity.[53]

These attempts to clarify the relationship of contemplation and apostolic activity occurred amid the expanding missionary activities of individual Jesuits on the one hand, and, on the other hand, the progressive structurization of the Society. In this context, Iparaguirre draws attention to the contrast between the liberty of action of those engaged in missionary work and the rigorous rules existing in Jesuit colleges.[54] Mary Ward's greatest support came, significantly, from those Jesuits who combined their missionary apostolate with the publication of devotional literature. Those involved almost entirely in administration either gave her little assistance or actively opposed her plans.

(ii) *Expressions of the Spirituality of the Society of Jesus*
Roger Lee and John Gerard

The importance of the Spiritual Exercises for Jesuit spirituality is reflected in the spirituality of Roger Lee and John Gerard, two Jesuits who played a significant role in Mary Ward's developing spirituality. As a layman Lee had been given the Exercises by Gerard and often gave them to his students. Both evinced in their lives and in instructions to Mary Ward and her companions that union of contemplation and apostolic zeal which is the essence of Ignatian spirituality.

In a letter of November 27, 1615, Mary Ward wrote to Roger Lee, her confessor for eight years, of the "content" (happiness) she experienced in following his direction. She also stated that knowing that he was ordained by Christ to be her director and helper was one of the most significant graces given her.[55] It was he whom William Baldwin, Vice-Prefect of the Jesuit English Mission, had nominated to give the Exercises to the members of the convent of Poor Clares she had founded in 1608.

Roger Lee, born in England in 1568, had been among the many young men who assisted John Gerard in his missionary work and visited him during his imprisonment. After spending some time in the English College in Rome, he entered the Jesuits in 1600 and was ordained in 1604. From 1605 to 1614 he worked at the English College in St. Omer. The historian Dodd and contemporary Jesuits record Lee's assistance to Mary Ward and her companions. It was rumored that Lee was moved from St. Omer at the end of 1614 for not having disapproved of Mary Ward's aims and work. He died in the last months of 1615 at Dunkirk while awaiting a boat to take him to England.

Lee's spirituality is found in the records of his ascetical instructions kept by Mary Ward's companions.[56] Emphasizing the essential relationship of contemplation and service of others, he describes "true devotion" as such "that we come to God for God, when obedience so requireth and be content to leave God for God." God's greater glory motivates our love of others. Referring to the opposition which Mary Ward and her companions were experiencing, Lee urges them to avoid "pusillanimity" for virtue does not lie in fleeing from opportunities or liberation from difficulties. Rather, the Institute's security lies in its members' fidelity to God's will. Lee describes true holiness as manifested in the interior disposition of "indifference" - being utterly at God's disposal - purity of intention, trust in and gratitude to God, humility - the antidote to pride - and prudence. Mary Ward's writings echo these sentiments.

Faithful to Loyola's spirituality and contrary to prevailing tendencies, Lee stresses that love not fear should motivate all actions and desires for virtue, for God requires "nothing of you but your heart." His references to intimacy with the persons of the Trinity, and especially to Christ, are typically Ignatian and admit of a more mystical tone than is found in most devotional literature.

Lee's concept of perfection as consisting in "the perfect contempt of the world, the flesh, and the devil" and the "continual denial and abnegation of oneself" to follow Christ crucified, is in tune with the spirituality formulated in the devotional literature of the period. Likewise, he extols meditations on the Passion and the value of the sacrament of Penance. In view of the fact that he was a product of recusant England and was preparing to return to England in 1615, it is not surprising that he speaks a great deal of courage to endure in the face of suffering. In tune with the Jesuit Constitutions he refers to his mission "under the standard of the Cross."

In treating of discernment of the temptations of the "spiritual enemy" which Lee likens to "papers diversely painted of which, if one do not please the nature of man, commonly another doeth," he follows the rules set down in the Exercises. He points to the value of "consolation" in making its recipients "fit to undergo greater matters for God." "Concurrence with God's grace" is shown in "tranquillity" and "good going forward."

At the same time, Lee's stress on obedience to one's "ghostly father" reflects the similar emphasis in the *Directory* and appears to go further than the advice given in the Exercises. Between 1612 and 1614 he played an influential role in the drawing up of a Plan for the Institute which diverged from Mary Ward's intentions to model her Institute on the Society of Jesus. Her spiritual notes of 1612-1614 reflect the tension she experienced between obedience to what she saw as God's will and obedience to her confessor.[57]

Recognizing the depth of her spiritual insights Roger Lee had asked Mary Ward to put in writing her mystical experiences and her enlightenment regarding her Institute. At the same time, he was forced to tread a fine line between obedience to his Superiors and belief in her insights. Mary Ward's last letter to Lee (November 27, 1615) testifies that Jesuit administrators strictly controlled his contact with her and that he had to submit to their opposition to her plan. Since many of her opponents linked her Institute to the Jesuits Mary Ward wisely disguised her letters to Lee.

Mary Ward's vision for the Institute went beyond Roger Lee's. In his encouragement to her companions he speaks of the future advantages of the Institute in terms of its works. In contrast, she looks to the source of these works. She sees the Institute as arising from the will of God and the prerequisites for its accomplishment of good as lying in the disposition of its members. After Lee's death in 1615 she abandoned the early plans he gave her; her subsequent formulations resemble the Jesuit Constitutions far more closely.

As was the case with Roger Lee, John Gerard was also a product of recusant England and attended the English College in Rome. After his ordination in 1588 he returned to England where his ministry (1588-1594) consisted of hearing general confessions, giving the Exercises, assisting young men and women to discern their vocation in life, teaching his penitents methods of meditation and reading ascetical books with them. His aim was to win over heretics and schismatics, first among the gentry and their servants and then among the poor who came to their households.

During his imprisonment in England in 1594 and 1597 Gerard made the whole of the Exercises from memory. References have already been made to his translations of the *Spiritual Conflict*, and *Epistle of Christ to the Devout Soul* for the use of English Catholics. In addition, he was well read in the ascetical writings of Saints Bonaventure and Bernard, and used Luis de Granada's *Memorial* with those he was directing.

After leaving England in 1611 he held the position of rector and master of novices at Liège, and had charge of the Tertians at Ghent. In 1627 he was recalled to Rome and resided at the English College until his death in 1637.[58] Peters notes his "modern" views with respect to the position of women.[59] This, I suggest, is due in part to his contact with recusant women and his experiences as a recusant, and in part to the flexibility he derived from the Society of Jesus.

In a letter to Henry Lee, March 8, 1627, John Gerard, under the alias of Tomson, refers to Mary Ward as "your best friend and mine."[60] Writing to Mary Poyntz in 1629 he refers to Mary Ward's readiness "in doing good to all," great love for friends and enemies, "immovable firmness" in all essential points concerning the Institute, "that neither threats nor flatteries could cause her to deviate from that which she recognised as the will of God."[61] Aware of the opposition to the Institute he urges its members to "engrave all her words, works and maxims" in their hearts. Gerard sees the "two greatest ends" of the Institute as the "glory of God and the good of souls."[62]

Mary Ward's high regard for Gerard is indicated in a letter to Winifred Wigmore, one of her first companions. In 1624 Mary Ward sent one of Gerard's letters to Winifred and advised her to recommend him to Lucy Knatchbull who was opening a new monastery at Ghent. She stated that one who receives Gerard's friendship and help "may esteem herself very happy."[63] From 1618 till at least 1620 Mary Ward made the Exercises under Gerard's direction and in 1626 received permission from Mutius Vitelleschi to make another retreat under his direction. She refers to her significant insights during these years as ranking among her greatest graces. The depth of Mary Ward's reflections suggests that Gerard's direction allowed a great measure of freedom to the exercitant.   John Gerard also played a significant role in Mary Ward's practical adaptation of the matter and manner of the Society. He was one of the strongest supporters of her Institute. The evidence suggests that Gerard gave her a copy of the Jesuit Formula and an English translation of the Constitutions, at least in part. From the time he became Mary Ward's advisor the Institute's plans bear a far more radical resemblance to the Society of Jesus. The final plan was drafted between the end of 1620 and February 1621. In the following September Gerard was forbidden by Vitelleschi to give further help to the "English Ladies" and was removed from his position as rector in Liège. Blount was asked to ensure that the copy of the Constitutions was returned since it would do no good to leave them in the hands of women.[64]

In 1619 when some of her members were questioning her aims, Mary Ward wrote to John Gerard seeking his advice. This letter is found in what is known as the "Parchment Book" and is placed between her notes on her meditations on "Death" and on the "Comparison of Christ with an Earthly King." These two meditations formed part of the Exercises which she made April 1619 under Gerard's direction.

Her letter reflects both the growth in her own inner freedom and the trust she placed in Gerard. She describes the directive given her in 1611 to take the "same of the Society" as: "words, whose worth cannot be valued, nor the good they contain too dearly bought; these gave sight where there was none, made known what God would have done, gave strength to suffer what hath since happened, assurance of what is wished for in time to come."[65] She adds that through this enlightenment she was "brought home," that is, to the Society of Jesus and to the "matter and manner" found in the Exercises and in the Formula.

Ravier after sifting through the varied and often conflicting views of what constitutes Jesuit spirituality concludes that its two fundamental sources are the Spiritual Exercises and the Formula. He describes the latter as the means through which one gains access to the experience of Loyola and his first companions. It establishes the point of reference essential for living by the spirit and plan of the first Fathers "through the changes of mentality and vicissitudes of history."[66] Mary Ward's lived and formulated spirituality and her plans for her Institute indicate that it was in the Exercises and in the Formula that she found the essentials of the spirituality of the Society of Jesus. Eighty five percent of the *Ratio Instituti* which she presented to Gregory XV corresponds word for word with the Formula. As in the Formula, the end of the Institute is the glory of God through love of God and neighbor. Its apostolate is concerned with the defence and spread of the faith and has a world-wide scope. Her third and final plan, the Institutum, takes over large parts of the Formula verbatim and follows its order.

(iii) *Devotional Works published by the Jesuits*

Reference has been made to the tension in Jesuit spirituality between ascetical and mystical elements. In 1575, Mercurian proscribed certain books "not suitable for ours." Included were the works of Erasmus, Tauler, Ruysbroeck, Suso, Saints Gertrude and Mechtilde and certain parts of Alonso de Madrid's *Art of Serving God*. Stressing the practical character of the spirituality of the Jesuits, he took measures against Balthasar de Álvarez who had been confessor to Teresa of Avila and numbered Luis de la Puente and Louis Lallemant among his disciples.[67]

At the same time, however, as de Guibert points out, Mercurian's choice of works was not entirely anti-mystical. Recommended in 1581 for the use of the novice masters were many authors mentioned in the *Directory*, such as St. Augustine, St. Bernard and Thomas a Kempis. In addition certain writings of St. Basil, St. Bonaventure, St. Gregory, Hugh and Richard of St. Victor, Ludolf the Carthusian, and Louis de Blois were recommended. Instructions on reading at meals about this time indicate a preference for the writings of the Fathers and church histories.[68]

Changes in the reading matter chosen by the Jesuits are apparent in a catalogue drawn up at the end of 1618 or early 1619 listing works left behind at Douay seminary when Kellison took over as President. As well as old favorites such as Thomas à Kempis, Gaspare Loarte, Luis de Granada, and Robert Persons, one finds works of Luis de la Puente (in French), of Vincenzo Bruno and Robert Bellarmine (in Latin and English), the Life of St. Teresa and the *Breve Compendio*.[69] With the exception of the last two works the General Congregation of 1615 recommended these authors together with Francesco Arias and Alvarez de Paz to Jesuit Tertians.[70] De Guibert describes de Paz as a theologian and a contemplative. Included in his three volumes on the theology of the spiritual life is a treatise on mysticism. Other works which appeared after 1609 and contain mystical elements are those of the lay-brother Alphonsus (Alonso) Rodriguez, Léonard Lessius, and Pierre Coton.[71]

During Aquaviva's time as Superior General the writings of Jesuits became dominant. Of the five hundred Catholic books in English printed between 1615 and 1640, over half were spiritual works and a quarter were written or translated by Jesuits.[72] These works stressed service of one's neighbor, the close following of Christ, and an optimistic view of creation and of humanity which reflects Loyola's "Contemplation for Attaining Divine Love."

Such optimism is found in the spiritual writings of Robert Bellarmine. His treatise, *Framing a Ladder Whereby our Mindes may Ascend to God by the Stepps of his Creatures*, was translated into English in 1616. Bellarmine stated that his book arose out of his own contemplation. His anthropology is reflected in his description of the dignity of the human being endowed with reason. By meditating on this dignity one comes to an appreciation of God's greatness.[73] The focus on finding God in human beings and creation which characterizes Loyola's thought harmonizes with the Christian humanism of the Renaissance.

The previous chapter made reference to the Eucharistic devotion in the large gentry households, especially when the Mass was outlawed. Jesuit literature likewise placed great emphasis on the value of the Eucharist. Mary Ward's writings and practice evince this same emphasis. In 1612-1614 she recorded her resolve to receive the sacraments as often as permitted; she communicated daily after 1617 and felt deeply the loss of the Eucharist when imprisoned in 1631.[74]

In 1547 Loyola had formed a group of lay men in Rome which later became the Company of the Blessed Sacrament in the Church

of the Twelve Apostles. Peter Favre's programme for the Company of
the Most Holy Name of Jesus included weekly communion. Francesco
Arias' work on the use of the sacraments published in England in
1602 and 1620 encouraged frequent communion, namely "once in
eight or fifteen days, or at least once a month." Arias extols the Eucharist as a source of grace and virtue and essential to enable human
beings to "become fit instruments to set forth God's glory and to
advance the good of his Church."[75] In general, Jesuit writers suggest
weekly communion as the norm, a recommendation which stands in
stark contrast to the rigorous stance adopted later by Jansenists.

So far we have said little about Cardinal Bérulle's influence on the
French Jesuits. Cultural factors and the more abstract style of his
spirituality may account for the absence of English translations of his
works during this period.[76] The case was very different with respect
to Francis de Sales, a dominant figure in seventeenth century spirituality. The first edition of his *Introduction to the Devout Life* appeared
in 1608, with five English editions 1613 and 1637. So popular was
the work with Protestants and Catholics that in 1637 Charles I ordered all copies to be burnt.

De Sales' spirituality urged that apostolic works and christian perfection were compatible with every state of life. In his anthropology
God's love defines human nature so that despite the effects of sin the
desire to love God above all and the light of reason remain in human
nature. Although differences from Ignatius can be detected in his
tone and imagery and in his treatment of contemplation his anthropology has affinities to the Exercises.

Comparisons could be made between Mary Ward's insights into
the estate of justice and de Sales' treatment of the need for harmony
between reason and desire. Both extol human reason and see excessive self-love as opposed to reason. Mary Ward, however, places no
opposition between contemplation and apostolic activity, whereas
he speaks of advancing from virtue to either contemplation or good
works.[77] No written evidence exists of her being familiar with his
works. Until 1638 when she spent the winter in Paris, she passed
through France only on her journeys to Rome and her visits to England were brief prior to 1639. De Sales' ideas may have come to her
indirectly through Jesuits with whom his works were popular.[78] De
Guibert sees similarities between de Sales' approach and Pierre Coton's
endorsement of affectivity in the spiritual life.[79] Mary Ward's Insti-

tute in York possesses an early copy of the latter's *The Interior Occupation of the Soul.*

We have explored the spirituality of the Society of Jesus because of its formative influence on Mary Ward's spirituality. Its charism allowed the Jesuits to play a dominant role in this era. Jesuits were influential at the Council of Trent and took up the work of reconciliation and reform demanded just when Catholicism faced the breakdown of Christian unity. In this context they also exercised a major influence on the development of the moral theology of Mary Ward's era.

Notes

[1] *AB*, cited by Orchard, 9.

[2] Memorial from Mary Ward to Pope Urban VIII, November 28, 1630, letter no.55, held in Archives of the Institute of the Blessed Virgin Mary, Munich, cited in full by Chambers, vol.II, 330-331.

[3] Dominic Aidan Bellenger, ed., *English and Welsh Priests 1558-1800: A Working List*, (Bath, England: Downside Abbey, 1984), 247.

[4] Ibid., 194-202. Records from the English College list William Ward as a brother of George and Mary Ward (Foley, *Records*, VI, 269). Peters and Chambers consider this is incorrect, the latter suggesting William was her cousin (Chambers, vol. I, 427). Mary Ward in a letter to Winifred Wigmore, May 6, 1628, refers to "My faithful friend and most dear cousin Wi". (Letter 50, cited by Chambers, vol.II, 255, 256).

[5] Geoffrey Holt, S.J., ed., *St. Omers and Bruges Colleges, 1593-1773: A Biographical Dictionary*, (*CRS* Record Series, vol. 69, London, 1979), 277.

[6] Foley, *Records*, VII, (2), 1253, (from the pastoral letter of James Blaise, bishop of St Omer, 1615); Chambers, vol.I, 162, 194.

[7] Augustine Baker, *Sancta Sophia or Directions for the Prayer of Contemplation*, (Douai, 1657), chapter 3; Hywell Wyn Owen, "Another Augustine Baker Manuscript," known as "The Upholland Baker Manuscript," from *Studien en Tekstuitgaven van ons geestelijk Erf,* vol. 16, (1964), photocopied material.

[8] *The lyf of the Mother Teresa of Jesus*, trans., M.W., S.J. (Antwerp: Henrie Jaye, 1611), 12, 15-17.

[9] Taken in its wide sense Quietism is a tendency dangerously to exaggerate the role of passivity and repose in spiritual life. It is often allied to a certain illuminism, that is, to an excessive readiness to see the inspirations of God everywhere, or to guide oneself by these inspirations rather than according to the principles of reason enlightened by faith (De Guibert, *Jesuits*, 402,403).

[10]Lunn, *The English Benedictines*, 199. This work is not listed in Clancy's
  bibliography of English Catholic books published between 1641 and
  1700. Allison has located only one copy of this edition, which is at the
  English College in Rome. See: Thomas H. Clancy, *English Catholic Books
  1641-1700: A Bibliography* (Chicago: University of Loyola Press, 1974);
  A.F. Alison, "New Light on the *Breve Compendio*, The Background to
  the English Translation of 1612," *Recusant History*, 4 no.1 (January
  1957):4-7, 16.

[11]Morey, 149.

[12]Noreen Hunt, "Enclosure," *Cistercian Studies* 22 (1987): 127, 136-137.

[13]James R. Cain, "Cloister and the Apostolate of Religious Women," *Review for Religious*, 27 no. 2 (March 1968): 262.

[14]Cited by Cain, 262, and Hunt, 150.

[15]Council of Trent, Session 25, chapter 5, "Decretum de regularibus et
  monialibus", English translation by Rev. J. Waterworth, (*The Canons
  and Decrees of the Sacred and Oecumenical Council of Trent celebrated
  under the Sovereign Pontiffs, Paul III, Julius III and Pius IV to which are
  prefixed essays on the External and Internal History of the Council.* (London: Burns and Oates, 1848).

[16]Grisar, 90, 104.

[17]Cited by Guilday, 199.

[18]Pastor, *The History of the Popes*, vol. XXIX, 31; Peters, 560-561.

[19]See: Chambers, vol. I, 319; Peters, 147-154.

[20]Burton and Williams, *The Douay College Diaries: Third, Fourth and Fifth,
  1598-1654 with the Rheims Report 1579-80*, vol.I, 397, 398; Peters, 342-345.

[21]*The lyf of the mother Teresa of Jesus*, preface by Fr. Lewis of Lyons.

[22]See: *Autograph Directories of Saint Ignatius Loyola*, trans., Bernard Bush
  and Aloysius Owen, (Jersey City: Program to Adapt the Spiritual Exercises).

[23]William Broderick, "One Mission: Many Ministries," *The Way*, 53, Supplement (Summer, 1985): 39. Evennett, "Editor's postscript" (by Bossy), 144.

[24]*AB*, cited by Chambers, vol. I, 49; Orchard, 9.

[25]*AB*, cited by Orchard, 19.

[26]Mary Ward, "Letter to Roger Lee," November 1615. See Appendix A.

[27]Ibid.

[28]From Mary Ward's addresses to her companions at St. Omer, December
  1617 to January 1618, cited by Chambers, vol. I, 409.

[29]"The Third Plan of the Institute", presented to the Congregation of Bishops and Regulars, February-March 1622, manuscript, Vatican Library,
  Capp.47, ff. 57-62, Wetter (IV): 19 (unpublished material). Of interest
  are documents from the seventeenth century with respect to the educa-

tion offered by the English Canonesses Regular of St. Augustine. Although they offered an innovative education for women, the Canonesses frequently reminded their students, wealthy English girls who were enclosed within the monastery for their education, of the "wicked world" which they had been fortunate enough to have left for the period of their schooling, and imposed upon them a rule according to the spirit and in imitation of that of the religious. (C.S. Durrant, *A Link Between Flemish Mystics and English Martyrs*, 423).

[30]André Ravier, S.J., *Ignatius of Loyola and the Founding of the Society of Jesus*, trans., Maura, Joan and Carson Daly, (San Francisco: Ignatius Press, 1987), 14.

[31]Grisar, 11.

[32]Evennett, 67.

[33]These communities were threatened with suppression by the same edict which condemned Mary Ward's Institute. Compare: Guilday, 198.

[34]Grisar, 91.

[35]Ibid.

[36]Complete enclosure was not intended for the Ursulines founded by Angela de Merici and confirmed by Charles Borromeo. The Ursulines of France, aware of the necessity of education, had opened almost fifty houses between 1612 and 1625. Unlike the Paris sisters, the Ursulines of Dijon who were working in the Spanish France Comté remained free of strict enclosure. That many Ursulines were unhappy with imposed enclosure is seen in the petition sent by the community of Narbonne. (Grisar, 268,269).

[37]Elizabeth Rapley, *The Dévotes: Women and Church in Seventeenth Century France*, (Montreal & Kingston, London, Buffalo: McGill-Queen's University Press, 1990),46, 47; Pastor, vol. xxvi, 62-73; King, 110-111.

[38]Letter to Winifred Wigmore, April 22, 1627, excerpts from Orchard, 91-92.

[39]*Constitutions of the Society of Jesus*, trans., George E. Ganss, S.J., (St. Louis: The Institute of Jesuit Sources, 1970). Ganss describes the "Formula of the Institute of the Society"as containing the supreme authority and dignity of all legislative documents of the Society. It consists of the "five chapters" found in paragraphs 3-8 of the Bull of Paul III, *Regimini militantis Ecclesiae* of 1540, and in slightly revised form in paragraphs 3-6 of the Bull of Julius III, *Exposcit debitum*, of 1550. Arising from the deliberations of Ignatius and his companions in 1539, it established the fundamental structure of the new order and authorized the establishment of more detailed statutes called constitutions (Ganss, 36). This document will be referred to subsequently as the "Formula."

[40]Compare: O'Malley, "Early Jesuit Spirituality: Spain and Italy," 17.

[41]Heinrich Bacht, "Early Monastic Elements in Ignatian Spirituality: Toward Clarifying Some Fundamental Concepts of the Exercises," in *Ignatius of Loyola His Personality and Spiritual Heritage 1556-1856*, ed., Friedrich Wulf, (St. Louis: Institute of Jesuit Sources, 1977), 235.

[42]"Directoria Exercitiorum Spiritualium (1540-1599)," ed., Ignatius Iparraguirre, *Monumenta Ignatiana*, Series Secunda, Exercitia Spiritualia Sancti Ignatii de Loyola et Eorum Directoria, nova editio, Tomus II. *Monumenta Historica Societatis Jesu*, vol.76 (Romae, 1955), 562-564.

[43]See: George E. Ganss, S.J. "The Authentic Spiritual Exercises of St. Ignatius: Some Facts of History and Terminology Basic to Their Functional Efficacy Today," *Studies in the Spirituality of the Jesuits*, (St. Louis Missouri, 1969), 14.

[44]James A. Donohue, *Tridentine Seminary Legislation: Its Sources and Its Formulation* (Louvain University Publications, vol IX, 1957), 82-84; Bernard Basset, S.J., *The English Jesuits*, (London: Burns & Oates, 1967), 148. Thomas Francis Knox, ed., *Records of the English Catholics under the Penal Laws*, vol. I, *The First and Second Diaries of the English College, Douay, and an Appendix of Unpublished Documents* (London: David Nutt, 1878), xxix; Michael E. Williams, *St. Alban's College Valladolid: Four Centuries of English Catholic Presence in Spain* (London: C. Hurst & Company, New York: St. Martin's Press, 1986), 235-239, 242. Cardinal Allen, who was instrumental in founding Douay College and the English College in Rome, endorsed the value of prospective English missionaries making the Spiritual Exercises "under the fathers of the Society" (Knox, xxix). Documents of 1600 from the English College at Valladolid indicate that the material selected from the Exercises included the "Foundation" and "some meditations on sin etc to prepare them for their general confession and to throw light on the road they must tread towards their salvation and that of many others" (Williams, 235-242).

[45]Clancy, *Introduction to Jesuit Life*, 127. Their opponents accused the Jesuits of using the Exercises for recruiting purposes. See: Christopher Bagshaw, *A Sparing Discoverie of our English Jesuits and of Fa. Parsons proceeding under pretence of promoting the Catholike faith in England: For a caveat to all true Catholikes our very loving brethren and friends, how they embrace such very uncatholike, though Jesuiticall deseignments*, (London: J. Roberts, 1601), 21-27.

[46]*Spiritual Exercises*, annotation #18.

[47]Ganss, "The Authentic Spiritual Exercises of St. Ignatius," 6,15.

[48]De Guibert, *The Jesuits*, 246. Iparraguirre sees this move as a "product of the tastes of an epoch" and criticises it as curtailing the doctrinal base of the Exercises as envisaged by Ignatius. Ignacio Iparraguirre, *Historia de los Ejercicios de San Ignacio*, vol 11, (Bilbao - Rome, 1955): 446, cited by

Brian O'Leary, "Third and Fourth Weeks: What the Directories Say," *The Way*, Supplement 58 (Spring 1987), 14-15.

[49]The *Directory* gives detailed instructions regarding the obedience required of exercitants to their directors (II:7;III:5; VII:1,2). The emphasis on method and procedure appears to leave exercitants with less freedom in prayer than is the case in the *Spiritual Exercises* themselves. This may be indicative of Aquaviva's fondness for order and method. A similar emphasis is evident in the *Ratio Studiorum* which Aquaviva issued in the same year.

[50]De Guibert, *Jesuits*, 305.

[51]Ganss, S.J., "The Authentic Spiritual Exercises of St. Ignatius," 19.

[52]*AB*, cited by Chambers, vol I, 165; *Retreat Notes*, 1616, excerpts given by Peters, 210, n.51, and Wetter, *Letters of Instruction.*

[53]Robert McNally S.J., "St. Ignatius, Prayer and the Early Society of Jesus," in *Jesuit Spirit in a Time of Change*, ed., Raymond A. Schroth, S.J. (Westminster, Md: Newman Press, 1968), 86,95. St. Ignatius had made no rigid stipulations with respect to the amount of time to be spent in prayer, but desired each member of the Society to have that union of contemplation and action which results from striving to find God in all things.

[54]Ignace Iparraguirre, "Élaboraton de la spiritualité des Jésuites 1556-1606; Jalons d'une Histoire," monograph issued in liaison with the *Dictionnaire de Spiritualité*, "Jésuites", vol. VIII, cols, 977-978, (Paris: Éditions Beauchesne; Rome: Centrum Ignatianum), 38-39.

[55]Mary Ward, "Letter to Roger Lee," November 27, 1615, letter no.2; "Reflection," 1624, Wetter, (IX): 19. Cited by Chambers, vol. I, 353-354, 356.

[56]Roger Lee's allocutions to the early members of the Institute in Saint Omer are collected in what is known as the *Liber Ruber*, kept at the Archives of the Institute of the Blessed Virgin Mary in Munich. The excerpts cited below are to be found in Chambers, vol. I, 311-317, 339, 340-343, 349-352, 374-375 and Peters, 131-132; 137-138,141.

[57]See Mary Ward's "Resolutions," 1612-1614, given in full by Chambers, vol. I, 357-361 and by Wetter (VII). Excerpts are found in Peters, 134-137.

[58]Thomas M. McCoog, S.J., *English and Welsh Jesuits 1555-1650*, (*CRS*, Record Series, vol. 75, London, 1995), 311-312; Foley, *Records*, VII, 294-295.

[59]Peters, 220.

[60]Excerpts cited by Chambers, vol. II, 227-229.

[61]Excerpts cited by Chambers, vol. II, 308-318.

[62]Letter to Father Henry Lee, cited by Chambers, vol. II, 227-229.

[63]Letter of September 10, 1624, cited by Chambers, vol.II, 109.

[64]Letter from Mutius Vitelleschi to Richard Blount, ViceProvincial of the English Mission," September 2, 1621, cited by Peters, 289, 291, 361; Wetter, (III): 3.

[65]Letter to Father Tomson, (John Gerard), April 1619, cited by Chambers, vol. I, 453; Orchard, 61; Wetter (V).

[66]Ravier, 111-112.

[67]De Guibert, *Jesuits*, 218; O'Malley, 15.

[68]*Instituti Societatis Jesu*, vol. 3, (Florence, 1893): 121, 144; De Guibert, *Jesuits*, 217.

[69]Willem Schrickx, "An Early Seventeenth Century Catalogue of Books from the English Jesuit Mission in Saint-Omer", *Archives et Bibliothèques de Belgique Brussels*, 45-47 (1974-5), 595-596.

[70]Clancy, *Introduction to Jesuit Life*, 124-125.

[71]De Guibert, *Jesuits*, 251, 264-265, 273, 276, 277. De Guibert describes Alphonsus (Alonso) Rodriguez as one of the Society's greatest mystics.

[72]Thomas H. Clancy S.J., "Spiritual Publications of the Jesuits, 1615-1640," *Recusant History*, 19 no.4 (October 1989): 426.

[73]Bellarmine, *A Most Learned and Pious Treatise, full of Divine and Humane Philosophy, framing a Ladder*, the Author's Epistle, 264, 265, 269, 270.

[74]See: Mary Ward's "Resolutions," 1612/1614, Chambers, vol. I, 357-361; Wetter (VII); Letter to Pope Urban VIII, March 27, 1631, Chambers, vol. II, 381-382.

[75]Francisco Arias, *The Little Memorial Concerning the Good and Fruitfull Use of the Sacraments*, anonymous translator, (Roan: 1602): 4, 16.

[76]Bossy cites the advice given to Benedictine missioners in the 1760s, that their sermons "be such as suit the Genius of the English people, that is, let them be wrote in a rational, concise manner, pathetic, and keeping close to the subject" and that they should "carefully avoid the French verbosity". (Bossy, *English Catholic Community*, 267-268).

[77]Ibid., 37, 209.

[78]Jean Fourier, S.J., for instance, persuaded de Sales to publish his works.

[79]De Guibert, *Jesuits*, 276-277.

Chapter 3

The Moral Theology of Mary Ward's Era

This father... guided my conscience entirely by way of fear,' for instance that I ought to hate myself, to fear the judgement of God, to tremble at the pains of hell, in all of which I was most inept.... To labour through love, even death appeared to me to be easy, but fear made but little impression. Hell I was resolved, by the assistance of God's grace, never to merit, and of the doings there I could form no conception as vivid as the father wished... finding myself so differently disposed from what he required... .Through this occasion I have sometimes thought... that there are some souls not the less fit to arrive at more than ordinary perfection who in their commencements, it would be well to treat with great generosity, giving them better things before taking away that which is less good, changing the object without destroying the nature... . I could easily enlarge on this and perhaps not without reason, having experienced much in this particular.[1]

The priest to whom Mary Ward refers above is George Keynes, professor of moral theology at the English College in St. Omer, (1595-1611) and her confessor from May to October 1616. Although Roger Lee and John Gerard reflected a very different approach, Mary Ward's experience and subsequent reflection throw considerable light on the content and orientation of the spirituality of her period and its moral theology.

Catholic readers whose life experiences predate the second Vatican Council, may find echoes of their experiences in Mary Ward's reflection. They will be familiar with formulations of morality which appeared to equate moral rectitude with avoiding sins and performing a multitude of "good" actions. Practical examples can be found in the numerous "examinations of conscience" which aimed to enable penitents with their confessors' help to assess the gravity of their sins, sins being viewed primarily as contraventions of the law, divine and ecclesiastical. Many will also recall the "missions" with their vivid presentations of the torments of hell, designed to move the more intransigent to conversion.

The *Oxford Dictionary of the Christian Church* defines moral theology as "the science of Christian conduct, treating of God as man's last end, and of the means by which He may be attained."[2] While moral theology as a systematic discipline is not to be confused with morality or moral practice, the manner in which it communicates the constituents of moral conduct is significant for the Christian's moral formation and understanding of the demands of the moral life. An excessive focus on moral rectitude as lying in the avoidance of "sins" (rather than "sin") tends to enforce a negative view of the human person and to obscure the importance of the interior disposition from which morally good acts flow.

In view of moral theology's history and the various theological pre-suppositions, methods and moral theories propounded with respect to its content and orientation, the broad definition given above may appear deceptively simple. Indeed, during the last decades of the sixteenth century the relationship of moral theology to theology as a whole and its place within theological courses was the subject of considerable debate. Today, over four-hundred years later, moral theology is experiencing the tensions which accompany significant changes in content and methodology.

Different emphases and varieties of approach reflect and endorse the Church's duty in its task of forwarding the work of Christ to scrutinize the "signs of the times."[3] Moral theology, while necessarily affected by its historical situation, must also address and contribute insights to this situation. In this context John Mahony's approach is singularly apt. His title: *The Making of Moral Theology*,[4] suggests a task in process, one which takes place in history, both secular and ecclesiastical, and reflects the religious, economic, social and cultural factors of its Age. Such an approach facilitates both an examination of the moral theology of a particular age and the evaluation of its insights into and response to that situation.

Mary Ward's life (1585-1645) coincided with a significant period of moral theology, namely, its emergence as an independent discipline, systematically different from other branches of theology. Significant in this development were the doctrinal and reforming decrees of the Council of Trent and the legacy left to the Council by the changing philosophical and historical climate of the late middle Ages.

3.1 The Legacy left to Moral Theology by the Changing Philosophical and Historical Climate of the Late Middle Ages
Johann Theiner points out that the expression "moral theology" was not entirely foreign to the Middle Ages. It would be anachronis-

tic, however, to understand the term as either a branch of study or a manual of instruction in the modern sense.[5] In the late Middle ages, four different, albeit not fully articulated, approaches to the content and orientation of moral theology and its place within theology can be detected.

The first approach is epitomised by St. Thomas' *Summa Theologiae* which considered moral matters within theology. His treatment of the human moral act was within the context of "beatitude," the virtues, the decalogue, the new law of Grace and the following of Christ. Although later writers on the decalogue, virtues and vices adopted St. Thomas's primarily "speculative" orientation and emphasized the principles underlying moral action, no further synthesis of such comprehension was produced within this period.

A second and markedly different approach is apparent in the "summas" for confessors (*Summae Confessorum*). These works were practical in orientation. Raymond of Pennafort, author of the *Summa de Poenitentia* (c. 1235) and a contemporary of St. Thomas, studied the human moral act from a canonical point of view within the context of the decalogue. His methodology of treating cases, "case" itself being a legal term, was taken up by later summists culminating in the fifteenth century with the works of Antoninus of Florence, Sylvester de Prierio, and Angelo Carletti. Their works made available to priests the decrees of Popes and councils and the doctrines developed by canonists regarding aspects of domestic, social and economic life.

A third approach, that moral theology is inherently pastoral in orientation and related to the administration of the sacrament of Penance, underlay the production of manuals for confessors and examinations of conscience for the penitent. The range of this literature extends from anonymously written, simple handbooks and penitentials to the more sophisticated works of John Gerson in the fifteenth century. It reflects the influence of the early penitentials which had stressed acts and decisions as central elements in moral life and of the decrees of the Fourth Lateran Council (1215) regarding the sacrament of Penance. A fourth "approach" which influenced later works dealing with the Christian moral life is reflected in the writings of Bernard of Clairvaux (died 1153) and Thomas à Kempis (died 1471) with their stress on moral asceticism.

The different literary genres reflect their cultural and institutional settings. While the medieval handbooks were the product of the monastery, the canonical and casuistic works of the summists reflected the growing scholarly interest in law and the embryonic systematisation of Canon Law, itself a practical discipline. They also coincided with the movement of the papacy between 1073 and 1302 for political and legal supremacy. The *Summa Theologiae* emerged within the context of the university, as did the revival of Thomism in the sixteenth century.

Post-Tridentine moral theology inherited the tensions within the late Middle Ages' literature. In both speculative and practical works emphases oscillated. Concentration on the virtues and vices vied with the focus on the commandments. The latter had gradually superseded the seven deadly sins although these still retained a certain artistic appeal! The summists wanted to provide a critical analysis of the new moral and legal issues which had arisen subsequent to the changing political and economic situation. Although some misgivings were expressed at the close relationship established between morality and law,[6] their works continued to be valued as systematic studies of Christian conduct in terms of divine and ecclesiastical laws.

In addition, post-Tridentine moral theology inherited the effects of philosophical, economic and political developments within the late Middle Ages and Renaissance. These effects were compounded by the breakdown of Christian unity. The late Middle Ages and Renaissance saw the emergence of conflicting views about the nature of the human being and of the universe. Doubt about human reason's ability to reach truth in philosophy competed with the conviction of the human being's dignity and autonomy. There was criticism of scholasticism and scepticism regarding philosophy. Specifically there was criticism of Aristotle and resistance to the theology and philosophy of St. Thomas who related Good to Being and proposed natural law as a fundamental source of moral knowledge.

William of Ockham (c.1285-1347) and the general movement of nominalism played an important role in the broad current of philosophy and theology during this time. Ockham interpreted human moral rectitude in terms of obedience to the obligations of law. Later moral theology reflects Ockham's rejection of universals and emphasis on the significance of each individual act.[7] Nominalism pervaded university circles in England, Germany and France.

Renaissance humanists, whose philosophy helped bring into prominence a conception of the human being as autonomous, added their flavor to the general mixture of philosophical scepticism and ethical individualism to which the nominalists had contributed. Renaissance humanism comprised various theories and formulations. Erasmus (c. 1466-1536) typifies one trend: humanism's general lack of sympathy for scholasticism. His focus on the primacy of Scripture and his questioning of metaphysics with its "crafty and tedious perplexity of words of relations, quiddities and formalities"[8] was more representative of the literary Renaissance in northern Europe and in the England of Thomas More. Here the emphasis was less individualistic and characterized by efforts to achieve moral and social reformation.

In the early years of the fourteenth century, Dominicans and Jesuits in Spain and in the German universities were instrumental in reviving interest in the works of Saint Thomas. This renewal centered around the ethical sections of the *Summa Theologiae*, with the *Secunda Secundae* arousing most interest. While St. Thomas dealt with moral questions within the context of a unified view of theology, commentators on his works adapted his principles to their own practical concerns. Thomas de Vio (Cardinal Cajetan) for instance, blended discussion of ethical questions with themes from the area of law. Francisco Vitoria and Francis Suárez produced commentaries on the *Summa Theologiae* and treatises on Law.[9]

Coincidental with the changed philosophical context in which individualism and the interpretation of morality in terms of the law, either divine or human, were significant features, the growing strength of the mercantile class after the breakdown of feudalism necessitated the drawing up of laws of justice and equity. The subsequent growth of the nation-states resulted in an increased development of political theory and philosophy of law that challenged the temporal power of the Papacy. The arena in which the conflict between Catholics and Protestants was fought out covered religious, social, political and economic ground. Between 1620 and 1660 this conflict resulted in the move of the dynamic center of Europe from Catholic Spain, Italy, Flanders and Southern Germany to Protestant England, Switzerland, Holland and the cities of the Baltic. Meanwhile, the Papacy, allied with the Catholic princes and monarchs, and placed in a defensive position, sought to maintain the *status quo* regarding its spiritual and temporal power.

This was the legacy left to the Church when the Council of Trent, itself disrupted by political and religious conflict, opened in 1545.

For post-Tridentine moral theology this legacy included: the focus on sin and acts of the early penitentials and medieval handbooks of penance; the association of law and morality reflected in the study of cases of the summists; the morality of obligation of Ockham and the nominalists; the individualism of Renaissance humanism; the effects of political and economic changes in Europe; and renewed interest in the works of St. Thomas, this interest itself being affected by the above factors.

The breakdown of Christian unity, and the changed social, political and economic conditions raised new moral issues for moralists and canonists. The study of "cases" taken up by the summists of the late Middle Ages, that reached its maturity in the period 1556-1656, resulted in a close alliance between moral theology and canon law. At the same time, the pervading influence of nominalism, combined with the value accorded to human activity characteristic of the age, led to moral conduct being viewed primarily in terms of individual actions which were in conformity to the law, divine and human, ecclesiastical and civil.

3.2 Effects of the Council of Trent

The Council of Trent fostered two responses over the breakdown of Christian unity and the Protestant challenge. One was doctrinal clarification; the other was the reform of Christian conduct, in particular, "the restoration of the tottering and well-nigh collapsed ecclesiastical discipline."[10] The effects of the Council's decrees in these areas were significant to the emergence of moral theology as a distinctive science. These decrees also, together with the formulation of the Jesuit programme of studies (the *Ratio Studiorum*), played a decisive role in moral theology's content and orientation.

In the area of doctrinal clarification, the Council gave greatest attention to the doctrine of Justification and to the sacraments. The decree on Justification made clear the essential nature of grace. At the same time the Council stressed the sacraments as sources of grace and the validity of good works in the human being's co-operation with grace. With respect to the sacrament of Penance the Council emphasized the necessity for enumeration of all mortal sins. Careful delineation of all circumstances of such sins was required so that confessors could determine the type of sin, its gravity, and the penalty which should be imposed.[11]

The implementation of the Council's decrees required a committed and educated clergy. In the area of reform the Council focused on the renewal of the life and conduct of clerics and their education. Influenced by the opening in Rome (in 1552) of a Jesuit college for the training of German clergy, and of Cardinal Pole's seminary legislation,[12] the Council decreed in 1563 that seminaries were to be set up in each diocese. The Council emphasised instruction in Scripture and administration of the sacraments, with particular emphasis on matters pertaining to the sacrament of Penance. Teachers were to be have expertise in canon law, and prior to ordination, candidates were to be examined by men "skilled in divine and human law."[13]

This was the immediate context for moral theology's development as a distinct branch of theology. Its center moved to the seminary where, identified with the pastoral and ministerial, it became separated from dogmatic theology which continued as an academic discipline.

(i) *The Establishment of Seminaries*

In 1564 the Roman seminary was founded by Pius IV and placed under Jesuit direction. Cardinal William Allen, with Jesuit assistance, was responsible for the foundation of English seminaries at Douay (1568), Rome (1576) and Valladolid (1589). Jesuits retained influence at Douay until 1613 and were rectors in Valladolid, Seville (1592), and, after 1614, in Madrid. In 1579 Gregory XIII placed the English College in Rome under their control. Only Lisbon, founded in 1622, was governed by secular priests. The Jesuit college in Louvain, transferred to Liège in 1615, offered courses in philosophy and theology. Introductory courses in moral theology and philosophy were taught at St. Omer College which had been established by the Jesuits Robert Persons and William Flacke in 1592-1593.

Between 1558 and 1603 eight hundred priests, many from Yorkshire, received their training from these colleges. By 1576 more than two hundred had studied at Douay, its first priests going to England in 1574. Vallodolid had seventy-five students by 1592. Thirty-three English missionaries had been sent from Rome by 1585. While secular priests formed the majority of the English Catholic clergy, by 1619 there were over one hundred Jesuits in England.[14] In addition, despite the disastrous effects of the English reformation on the older religious Orders, monasteries in Italy and Spain provided training for English Benedictines, Friars Minor, Dominicans and Capuchins.

(ii) *Moral Theology in the Seminaries*
(1) *The Ratio Studiorum*

The Society of Jesus played a major role in the direction of the seminaries established under the directives of the Council of Trent, and determined the content and orientation of courses in moral theology given in these seminaries. Contemporary documents indicate that seminary teaching generally followed that set down in the Society's *Ratio Studiorum* (order of studies).

The basic orientation of the *Ratio Studiorum* is set out clearly in the fourth part of the Jesuit Constitutions in terms of "the end of the Society and its studies," namely "to aid our fellow men to the knowledge and love of God and to the salvation of their souls." Theology is seen as "the means most suitable to this end."[15] The *Ratio* was issued in response to Loyola's prescription that "the hours of lectures, their order and their method be treated in a separate treatise."[16] It also represented attempts to set out clearly the place of theology, and in particular of moral theology in Jesuit colleges and seminaries.

In 1583 Aquaviva, Superior General of the Society and former rector of the Roman College, decreed that a commission be set up to draw up an order of studies. In 1599, after two preliminary drafts (1586,1591) were examined, a definitive plan was issued "to be observed in the future by all of ours."[17] This plan and the decrees of the General Congregation of the Society (1615) were responsible for the establishment of two distinct courses pertaining to morals: the moral theology of the *cursus maior* (longer course) and *cursus minor,* (shorter course). This distinction was important to the content and orientation of moral theology.

In the *cursus major* moral theology was included in the four years of scholastic theology. It relied for its content on the ethical sections of the *Summa Theologiae*. In keeping with the Council of Trent's decrees and the Society's aims that theology be taught as a speculative science in the service of the direction and care of souls, all Jesuits received training in Cases of Conscience.[18] Here, professors had to limit their courses to the basic principles of moral teaching. No separate chair of canon or civil law was set up. Rather, within the theology course one professor was to devote a year to matters of justice and law.[19]

In the *cursus minor,* moral theology became identified with casuistry, the study of cases of conscience. Following Aquaviva's decision in 1580 that, in the future, students from the Roman seminary were to study primarily cases of conscience, and only by way of exception philosophy and theology, the moral theology offered in the seminaries was the *cursus minor*. It was also the course for those members of the Society who were determined "unfit for philosophy," or "mediocre in letters, and endowed with no other talent."[20]

The duty (*finis*) of the Professor of Cases of Conscience was defined as the training of skilled parish clergy and administrators of the sacraments. Two professors were assigned to this two year course. One taught the sacraments and censures, and the different states and duties of life, while the other taught the commandments and the matter of contracts. Treatment of aspects of canon and civil law were thus included. Only those theological principles on which the cases depended were to be discussed and only briefly.[21] The *cursus minor* did not include specific treatment of passions and habits, the virtues, gifts or beatitudes (*ST*: 1a.2ae, 22-54, 55-70). Moreover, at least until 1615, the *Ratio* allowed for these topics to be curtailed or entirely omitted from the *cursus maior* when a third professor was not available.[22] St. Thomas' treatise on Grace was allocated to the scholastic theology of the *cursus maior*. This treatise was not taught as a unit, however, but spread over the several parts of the theology course.[23]

This period's Jesuit theologians provide further insights into the content and orientation of courses in moral theology and reflect the specialization of professors. Häring identifies four distinct groups among the Society's theologians. The first consisted of commentators on the *Summa Theologiae* such as Suárez, Francisco de Toledo and Gabriel Vasquez, all three with a legal approach. The second devoted their efforts to a study of select questions notably concerning the morality of the law. Among these were Louis Molina (1545-1600), Leonard Lessius (1554-1623), John de Lugo (1583-1660) and Thomas Sanchez (1550-1610). The third group provided theological manuals: Sanchez, John Azor (1536-1603), John de Lugo (1583-1660), Paul Laymann (1575-1635) and Herman Busenbaum (1600-1668).[24] Handbooks for confessors were the work of the fourth group, de Toledo's *Summa Casuum Conscientiae* being published in 1569. His *De Summulis*, was recommended by the *Ratio* as a reference text for philosophy.[25]

Since Mary Ward and her early members had close contact with and received instruction from members of the English clergy, information on their background and training is valuable.[26] Contemporary records indicate that the majority of the secular clergy began their studies at Douay and, in general, took shorter theology courses. For the scholastic theology course they were sent to Douay University or colleges in Rome or Spain.

Among this group were Richard Holtby and John Mush, Mary Ward's early confessors, her cousin William Ward (Ingleby), Henry Vines (Lee), her chaplain during the 1620s and 1630s, James Sharp (Pollard), well known in Yorkshire, John Wilson who assisted her community in St. Omer, and Henry Ansley, canon of Munich, who was recommended to her by John Gerard. Holtby and Sharp, both Oxford graduates, later joined the Jesuits. Henry Vines (Lee), Wilson, and Mush attended the English College, taking only two years of theology.[27]

After a year at Oxford, George Keynes joined the Society in Tournay in 1593. He was sent to study moral theology at St. Omer. [28] Roger Lee and John Gerard took shorter theology courses in Rome, the latter studying both moral and positive theology (the study of biblical history, the Fathers, definitions and decrees of the Councils and canon law).[29] Jesuits studying scholastic theology in Rome or Valladolid include Robert Southwell, George Ward - Mary's brother - who was esteemed by his peers as an "able theologian,"[30] Thomas Coniers, her cousin,[31] and many who acted as confessors or gave other support: William Baldwin, Henry More, William Flacke, John Floyd, Edward Coffin, Edward Catcher (Burton), Thomas Owen, Anthony Hoskins, Richard Gibbons, Edward Bedingfield (Silesdon), George Holtby (Duckett) and Andrew White.[32]

Alumni of the English College in Rome who opposed her work include George Mainwaring, S.J, Richard Blount, S.J, Richard Banks, S.J, Henry Bedingfield (Silesdon), S.J., Matthew Kellison, later President of Douay College, and Richard Smith, appointed bishop to England in 1625. William Harrison earned his doctorate from Douay University while his secretary William Harewell (Farrar), Robert Sherwood, O.S.B., John Bennet and Thomas White (Blacklow), who held the position of agent of the English clergy in Rome, studied at Douay seminary.[33] This last group was bitterly opposed to both Mary Ward and the Jesuits.

(2) *Courses at the English Colleges and Seminaries*

In 1581 William Allen described the mission of the colleges at Douay and Rome as the salvation of souls, instruction in "Cases of

Conscience and Controversies" and the fostering of priestly vocations.[34] Allen was a graduate of Oxford University as were Richard Barrett and Thomas Worthington, subsequent presidents of Douay, Richard Bristow, professor of casuistry, Owen Lewis, professor of civil and canon law, Thomas Stapleton, professor of divinity and translator of Bede's Ecclesiastical History, and Gregory Martin, professor of Scripture and translator of the Bible.[35]

Aveling is critical of the training given at Douay and describes Allen as "a complete academic traditionalist" who shunted the "less capable or more fractious" students into "improvised crash courses" within the college.[36] His comment, however, reflects his desire to deromanticise what he believes is an overly enthusiastic view of the role of Douay seminary and needs qualification. Writing to the Prior of the English Carthusians in August, 1577, Allen admitted that the shortage of priests in England necessitated the ordination of students "of moderat knowledge." He defended the courses given, however, on the grounds that they met the Council of Trent's requirements and were similar to the Jesuits'.[37]

Contemporary documents provide insight into the content and orientation of these courses. The Rheims report of 1579-1580 asserts that courses on the *Summa Theologiae* were given "according to the dictates of the Society of Jesus."[38] These courses were reduced to cover questions of controversy and to meet the needs of priests preparing for England. They were supplemented by the works of the Fathers against heresy, Bede's Church History, the documents and Catechism of the Council of Trent, and the *Treatise of Schism* published in 1578 by Gregory Martin. Kellison, later president of the College, lectured in scholastic theology from 1591 using the third part of the *Summa Theologiae* as his text. Lecturing in theology and Aristotelian philosophy was Thomas White (Blacklow), later head of Lisbon College and friend of the English political philosopher Thomas Hobbes.[39]

Professors of casuistry at Douay included Thomas Worthington, Lawrence Webbe, Richard Bristow, Thomas Coniers, Richard Gibbons (1605), James Sharp (1606-1607), Edmund Arrowsmith, (1591) and Edward Weston (1599-1603). John Hungerford Pollen, who has spent many years in researching the recusant era, has located a contemporary manuscript containing the content of Arrowsmith's lectures at Douay/Rheims during the first half of 1591.[40] For the most part, Arrowsmith's course follows the pattern set down by the *Ratio Studiorum* of 1586 for Cases of Conscience. Edward Weston's literary works focus on the defence of the Church's authority in matters of faith and morals. His comprehensive knowledge of the Church fathers and St. Thomas is, unfortunately, overshadowed by polemic against Protestant ministers as the agents of Antichrist.[41]

The Constitutions of the English College at Rome prescribed three years for philosophy and four for theology but allowed certain students to replace philosophy with courses in controversies and casuistry.[42] In 1596 the Jesuits at the College reported to Cardinal Sega that they followed the practice "usual in every Seminary" of applying "to the study of moral theology those who are unfit for scholastic divinity."[43] Lukács records that from 1573 to 1580 the number of Jesuit spiritual coadjutors who were not required to take the full four year course in theology rose to forty-six percent.[44] According to Aveling of fifty-three Jesuits working in England in 1610 thirty seven had done the scholastic course and fifteen were *positivi.*[45]

Professors in scholastic theology at the Roman College who provided instruction for English College students included many of the Jesuit authors mentioned above, such as de Toledo (1562-1568), Suárez (1580-1585), Gabriel Vázquez (1585-1591), Azor (1584-1603) and de Lugo (1620-1624).[46] Robert Bellarmine lectured in controversial theology from 1576 to 1588. His lectures were transcribed at Douay and were required reading at the English College. Many Jesuits, with whom Mary Ward came into contact, were also involved in teaching moral theology at either Louvain or Liège. Among these are: William Baldwin (1594), Andrew White (1626), George Mainwaring (1630), Thomas Babthorpe (1633,1634) and George Ward (1639).[47]

The seminaries for the English clergy aimed to prepare them to deal with the new moral issues concomitant with the breakdown of Christian unity. Controversial theology and casuistry formed a major part of theological studies. The former treated such topics as Scripture and Tradition, papal power, the councils of the church, the sacraments, the Eucharist and the Mass, the doctrines of justification, predestination, concordance of grace and free will, merits of good works, purgatory, indulgences and reverence paid to the saints.[48] The most frequently used text in the teaching of casuistry was Martin de

Azpilcueta's *Enchiridion*. It was later superseded by John Azor's *Institutiones Morales*.[49]

(3) *Manuals of Moral Theology*

These manuals drew their theological principles from and closely followed the framework of the *Summa Theologiae* (1a.2ae). Their orientation, however, was very different, their focus being on practical issues. The manuals also relied on the *Summas* of the late Middle ages and reflected the close alliance which had come to exist between morality and law, both canonical and civil.

Martin de Azpilcueta's *Enchiridion* served as a model for later instructional texts. Jacob Lainez, second General Superior of the Society of Jesus, recommended it to his colleagues at Trent because in order to decide all cases, confessors required knowledge of both "theology and law."[50] Azpilcueta opens with ten preludes which serve as a theological foundation for his subsequent exposition of the sacrament of Penance. Here his portrait of human nature is in terms of its sinfulness and need for God's mercy. Painting a vivid picture of hell, Azpilcueta proposes consideration of one's last end as an effective means of moving one to contrition and amendment.

Azpilcueta addressed theological issues only to the extent necessary for the resolution of cases. His seventh prelude illustrates this. Here, only two of twenty eight sections are allotted to grace and to the human act considered insofar as it is morally good. The remaining sections and the next two preludes concentrate on sin and its distinctions. Mortal sin receives most attention. Unlike St. Thomas who emphasizes the essential nature of mortal sin as a turning away from God to whom the soul is united in charity, Azpilcueta focuses on mortal sin as a transgression of law and on the eternal punishment which it incurs. His remaining chapters are devoted to practical aspects of the Sacrament of Penance: including the prerequisites of the confessor; the matter on which the penitent is to be questioned; satisfaction (penances to be imposed, censures and excommunication), doubt and scruples, and obligations to one's neighbor.

With his background in canon law and his aim to provide a handbook for confessors, Azpilcueta focuses on the circumstances related to human action and on assessing in particular cases when the law does or does not apply. Probable opinions of the summists are cited and their merits discussed. Emphasis on law as external to the hu-

man being overrides attention to personal disposition and virtue. As
will be seen later in this chapter, English priests found the *Enchiridion*
useful in relieving the consciences of their penitents. At first glance,
however, the phrase *qui peccat* occurs far more frequently than *qui
excusatur*!

Azor's *Institutiones Morales* differs from the *Enchiridion* in that its
purpose goes beyond that of a handbook for confessors. Azpilcueta
did not try to provide a method for the treatment of all dimensions
of ethics. He concentrated on the negative aspect of morality. The
work's introduction and structure suggest that Azor's aim was to provide a text which would assist professors of casuistry to explain more
fully the general principles on which cases depend.

Given Azor's role in the production of the *Ratio* it is not surprising
that his methodology is consistent with the Rules laid down for the
Professors of Cases of Conscience. His first seven books and the in-
troductions to subsequent books are devoted to laying a theological
foundation for the discussion of particular cases. The *Ratio's* recommendation to cite probable opinion is adhered to, albeit less briefly
than suggested!

Even a cursory examination of the *Institutiones Morales* reveals Azor's
practical orientation and emphases. His treatment of law is dominated by discussion of the Old Law. Only one chapter is devoted to
the precepts of the new law and the Gospel. Azor's treatment of the
second precept of the Church includes exhaustive consideration of
regulations about fasting. The main part of his treatment of sin, book
four, is concerned with its distinctions: mortal and venial; omission
and commission, sins of thought, word and deed and the various
kinds of each and the seven capital sins. It also contains a defence of
the doctrine of original sin against the errors of heretics.

Theiner, while recognizing the strengths of Azor's work, points to
the limitations of his canonical-juridical orientation.[51] Azor's practical orientation and concentration on morality in terms of acts, however, tends to obscure his positive view of human nature. His sound,
albeit brief, treatment of grace indicates that he sees a fuller discussion as belonging to dogmatic theology. Moreover, although only
one chapter is devoted to each of the theological virtues, his treatment of charity emphasizes both the need for grace and the dignity
of human nature. Azor portrays God's love as embracing all human

beings, including sinners. Each person is created as good, both by nature and by God's goodness in calling each to eternal glory.[52]

Azor's expertise was in frequent demand from his contemporaries.[53] His work exercised a significant influence on the content of moral theology. In Häring's opinion, Azor's *Institutiones Morales* established such a pattern for moral theologians that later moralists made little change to its form.[54]

The separation of the study of cases of conscience from the scholastic theology of the *cursus maior* meant that conscience was no longer treated within the synthetic context provided by St. Thomas. Rather, the concern of Cases of Conscience was to assess the extent to which conscience was bound by law in particular circumstances. The conviction that circumstances are significant in defining the moral act and assessing the gravity of sin allows for discussion of questions of doubt about the law and its application. Casuists of the post-Tridentine period sought reliable opinions to solve doubtful cases and to support their conclusions. This meant a reliance on a theory regarding moral deliberation which left room for a variety of opinions. Coincident, then, with the systematic development of casuistry was the development of the moral system of probabilism.

Azpilcueta and Azor discuss and use methods of resolving conflict through a survey of probable opinion. The way the English clergy of Mary Ward's era used the casuists' works to solve conflicts of conscience illuminates some difficulties underlying both casuistry and the system of moral probabilism.

(4) *Particular "Moral" Issues of the Period with respect to the Practice of Missionary Priests in England*

Late sixteenth century records of discussions at Douay College provide valuable information about the cases of conscience confessors met in their ministry. Peter Holmes, whose doctoral studies (Cambridge, 1976) focused on the political thought of the Elizabethan Catholics, has collated and translated original documents held by the *Bibliothèque Municipale* of Douay, Lambeth Palace and the Bodleian Library.[55] The first set of documents edited by Holmes contains reports of 172 cases discussed in 1578 and 1579 by seminary students at Douay College and then arranged in booklet form. The second document, written in part by William Allen and Robert Per-

sons, is entitled *Resolutiones quorundam casuum nationis Anglicanae.*
A copy was held by the English College in Rome as early as 1603.[56]
Composed before 1585 but after the anti-recusant legislation of 1581,
this document consists of sixty cases discussed at Douay and focuses
specifically on moral problems facing English priests.

Authorities cited in the "Douay" documents reveal the casuists'
reliance on canon law. 143 references are made to the *Enchiridion*,
and forty-four to other canonists, including nineteen to Lyndwood.
Cajetan is cited on nine occasions, St. Thomas on six, and sundry
references are made to other authors and to the decrees of Trent. The
"Allen-Persons" document makes fewer references but relies on arguments used in the earlier documents. Although publication of the
Institutiones Morales post-dates these documents, Azor clarified and
developed many of Azpilcueta's arguments and influenced later casuists faced with the same problems. Moreover, his stand was known to
Persons, a former rector of the English College in Rome, and to his
students.

A. *Cases of Conscience Involving Communication with Protestants*
   (a) Attendance at Protestant Church Services

In 1562 the Council of Trent decreed attendance at Protestant
church services sinful, and in 1606 Pope Paul V forbade English
Catholics to obey the state's laws regarding church attendance. Writers such as Garnet, Persons, Gerard and Bristow taught that the Protestant service was heretical and encouraged Catholics to be identified by their non-conformity. At the same time, the English clergy
used the protection provided by schismatics. Many seminarians came
from families divided by schism. Mary Ward refers to relatives and
acquaintances who were schismatics such as Ralph Babthorpe and
John Wright.[57] Moreover, problems peculiar to England were raised
by the Anglican settlement of religion. Many of the gentry had property rights over Protestant churches or were tenants of episcopal landowners. At Ripon in Yorkshire, for instance, Marmaduke Ward was a
tenant of the Archbishop of York.[58]

Hence, the casuist documents used by the English clergy dealt
mainly with whether Catholics who attended "heretical" services were
to be admitted to Mass, to what extent the obligation to hear Mass
extended given that it was forbidden by Parliament, and whether

Catholics were permitted to maintain churches and pay tithes to heretics who held benefices. The English casuists based their arguments mainly on the respective obligations of divine, natural and human law, the immorality of cooperation in the sin of another, and the illicitness of using the end to justify the means.   The conclusions drawn are less clear. Arguments used to justify granting dispensations to Catholics, for instance, lead one to suspect that the English casuists were treading a thin line between pastoral concern and pragmatism. On the one hand, dispensations were claimed to be a just reward for those English Catholics who were "prepared to die a thousand times" for the defence of their faith. On the other hand, dispensations given to the "weaker and feebler" were asserted to be still "most holy."[59] Some clergy argued that Catholics should be allowed to attend Protestant services so that Catholicism was not destroyed as a result of the death or total penury of its members. Other clergy insisted on non-conformity as a sign of Catholic identity. The English casuists were able to find "probable" opinions supporting both views.

Douay casuists first distinguished schism and heresy and then specified types of heretics. Heresy was defined as recognising another head of the Church in England where it was considered a crime to believe that the Pope is the vicar of Christ. In a rare advertence to the importance of human disposition, the casuists made it clear that both heresy and schism involved the "heart," that is human will and intellect, and not only the action itself. They concluded that those who participated with heretics were not necessarily heretics or schismatics.[60] Following Azpilcueta and Azor they allowed commerce with those who had not been publicly excommunicated or known to persecute the clergy.[61]

In their considerations of law, the casuists argued that human law was essentially conditional and depended on divine law for its validation. This argument could justify both recusancy and religious conformity. Its main tenets were set out as follows. One, human law never "of itself" obliges but only when conjoined with divine or natural law. Two, the Pope interprets divine law but cannot dispense from it. Three, when two divine precepts have a bearing on a case and it is necessary to violate one of them, the more important prevails. Preservation of life and honor, for instance, were of more importance than restitution.[62]

On the basis of these tenets the casuists used the notion of "just fear" to exonerate from excommunication those who broke the (*human*) church law by frequenting heretic churches. Fear of death, did not excuse mortal sin, scandal, injury to the faith, or receiving communion at heretical services because these were contrary to *divine law*.[63] Prior to the Spanish Armada's defeat (1588) emphasis was placed on Catholic non-conformity as a means to distinguish Catholics from heretics. In 1592, however, Allen and Persons judged, as Bellarmine would in 1609, that although divine law forbade Catholics to attend Protestant churches, those who did so would be absolved.[64] They agreed that *natural law* forbad any person to enter Protestant churches who would be harmed by doing so, but noted such cases were rare.[65]

Indirect and *direct co-operation* were distinguished. Casuists considered that providing Protestants with prayer books was a "mortal sin" because these would be used in heretical worship. Paying taxes which could be used for unlawful purposes was permitted, however, provided the purpose was not known at time of payment. Elisha's concession to Naaman (II Kings, 5, 18-19) was the precedent cited to allow servants to attend church with their Protestant masters.[66]

The principle that *evil can never be done so that good may result* underlay the prohibition against building or endowing university colleges as these could be used by Protestants.[67] In some instances, however, principles seem to have been lost in tortuous reasoning or abandoned altogether. Dictates of etiquette, for instance, permitted Catholics to bare their heads when heretics "said Grace" and defrauding heretics of tithes could be "holy"![68]

(b) Questions Regarding Marriage and Baptism

The Council of Trent's Decree on the Reformation of Marriage had declared clandestine marriages valid but unlawful. At the same time Catholics were forbidden to marry those in heresy or schism, or to marry in non-Catholic churches. As a concession to English Catholics, Pius V dispensed with the obligation of banns and permitted them to contract marriage in the presence of a priest and two witnesses.[69] Marriages not performed in accordance with the prescriptions of state authorities, however, raised the question of the legitimacy of children born of the union.[70] Mary Ward's writings and other contemporary sources reveal her closeness to many who faced these dilemmas. Marmaduke Ward considered Edmund Neville, while still a schismatic, a possible husband for his daughter. In 1591 Mary Ward's aunt, Martha Wright, married Thomas Percy, who at that time was not fully reconciled to Catholicism. Another aunt, Alice Wright, secretly married William Readshaw in Marmaduke Ward's house in 1593.[71]

In contrast to concessions made regarding communication with Protestants the Douay casuists gave harsher decisions concerning marriage. Citing the *Enchiridion* (14,18;22,49) and the support of all theologians they asserted that Catholics who marry heretics sin mortally, as did parents who arranged such marriages and priests who conducted the ceremonies, by cooperating in another's mortal sin. Allen and Persons agreed with the Douay decision but at the same time allowed marriage between Catholics and schismatics in certain cases.[72]

The question of Baptism raised the issue of legitimacy, although it could be claimed that baptism had been administered because of danger of death. Ralph Babthorpe was forced to have his children rebaptised by Protestant ministers.[73] Casuists regarded Baptism of Catholics by Protestant ministers or schismatic priests as generally valid but always unlawful. Not surprisingly they did not discuss the issue of Catholic burial services. During Charles I's reign only two Catholic cemeteries existed in London, those belonging to Queen Henrietta Maria and her mother. In general, Catholics were buried by Protestant ministers after priests had secretly conducted ceremonies. Mary Ward's companions remarked on having found a minister "honest enough to be bribed" to conduct her funeral service in the Church yard rather than in the church itself.[74]

B. *Confrontation with Authorities*
(a) The Obligation of Oaths

Among strategies recommended to recusants confronting the authorities was the claim that penal laws did not oblige morally because they were police measures to encourage an essentially indifferent act. Azor and Azpilcueta both opined that a law which had a set penalty had no higher purpose and that by being prepared to accept the penalty one was obeying the law according to its real intention. Azor, however, found it difficult to be prescriptive because few laws were purely penal. He concluded that, in general, human laws were binding insofar as they were just.[75] It remained for Suárez to elaborate further the moral theory of the "purely penal law."

Elliot Rose has undertaken extensive research into the Catholics' and Puritans' conflicts of conscience during the Elizabethan age. Rose cites a Winchester diocesan court book of 1598 which records that the recusants' usual answer to why they had not attended Church was a formula "their conscience would not serve them to go."[76] The issue of conscientious objection was not dealt with by the casuist documents. Implicit in their discussion of the extent to which law is obligatory, however, was the recognition of the inviolability or freedom of conscience. In a treatise written in 1580, Persons attempted a consistent treatment of freedom of conscience as justifying recusancy.[77] He dealt with the problem of the erroneous conscience by allowing freedom of conscience to Jews and infidels, but disallowed it to heretics because having left the Church, their ignorance was vincible. Ultimately, he decided that one had to follow one's conscience but went no further in trying to resolve the conflict between the subjective and objective moral order.[78]

The most difficult problem for English priests arose when pleas of conscientious objection failed and the recusant was faced with martyrdom, imprisonment, or loss of property. The casuists allude only once to the role of personal discernment in making moral decisions. Their brief explanation of discernment was based on the Ignatian rules of discernment and occurred within the context of their discussion of choice of martyrdom.

The Douay casuists devoted their attention mainly to cases where conflict existed between the obligation to speak the truth and self-preservation. Here they stressed that the common good must be put before individual good and that pastors must speak out before a tyrant. The decision of Allen and Persons, however, suggests that they found the common good was rarely served in such cases. Answers to be given to the authorities were distinguished from those to be given to lesser officials or curious travellers. All English casuists considered that priests who refused to give their names or professions when questioned by the authorities could be in danger of denying their faith. Where no dishonour to God or scandal to their neighbours was involved, priests were permitted to use mental reservation and ambiguity.

(b) "Equivocation" and Mental Reservation
The authorship of a pamphlet entitled: *A Treatise of Equivocation or Against Lying and Fraudulent Dissimulation*, written in 1585 shortly

after Southwell's trial, has been attributed to Henry Garnet.[79] Garnet's defence of Southwell corresponded with Azpilcueta's arguments in his commentary on a question from Gratian's *Decretals* (II,c.22,q,5). In this work, published in Rome in 1584, Azpilcueta argued in favor of the truthfulness of a statement which consists in part of vocal enunciation and in part of mental enunciation.[80]

John Gerard's report of Garnet's defence at his trial provides an understanding of how he viewed mental reservation and equivocation in practice. Garnet rejected any equivocation in matters of faith, stating that it may not be used in matters of contract or testimony, or before a competent judge. He saw it as lawful only when it was used for one's own or another's good, or when one was urged to reveal such matters as the secrets of confession, which were "not liable to any external court."[81]

The criticisms levelled at casuists for their espousal of equivocation need to be seen in their proper context. They reflect the Elizabethan state authorities' hostility to the clergy and many secular priests' hostility to the Jesuits.[82] It is significant that Garnet and Southwell, who defended equivocation, gave up their lives for their faith. Moreover, casuists such as Azor and Laymann were adamant in their condemnation of lying as "intrinsically evil."[83]

The so-called "bloody questions" were the most serious to be faced by priests under interrogation. These required them to reveal their position concerning loyalty to the Queen. Patrick McGrath's claim that these questions were reasonable demands from rulers concerned with the safety of the realm, overlooks the fact that they were the usual prelude to execution. Catholics, by objecting to questions about where their allegiance would lie if the Pope sent an army against the Queen, revealed the question's hypothetical nature and showed that the authorities sought to condemn individuals on the basis of their intentions. In many cases such questions were answered equivocally because of the priests' unwillingness to deny the Pope's supreme power in matters of faith and temporal affairs.[84]

(c) Obedience to Pope and Civil Rulers

In 1570 Pius V issued the Bull *Regnans in Excelsis* that excommunicated and deposed Elizabeth I, declared that she and all her adherents were no part of the Body of Christ, and released all her subjects from allegiance to her. In 1580 priests who set out for England were told by Pope Gregory XIII that this Bull did not bind Catholics in present circumstances. The Bull, however, not only led to reprisals against English Catholics but divided them and caused them conflicts of loyalties.

Allen and Persons, whose support for the Armada did not help the English priests' situation, agreed with the Douay casuists that since a "heretic Queen" was not a legitimate ruler interrogation by her officials was not lawful. Douay casuists in general advised Catholics to remain silent or give indirect answers. They wanted to show that Catholics were not executed for treason but because of their faith.[85] Azor, in his list of monarchs, described Elizabeth I as "depraved and infamous" because of her heresy and schism.[86] He was explicit on the Pope's right to depose but placed limits on the people's right to rebel. In his view the just commands of a monarch, even a tyrant, were to be obeyed.[87]

The situation was compounded further in 1606 after the Gunpowder Plot when James I introduced the Oath of Allegiance. This oath, based on the theory of the divine Right of Kings, was condemned by Paul V in 1606. It raised the question of Papal power in temporals and the theological problem about how one could be a loyal Catholic and a loyal subject simultaneously. Bellarmine incurred the wrath of both Pope and monarchs. He claimed that Popes had only indirect power over temporalities, that is when spiritual values were in question, and that monarchs' power comes directly from God and resides immediately in the whole state.[88] The Jesuits' position was damaged by one of their members' support for tyrannicide and a former pupil's attempt to kill Henry IV!

Moral theology's emergence as an independent discipline occurred during the counter-Reformations' post-Tridentine era and as such was affected by religious conflict. It is in this context that casuistry's relationship to the moral system of probabilism must be viewed. While probabilism represented an attempt to deal with the question of individual moral responsibility, the onus of decision-making tended to be removed from the individual. The responsibility of the confessor or "ghostly father" (the two roles being virtually synonymous) was not only to determine the degree of penitents' guilt but to guide their conscience. Prudence was defined as seeking the counsel of experts, with expertise including both goodness and learning.

With the two exceptions noted above, that heresy and schism involve the "heart" and choice of martyrdom requires personal discernment, the casuists and authors of the manuals centered their attention on the law and the opinions of the experts who deciphered it. The objective moral order and significant issues in moral life had come to be understood for the most part in legal rather than ethical terms. Paradoxically, this was both responsible for and the result of the close alliance between moral theology and canon law. Moral theology's task became the resolving of cases of conscience in terms of the law's demands.

At the same time, the cases discussed were actual dilemmas faced by English Catholics and their confessors. The Council of Trent's decrees on reform, establishment of seminaries, the pastoral orientation of the Jesuits' educational program, the works of theologians. and the casuist manuals made it possible for moral theology to deal with objective reality and with the situations Christians would meet in daily life. Moreover, the climate of the age endorsed the value of secular life.

3.3. Anthropology and Theological Principles underlying Moral Theology

The philosophical movements of the late Middle Ages and Renaissance had raised questions for moral theology, such as *human reason's power* to reach moral knowledge and *human nature as a source of moral knowledge.* Answers to these questions were influenced by views taken about human nature. In this context the theological anthropology underlying the moral theology of Mary Ward's time reveals certain anomalies.

On the one hand, one finds themes common to Renaissance humanism in the endorsement of the dignity of human nature, the capacity of human reason to comprehend moral values, individual responsibility and freedom. The decree on Justification of the Council of Trent endorsed that human nature after the Fall is not totally corrupted and that although concupiscence (the inclination to sin) remains, free will is not extinguished.[89] In tune with the Council and with St. Thomas, Bellarmine defended the dignity of human nature and the power of human reason to come to the knowledge of some moral truth.[90] Mary Ward supported Bellarmine's positive view. She

saw the "darkness of understanding and the propensity to sin" which
remain after justification as "sufferings not sin," although sin may
happen as a result.[91]

Moral theology's focus on sin and law within the context of the
sacrament of Penance threatened to place its emphasis on the negative aspects of human nature. Its starting point became almost exclusively a consideration of the human being as a sinner. Mortal sin
appears to have been regarded as a frequent occurrence and sacramental absolution as an act of judgement. This pessimistic view resulted in part from the effects of the Council of Trent's decrees with
respect to the Sacrament of Penance and in part from the minimal
attention given by casuists to grace and the new law.

While the Council of Trent used Scriptural references rather than
citing works of scholastics, its understanding of grace was consonant
with that of St. Thomas. His treatise on grace stands at the end of his
treatment of beatitude as the destiny of the human creature (1a2ae.1-
5) and human moral activity as it relates to reaching that end. He
saw grace as elevating and regenerating human nature, enabling human beings to reach the end to which they are called. The new Law is
a law of freedom based on the grace of the Holy Spirit obtained for
us by Christ in redeeming humanity (1a2ae. 106,3;108,1). This law,
while not necessarily inconsistent with external laws, interiorises them,
such that the primary motivation for obedience is love.

Specific treatment of grace was not part of the *cursus minor*. Certain aspects which related to original sin, justification and the relationship of grace and free will were, however, treated in controversial
theology. Even so, in formulations of moral theology one does find
implicit recognition that grace and nature are in harmony. Azor, for
instance, accepted St. Thomas' elaboration of the supernatural character of grace and the need for elevating grace even in the state of
innocence. Suárez who was both an exponent of probabilism and a
professor of scholastic theology, saw the supernatural obligations of
divine law as in harmony with human nature in that one who turns
away from one's supernatural end through sin is at the same time
diverted from one's natural end.[92] Moreover, the basically optimistic view
of human nature held by the Jesuits in general is evident in their opposition to Jansenism which arose in the mid-seventeenth century.

St. Thomas considered moral matters within theology as a whole,
his starting point being God and his conclusion being the Person of

Christ, through whom come the sacraments, sources of grace. The *Summa's* ethical sections open with an examination of the human creature, made in God's image and endowed with intelligence and freedom of judgement. In his subsequent treatment of human acts St. Thomas deemed it essential to include the intrinsic principles of these acts: passions and habits, virtues and vices, and the external principles: law, whereby God instructs us and grace, whereby God assists us.

The authors of casuist manuals used a predominantly practical mode of argument. Their emphasis was on the objective aspects of morality. Moral conduct was viewed in terms of human actions which were in conformity to the laws which regulate human conduct with reference to the human being's supernatural end. Actions were given more attention than habits and virtues. Sin and virtue were considered as acts rather than as states or dispositions resulting in acts. Hence, little explicit attention was given to the agent's disposition as a significant determinant of the goodness or malice of human action or to an explication of moral conduct in terms of fidelity to the teaching or example of Christ. Until 1615, when the Jesuits' General Congregation made a chair of moral theology mandatory, consideration of the passions and habits was not included as part of the academic teaching of moral theology within the *cursus maior*.

Casuists took their notion of natural law from St. Thomas and theologians' commentaries on his work. Noting that natural precepts are not equally well known or easy to understand, casuists undertook the task of interpretation. In so doing they placed considerable reliance on the teaching of the church Fathers, the councils, and experts in canon law. Their idea that prudence lies in seeking the advice of wise and good experts, however, failed to emphasize St. Thomas's emphasis that prudence arises from love and is a virtue which makes its possessor good (2a,2ae, 49:1,4,7). Nor was explicit attention given to charity as the motivation for morality. Rather, casuists focused on acts contravening the commandments and virtues. As a result, their emphasis appeared to be more on not disobeying God than on seeking and accomplishing God's will.

At the same time clergy using casuist manuals were aware that while casuistry had an important role to play in making moral decisions, moral rectitude was not synonymous with conformity to external laws. The importance of moral formation and growth in personal holiness was stressed both by Aquaviva and reports from the colleges and seminaries.[93] Significantly, however, moral theology was not specifically mentioned as contributing to this growth. Rather, the clergy turned to treatises on the Christian life. Here the emphasis was on love of God as the primary element of the moral life - this love was reflected in discipleship, love of neighbor, and the exercise of moral asceticism.

Hence, with the emergence of moral theology as an independent discipline systematically separated from other branches of theology, matters pertaining to morals came to be addressed in two different forms: manuals which conveyed moral theology in the strict sense, and ascetical works which dealt with the practice of the moral life. While authors of the latter were familiar with the former a rigid distinction of content was maintained between them. In the years immediately preceding the second Vatican Council Catholic moral theology came under increasing criticism. When the Council asked that special attention be given to the development of moral theology, many regarded it as an indictment of what they saw as moral theology's pre-occupation with casuistry. The real misfortune for moral theology, however, lies, not so much in its use of casuistry, which has a valid role in moral decision-making, but in its divorce from spiritual theology. In the centuries following the Council of Trent, moral theology and spiritual theology had continued to develop along parallel lines. Each presented different, although not necessarily opposed, views of morality. One consequence of this dichotomy can be seen in the moral theology of the late-seventeenth and eighteenth centuries which became almost exclusively preoccupied with debates over probabilism.

In contrast, convinced of the essential relationship between "matters pertaining to morality" and "matters spiritual,"[94] in her moral instruction and guidance Mary Ward sought to bring the two disciplines into harmony. Her insights flow from the theology and anthropology underlying her lived and formulated spirituality.

Notes

[1] *AB*, cited by Chambers, vol. I, 165,166.
[2] *The Oxford Dictionary of the Christian Church*, s.v. "Moral Theology".
[3] *Documents of Vatican II*, "Gaudium et Spes," #4.

[4]John Mahoney, *The Making of Moral Theology: A Study of the Roman Catholic Tradition* (Oxford: Clarendon Press, 1990).

[5]Johann Theiner, *Die Entwicklung der Moraltheologie zur eigenständigen Disziplin* (Regensburg: Freidrich Pustet, 1970), 38.

[6]Angelo Carletti, for instance, a canon lawyer and author of the *Summa Angelica* (c. 1476), pointed out that law and morality have different orientations and natures. Cited by Pierre Michaud-Quantin, *Sommes de Casuistique et Manuels de Confession au Moyen Age, (XII-XIV Siècles* (Montreal: Dominican Library, 1962), 100; see also: 105,107.

[7]Compare: L. Vereecke, "La Concile de Trente et l'enseignment de la théologie morale," *Divinitas*, 5 (1961): 361-374; S. Pinckaers, "La théologie morale au déclin du Moyen-Age: Le nominalisme," *Nova et Vetera* 52 no.3 (July-September 1977): 209-221; "Ockham and the Decline of Moral Theology," *Theology Digest*, 26 no. 3 (Fall, 1978): 239-241 (English Translation).

[8]Desiderius Erasmus, "Paraclesis," anonymous English translation, perhaps by William Roy, first published in Antwerp in 1529 and entitled "An Exhortation of the Diligent Study of Scripture", quoted in *English Humanism: Wyatt to Cowley*, ed., Joanna Martindale, (Dover, New Hampshere: Croom Helm, 1985), 276.

[9]Theiner, 77. Albert R. Jonsen and Stephen Toulmin, in *The Abuse of Casuistry: A History of Moral Reasoning* (Berkeley, Los Angeles, London: University of California Press, Ltd., 1988), include in their Catalogue of Casuists: Francisco Suárez, S.J. *Tractatus de Legibus et de Deo Legislatore* (Coimbra, 1612); Francisco Vitoria, O.P. *Relectio de Indis et de Iure Belli* (Salamanca, 1539). Vitoria was representative of the Salamanca school which embodied within the framework of Thomistic moral teaching the fruits of Nominalistic research (Bernhard Häring, *The Law of Christ Moral Theology for Clergy and Laity*, vol. 1, (New York: The Seabury Press, 1978), 17.

[10]Oration of Bishop Girolamo Ragazoni of Venice delivered in the last session of the Council, December 4, 1563, *Canons and Decrees of the Council of Trent, Original Text with English Translation*, trans., H.J. Schroeder, O.P.,(London and St. Louis, Mo.: B, Herder Book Co., 1950), 363.

[11]*Council of Trent*, session 6, 1547, *Canones de Iustificatione*, 9, 24, 26,29,32; *De Confessione*, canons 6-8.; session 14, ch.5, 1551.

[12]Donohue, Tridentine Seminary Legislation, 170-171. Donohue's thesis is that the immediate inspiration of the seminary legislation ratified by the Council of Trent was the seminary legislation of Reginald Cardinal Pole, copies of which were circulated to participants at Trent in 1555-1556. The remote cause of its adoption was the promulgation of such ideas as those of Claude le Jay, S.J. that the presence of a moral and learned

clergy could be properly assured only when each bishop was obliged to erect and supervise personally an institution dedicated to that purpose. (89, 115, 135-145, 167, 171). Donovan also finds similarities between the ideas expressed in the statutes drawn up under Protestant auspices for the re-foundation of the Canterbury Cathedral school and Cardinal Pole's proposals for seminary reform at the Legatine synod held in 1555-1556 during Mary I's ill-fated reign (108).

[13]Council of Trent, session 23, canons 7 & 8.

[14]Bossy, *The English Catholic Community*, 18; Morris, *Troubles*, third series, 109; Anstruther, vol. I, x,xi; vol.2, vii - x; Morey, 110,111; Guilday, 146, 147; Pastor, vol. XXIV, 8.

[15]Ignacio de Loyola, *The Constitutions of the Society of Jesus*, trans., George E. Ganss, part IV, chap. 12, no. 1.

[16]Ibid., part IV, chap. 13, no. 2, A.

[17]The final plan was issued after careful deliberation. It drew from the previous drafts and the recommendations and practice of previous years. These include Polanco's *Constitutiones Collegiorum*, successive plans of studies written prior to 1575 by the rectors of the colleges at Rome and Messina respectively, and recommendations from the Visitors of the Parisian and Belgian colleges. (*Monumenta Historica Societatis Jesu*, vol. 129, *Monumenta Paedagogica Societatis Jesu*, V, *Ratio Atque Institutio Studiorum Societatis Jesu (1586,1591,1599)*, ed., Ladislaus Lukács S.J., (Rome, 1986), V, 3*-7*, 13*, 17*, 356; vol.124, *Monumenta Paedogogica Societatis Jesu*, IV (1573-1580), (Rome, 1981), 194, 353 429. Henceforth these documents will be cited as *MonPaed*, V, and IV respectively.

[18]The integral part of Cases of Conscience in the programme of studies for Jesuits is evinced by the Constitutions of the Society and correspondence prior to the systematisation of the *Ratio Studiorum*. These endorsed that in keeping with the end of the Society all scholastics were to study cases of conscience and to be prepared for preaching and hearing confessions. (*The Constitutions of the Society of Jesus*, nos. 402-407, See also: *MonPaed*, IV, 195, 354, 429.

[19]*MonPaed*. V, 269, 387; "Regulae Professoris Theologiae," 1591, 1599.

[20]Ibid., "Regulae Provincialis," no. 19, #4,#5, 1599. (See also: *Constitutions of the Society of Jesus*, cons. 356, 461; *MonPaed*, V, 89, "De Casibus Conscientiae," 1586).

[21]*MonPaed*, V, 395, "Regulae professoris Casuum Conscientiae," 1599.

[22]Ibid., 387, "Regulae Professoris Scholasticae Theologiae," 1599, #1-#5.

[23]Certain questions (1a2ae.112:2; 113:4,7; 114:3,6) were treated in conjunction with other sections of the *Summa Theologiae* such as Charity and the Incarnation. The question of preparation for the grace of justification (1a2ae,112,3) was combined with a treatment of contrition as

part of the sacrament of Penance (*Mon. Paed.* V, "De Theologia Scholastica", 65, 392).

[24]Häring, *The Law of Christ*, vol.I, 19-20.

[25]*MonPaed* V, 398, "Regulae Professoris Philosophiae."

[26]The theology courses of individual Jesuits and members of the secular clergy mentioned below have been ascertained from an examination of the records given by Morris, Anstruther and Foley and in the following works: *Annales Collegii I (Liber Ruber Venerabilis Collegii Anglorum de Urbe,1579-1630*, edited by Wilfrid Kelly Ph. D., et al., (*CRS*, XXXVII, London, 1940); *Registers of The English College at Valladolid 1589-1862*, edited by Canon Edwin Henson, (*CRS*, XXX, London, 1930); Martin Murphy, *St. Gregory's College, Seville, 1592-1767* (*CRS*, London, 1992); Knox, *The First and Second Diaries of the English College*; Burton and Williams, *The Douay College Diaries*; Joseph Gillow, *A Literary and Biographical History or Biographical Dictionary of the English Catholics from the Breach with Rome, in 1534, to the Present Time*, vol.3, (London: Burns & Oates, 1887). Thomas McCoog, S.J. has collated much of the research of the above authors in his recent work: *English and Welsh Jesuits 1555-1650* (*CRS*, Record Series, vols. 74, 75,   London: 1994, 1995).

[27]Morris, *Troubles*, third series, 105-106, 112, 358-359, 443-444; Anstruther, vol.I, 9-10, 175, 240-241; vol.II, 240-241; 329, 358; *Registers of The English College at Vallodolid 1589-1862*; Foley, *Records*, V, 424-426; VI, 100, 140, 269; VII, 369-370, 703, 814.

[28]Gillow, vol.3, 30; Foley, *Records*, V, 297; VII, 416.

[29]Foley, *Records*, I, 456-466, VI, 526, VII, 446; Caraman, *John Gerard*, 6; *Liber Ruber Venerabilis Collegii Anglorum de Urbe*, I, no.188; Anstruther, vol.I, 130; Francis Edwards, S.J. ed., *Elizabethan Jesuits: Historia Missionis Anglicanae Societatis Jesu (1660) of Henry More* (Phillimore, 1981), 337-338.

[30]Foley, *Records*, II, 303; V, 681; VII (2), 814, 1457.

[31]Foley, *Records*, III, 210-214; Chambers, vol. II, 240.

[32]Foley, *Records*, I, 653-655; II, 416-424; III, 502, IV, 392-394, 403-407, 484-485; V, 681; VI, 159, 167, 173, 185, 240, 522, 524, 531; VII, 42, 299, 562, 814, 1444; *Liber Ruber Venerabilis Collegii Anglorum de Urbe*, I; Anstruther, vol I, 18; Peters, ch. XIV.

[33]Guilday, 185; Burton and Williams, *Douay College Diaries*, vol.I, 212, 216; Rev. M.A. Tierney, *Dodd's Church History of England: from the Commencement of the Sixteenth Century to the Revolution in 1688 with Notes, Additions and a Continuation*, vol. V, (London: Charles Dolman, 1843), 105,n; Anstruther, vol. I, 20, 31-32, 41, 152, 193-194, 321-322; vol.II, 145, 349-350; Canon Raymund Stanfield, contributor, "The Arch-Priest Controversy," Part 2 , "Papers Relating to Dr. Richard Smith, Bishop of

Chalcedon, and his Jurisdiction, 1625-1633," *Miscellanea XII*, (CRS, XXII, London, 1921), 146; Foley, *Records*, I, 654-655; V, 520-521; VI, 156, 163, 175-176, 209, 210, 254, 259; VII, 45, 64, 80, 278.

[34]Cardinal William Allen, *An Apologie and True Declaration of the Institution and Endeavours of the Two English Colleges, the one in Rome, the other now resident in Rhemes* (Rheims, Jean Foigny, 1581), fol.25. John Bossy points out that Allen wrote this description thirteen years after the founding of Douay and attributes the change in his frame of reference which was initially primarily academic to the influence of the Jesuits (*The English Catholic Community, 1570-1850*, 12-17).

[35] *Histoire du Collège de Douay à laquelle on a joint La Politique des Jésuites Anglois*, Ouvrages traduits de la Langue Anglaise (London: 1762), 8,180,181; Foley, *Records*, VI, 528, 532; Holmes, *Elizabethan Casuistry*, 6; Burton and Williams, *Douay College Diaries*, 14,20,70,73,81,198-200; *Liber Ruber Venerabilis Collegii Anglorum de Urbe*, I; *Registers of the English College at Valladolid*; Southern, 45,46,51.

[36]J.C.H. Aveling, *The Handle and the Axe: The Catholic Recusants in England from Reformation to Emancipation* (London: Blond and Briggs, 1976), 55,56.

[37]Thomas Francis Knox, ed., *Letters and Memorials of William Cardinal Allen*, no. XIII, in *Records of the English Catholics under the Penal Laws*. vol. 2, *The Letters and Memorials of William Cardinal Allen (1532-1594)* (London: David Nutt, 1878, 1882, New Jersey: The Gregg Press, 1965).

[38]Burton and Williams, eds. "Rheims Report (1579-1580)," in *The Douay College Diaries*, vol. II, (*CRS*, vol XI, 1911), 557-558, 564.

[39]Burton and Williams, *Douay College Diaries*, 198-200, 359-364; Aveling, *The Handle and the Axe*, 115. Guilday, 313.

[40]John Hungerford Pollen S.J., "A Relic in Times of Persecution," *The Month*, no. 433 (July 1900): 46-51; Burton and Williams, *Douay College Diaries*, vol. I, 198; Foley, *Records*, VI, 155. The Douay Diary refers to Arrowsmith as teaching Sacred Theology, whereas Foley and Pollen identify him as professor of casuistry. Arrowsmith commences his course with the consideration of general principles: *De actibus humanis*, Law, Sin and the Commandments, moving to a specific treatment of censures, *De Irregularitate*, the Decalogue, precepts of the Church, Benefices and finally Matrimony. St. Thomas' opinions are cited as decisive. Arrowsmith also taught theology at the Jesuit College for higher studies at Louvain.

[41]Edward Weston, *The triall of Christian truth by the rules of the vertues. The second parte, entreating of hope* (Douay, 1615).

[42]The studies of John Percy, cited by Foley, provide an illustration of the full seven years course. After two years of philosophy at Douay College, he

entered the English College in Rome in 1589. Here he took a further year of philosophy, three and a half years of theology, with one year of cases twice a week, and one year of Hebrew. After publicly defending universal theology at the Roman College, he was admitted to the Society and after two years novitiate was sent to the English mission. He was professed of the four vows in 1603. (Foley, *Records*, VII (1), 585).

[43]Foley, *Records*, VI, 46.

[44]Ladislaus Lukács, "De graduum diversitate," AHSJ, XXXVII (1968), cited by Ganss in *Constitutions of the Society of Jesus*, 81.

[45]J.C.H. Aveling, *The Jesuits* (New York: Stein and Day, 1982), 217.

[46]Riccardo G. Villoslada, *Storia del Collegio Romano dal suo inizio (1551) alla soppressione della Campagnia di Gesù (1773)*, Analecta Gregoriana, vol. LXVI, Series Facultatis Historiae Ecclesiasticae, Sectio A (n.2) (Rome: Gregorian University, 1954), 323-325.

[47]McCoog, entries arranged alphabetically.

[48]See Lessius' description of the content of the two-year course in controversies given at St. Omer in 1603. (*M.H.S.I.*, Vol. 141, (Rome, 1992), *MonPaed, VII: Collectanea de Ratione Studiorum Societatis Jesu (1588-1616)*, 54 VI A 1, 537-538).

[49]Jesuit correspondence prior to 1580 indicates that in addition to the *Enchiridion* works initially used in teaching "Cases" were Cajetan's *Summula Peccatorum*, (1523); the *Summa Armilla* of Bartolomeo Fumus (died 1545); and Juan Polanco's *Directorium* (1554). Douay students also used Cajetan's *Summa*, the *Provinciales* of William Lyndwood (c1375-1446), an English canonist, and Richard Gibbons and James Sharp lectured from de Toledo's handbook. A document written in part by Allen and Persons in the years 1581-1585 and kept at the English College at Rome evinces a similar content and orientation. ((*MonPaed*, IV, 197, 285, 304, 429, 476, 615-616, 798); Knox, *First and Second Douay Diaries*, 304 and *Letters of William Cardinal Allen*, 66; *Histoire du Collège de Douay à laquelle on a joint La Politique des Jésuites Anglois*, 8; Burton and Williams, *Douay College Diaries*, 73).

[50]H. Grisar, "Disputationes Tridentinae," II,440, cited by Theiner, 70,n.13. See also: 342.

[51]Theiner, 274.

[52]John Azor, *Institutionum Moralium* (Pars Prima Brixiae: Apud Io. Baptistam, & Antonium Bozzolas: Pars Secunda, Mediolani: Apud Haer. Pacifici Pontii, et Ioan. Baptistam, 1617), part 1, cols. 697, 698.

[53]*MonPaed*, IV, 615, - Letter of Cordeses to Mercurian, October 20, 1575.

[54]Häring, *Law of Christ*, vol. I, 19.

[55]Peter J. Holmes, *Elizabethan Casuistry*, (CRS, London: 1981), 6, 7.

[56]R. Walpole refers to this document in his work: "A brief and clear confutation" (Antwerp, 1603), 212 2v.

[57]*AB,* cited by Chambers, I, 10,11; Morris, *The Condition of Catholics Under James I,* 59.

[58]Aveling, *The Handle and the Axe,* 145.

[59]Holmes, *Elizabethan Casuistry,* 63-64.

[60]Ibid., 49.

[61]Azor, part 1, book 8, ch. xi. col 958; *Enchiridion,* 27: 56,57.

[62]Holmes, *Elizabethan Casuistry,* 61-62.

[63]Azor, part 1, columns 28, 958: *mala, quae ex sua natura peccata sunt...nulla metu excusari;* Holmes, *Elizabethan Casuistry,* 20, 62,75. The casuists follow the views of Azpilcueta and Azor in this matter. (Martin de Azpilcueta, *Enchiridion sive Manuale Confessariorum et Poenitentium ...* (Venice, 1604), 25:50; 27:56, 57, 63; Azor, part 1, book 1, ch. 10, cols. 25-26). Azpilcueta deemed that in Germany, England, Scotland and parts of Gaul many could be excused in conscience, and also in the external forum, because of fear, necessity and utility. Azor regarded fear of loss of all temporal goods as "just" fear. Citing St. Thomas (2a.2ae, 39,3), however, he considered Azpilcueta's allowance of the reception of heretical sacraments under certain circumstances as an extremely questionable opinion (pt.1, bk. 8, ch. xi. col 959).

[64]Holmes, *Resistance and Compromise,* 107; Letter of 1609 from the English College in Rome, 1609, cited by Foley, *Records,* VI, 119-120.

[65]Holmes, *Elizabethan Casuistry,* 76.

[66]Ibid., 22, 67, 102-103.

[67]Ibid., 118.

[68]Ibid., 72, 102.

[69]Council of Trent, *Canones super reformatione circa Matrimonium,* caput 1; *Elizabethan Casuistry,* 29.

[70]The writer of the annual letters from the English mission for 1614 states that the validity of all marriages which have not been contracted before ministers is called into question and thus, in addition to the heavy fine of 400 crowns, is added the stigma of concubinage. He adds that a fine is levied for having children baptised at home. (Cited by Foley, *Records,* VII (2), 1037).

[71]John Morris, S.J., ed., *The Condition of Catholics Under James I: Father Gerard's Narrative of the Gunpowder Plot* (London: Longmans, Green, & Co., 1981), 58; Chambers, vol.I, 18, 72; Peters, 17, 31, 34.

[72]Holmes, *Elizabethan Casuistry,* 29, 91, 107, 108.

[73]Foley, *Records,* III, 199. No records of Mary Ward's Baptism have been located.

[74]Poyntz, *A Briefe Relation.*

[75] *Enchiridion*, 23.56; Azor, part 1, cols. 470-473.

[76] Elliot Rose, *Cases of Conscience: Alternatives Open to Recusants and Puritans under Elizabeth I and James I* (New York: Cambridge University Press, 1975), 64; see also: 38, 53, 60-63, 81.

[77] Robert Persons, *A Brief Discours Contayning Certayne Reasons why Catholics Refuse to go to Church* (London: Greenstreet House, 1580).

[78] Clancy, *Papist Pamphleteers*, 156, 157.

[79] A.E. Malloch, "Father Henry Garnet's Treatise of Equivocation," *Recusant History*, 15, no.6 (October 1981): 388; Allison, "The Writings of Henry Garnet, S.J.," 14,15; Jonsen and Toulmin, 207. In a letter to Robert Persons in April 1598 Garnet stated that he had written a treatise justifying Southwell's defence of equivocation, and a copy was used against him during his trial. A copy of this pamphlet exists at the English College in Rome having been sent to Persons by either Holtby or Blunt.

[80] Martin de Azpilcueta, "Commentarius in cap. humanae aures xxii. De veritate responsi, Partim Verbo Expresso, partim mente concepto redditi," *Operum Martini ab Azpilcueta Doct. Navarri*, Tomus Secundus, (Romae: Iacobi Tornerii. 1560. 453-465).

[81] Morris, *The Condition of Catholics Under James I*, 243-244.

[82] Bagshaw, *A Sparing Discoverie*, 10-12.

[83] *per se intrinsice malum*. Paul Laymann, S.J., *Theologiae Moralis Compendium*, second edition, (1744), part 2, book 4, tract 3, chapter 13; Azor, part 1, col.28. See also: Johann P. Somerville, "The New Art of Lying," in *Conscience and Casuistry in Early Modern Europe*, ed. Edmund Leites, 171-173.

[84] Patrick McGrath, "The Bloody Questions Reconsidered," *Recusant History* 20, no. 3 (May 1991): 316; Burton and Pollen, *Lives of the English Martyrs*, xix.

[85] A. G. Petti, "Richard Verstegan and Catholic Martyrologies of the Later Elizabethan Period," *Recusant History*, vol.5, no. 2, (April 1989); 64-66; Holmes, *Elizabethan Casuistry*, 53, 65.

[86] Azor, part 2, book 11, ch. 5, col. 600.

[87] Ibid., cols. 685-687.

[88] Excerpt from Bellarmine's *Treatise on Civil Government*, 1586-1590, in *Readings in Church History*, Colman J. Barry, O.S.B., ed., vol. 2, *The Reformation and the Absolute States 1517-1789* (Maryland: The Newman Press, Westminster, 1965): 208. Suárez also took up the question of the temporal power of the Pope. He cites Azpilcueta, Cajetan, Bellarmine and de Soto to support his contention that supreme temporal jurisdiction is not possessed by the Pope. Nevertheless, in his comments on James I's Oath of Supremacy, he allows to Popes the use of coercive power against Kings, even to the point of deposing them, if there be a

valid cause, as, for instance, the defence of his charges against enemies. The Pope has directive force over all Christians and directive force is inefficacious without coercive force. (Francisco Suárez, *Defensio Fidei Catholicae, et Apostolicae adversus Anglicanae Sectae Errores*, (1613), ch. 23).

[89]Council of Trent, *De Iustificatione, Canones de Iustificatione*, canon 5.

[90]Cardinal Robert Bellarmine, "De Gratia et Libero Arbitrio," book 5, ch.2, from *Opera Omnia Roberti Bellarmini*, vol.6, Venetian edition revised and edited by Justinus Fèvre, (Paris: 1873), 37.

[91]"Reflection," April 1619, cited by Wetter (VIII): 7; Peters, 260,note 57.

[92]Suárez, *De Legibus, ac Deo Legislatore*, (1612), book 2. 9:10, 13.

[93]"Instructions given to Fr. Robert Persons and Fr. Edmund Campion, the Founders of the Mission," 1583, cited by L. Hicks, ed., *Letters and Memorials of Father Robert Persons, S.J.*, vol. I (to 1588), (*CRS* Volume XXXIX. London, 1942),

319. Accounts of the spiritual and moral formation given in the seminaries and colleges are given by William Allen: *Apologie of the English Seminaries* ((Rheims, Jean Foigny, 1581) and: Knox: *First and Second Douay Diaries*, xxix; Michael E. Williams, *The Venerable English College Rome: A History*, 1579-1979, (London: Associated Catholic Publications, 1979), 15-16, 220- 221 and *St. Alban's College Valladolid*, 235-239, 242; Donohue, 82-84; Foley, *Records*, VI, 81-82; VII, 1077.

[94]*AB*, 10, cited by Chambers, vol. I, 166.

Chapter 4

Mary Ward's Spirituality and Practice
The Estate of Justice

O how well ordered are thy deeds, my Lord God!
Then thou saidst that justice was the best disposition:
Now thou showest how such justice is to be gotten. (1636)[1]

These words form part of the last extant personal note left by Mary Ward and were written in 1636, five years after her release from the Anger prison in Munich and the suppression of her Institute. They echo her original insights in 1615 into what she termed the "estate of justice" and the increasing understanding she had in subsequent years about the "excellence" of this estate.

Mary Ward's description of the "estate of justice" is one of the oldest extant manuscripts we have of her writings. It repays careful examination since her understanding of and lived fidelity to this estate reveal the definitive aspects of her spirituality. The most complete account was given in a letter to Roger Lee, written on November 1, 1615, after she had completed a week's retreat.[2] She told him of an ongoing enlightenment of her "understanding" occurring over the previous two days. A prior account had been given in a letter of October 31 of which no copy remains. The purpose of her second letter was two-fold. First, in committing her reflection on her experience to writing she found herself better able to "discern" it, albeit less able to "declare" it. Second, although drawn to love this estate and "unable to choose but retain it," she sought Lee's approval before embracing it for "truly good."

Mary Ward's retreat and subsequent letters to Roger Lee also coincided with her finalizing of the *Ratio Instituti*, the plan approved by Bishop Blaise of St. Omer, which Thomas Sackville was going to present to Pope Paul V for approbation. Seeking to establish a new kind of religious order for women modelled on the Society of Jesus, she realized that in her day women lacked the opportunities and training possible for the Jesuits. Mary Ward's immediate concern, therefore, was to discern how her members could harmoniously combine love of God and the close following of Christ with the active love and service of others.

Towards the end of her retreat Mary Ward was given insights into the interior disposition which she considered as "altogether needful for those that should well discharge the duties of this Institute." Using the phrase "estate of justice" to denote this disposition, she first described its foremost characteristic, namely, the three-fold interior freedom from all that could take one from God, for the "entire application and apt disposition to all good works" and to "refer all to God."

Mary Ward's next statements indicate that the "estate of justice" refers fundamentally to the personal interior disposition ("a soul thus composed") and is manifested in "works of justice." Mary Ward identified this interior disposition as "the fountain, and best disposition for a soul to be in, that would perform all this well." To her mind, then, this disposition was fundamental for the validity of her Institute's apostolate.

Mary Ward's continued reflection on and lived expression of the insights she received in 1615 enriched her understanding of her original experience. In 1618 she described the perfection which comes from living according to this estate as bringing a greater resemblance to Christ, "the most perfect model of all virtue."[3] In 1619 she referred to this estate as " the excellent state of a soul wholly God's; that such only truly love, are strong and apt for all such good works as are in this world to be done."[4]

Mary Ward saw the terms goodness, justice and verity as primarily to be attributed to God, and only secondarily to be used with respect to human beings. Addressing God as: "all seeing Goodness, the Giver of truth and Worker of justice, Verity Itself," she prayed that those following the way of life of the Institute "would endeavour henceforward to become lovers of truth and workers of justice."[5] Her reflection on God's action in her life in the years between 1615 and 1636 made it clear that God reveals how justice must be manifested.

Mary Ward's exposition of the "estate of justice" in her letter to Roger Lee of November 1615 contains three key statements which are important not only for further clarifying her understanding of the justice, freedom and sincerity/verity, which are its essential characteristics, but also for providing insights into the anthropology and theological principles underlying her thought. First, she contrasted the estate of justice with the state of those whose holiness chiefly appears in that union with God, which "maketh them out of themselves." Second, she saw the estate of justice as integral to but not identical with the Original Justice of the first human beings. Third, she related the continuance of the Institute to its return to its source. A close analysis of her letter and of her subsequent writings and practice throws light on the meaning and significance of these three statements.

In contrasting the estate of justice and the state of saints whose holiness chiefly appears in ecstatic union with God, Mary Ward was explaining the form of holiness she considered necessary for the members of her Institute. That the "saints" to whom she referred were not the saints in heaven is made clear by the fact that she distinctly stated that she was referring to "a certain clear and perfect estate to be had in this life." It is important to note also that Mary Ward did not contrast the estate of justice with a holiness which has its source in a close union with God but with a holiness which consists *chiefly* in ecstatic union with God. The key to understanding this contrast lies, I believe, in her realization of the harmonious relationship of contemplation and apostolic activity made possible by the interior disposition and qualities she saw as comprising the estate of justice. For this reason she felt a preference for this state.

In the first place, this realization enabled Mary Ward to resolve the conflict she had experienced in the years prior to 1609. Writing to Albergati, the Nuncio of Lower Germany, in 1621, she described this conflict as between the value she saw in that "great quiet and continual communication with God which strict enclosure afforded" and the doing of good to others which she valued "above all,"[6] and which, given the then current views of religious life for women, she had not thought possible.

In the second place, her preference to love and desire this estate more than extraordinary favours in prayer arose from her conviction that such favours are the gifts of God and not to be sought out of self-interest. The union with God which she desired was the union of her will with God's. It was this desire which underlay her resolve that, when aware of any desire to seek her own content in "interior spiritual delights," she would offer that "content unto God," loving God and all other goods only for God.[7] For Mary Ward, true holiness lies in love and desire for and receptivity to whatever God wills.

The quality of Mary Ward's openness and receptivity to God's will stands out all the more strongly within the context of her own experiences of God in prayer. Her records show that she was no stranger to more than ordinary experiences of God's transforming love. She recalled in 1609 how as a novice within the English convent of Poor Clares, she experienced a "sudden alteration and disposition, as the operation of an inexpressible power could only cause, with a sight and certainty that there I was not to remain, that some other thing was to be done by me.... . The suffering was great because far beyond my powers, and the consolation was greater to see that God willed to make use of me in what pleased him more."[8]

While in London at the end of the same year Mary Ward received a similar intellectual illumination which she described as "a second infused light, in manner as before, but much more distinct, and with greater impetuosity, if greater there could be. I was abstracted out of my whole being ... . I did not see what the assured good thing would be, but the glory of God which was to come through it, showed itself inexplicably and so abundantly as to fill my soul in such a way that I remained for a short space without feeling or hearing anything, but the sound `Glory, glory, glory.'"[9]

In 1611, the directive to take the "same of the Society" was given in a similar manner: Mary Ward recorded hearing "distinctly not by sound of voice, but intellectually understood, these words "take the same of the Society." These words gave "so great light ... comfort and strength and changed so the whole soul" that it was "impossible" for her "to doubt, but that they came from Him whose words are works."[10]

In Mary Ward's account of these three experiences of God's extraordinary graces the joy brought by knowledge of God's will stands out clearly. In 1624-1626, when recalling the opprobrium and condemnation she received in 1609 when she left the Poor Clare convent, she described these as "trifles" not to be compared with the interior sufferings caused by her uncertainty as to God's will. In her words: "the pain was very great but very endurable, because he who laid on the burden, also carried it. Notwithstanding I could believe that there is no suffering greater than the uncertainty as to the Divine Will, to one who is resolved to seek above everything to serve God."[11]

Mary Ward's fidelity to her vocation is a living example of the harmonious relationship between contemplation and action and love of God's will which are concomitant with the estate of justice. Between 1615 and 1621 she founded houses in Liège (1616, 1618), Cologne and Trier (1620/1621), and was engaged in seeking approbation for the Institute. During this period of heightened activity her personal notes indicate that her manner of prayer was characterised by an immediate awareness of God and receptivity to God's will.[12] In 1619, in her contemplation on "comparing Christ with an earthly king" Mary Ward asked for the grace to leave all that was not agreeable to God's will. In the same year she recalled experiencing an extraordinary realization of what God was and of God's presence, and in 1620 described her heart being "holden with some power far above itself," the "least endeavour" bringing "increase of knowledge and love."[13]

Mary Ward's letters to her companions were permeated with expressions of love of God's will and her wish that they would have the same love. By 1624 Mary Ward had opened schools in Rome, Naples and Perugia and presented the final plan of the Institute to Urban VIII. In a letter of that year she urged Winifred Wigmore to seek to be "wholly God's." In 1627, when the Institute was facing opposition to its work in England and Munich and the threat of closure to its schools in Perugia and Rome, Mary Ward asked Barbara Babthorpe to pray that she "have one will with God's for then what happens will always be best welcome."[14]

Mary Ward's openness to God's will was equally evident in periods when she experienced God's apparent absence. According to Mary Poyntz, one of her first companions, between February 1629 and February 1631 Mary Ward "found herself disrobed of all that could either please or fortify her soul" and "wholly incapable of any practice, but to believe and hope in God." She attributed Mary Ward's courage and assurance at this time to her ability "to live most where herself was least," and her great capacity to give.[15] These same qualities are apparent in Mary Ward's own description of the "extreme aridity without intermission" which she experienced during the years 1607 and 1608. Despite the doubts and fears which resulted, her response was one of "great love and desire to labour without reward, that giving most satisfaction which was done unseen."[16]

During her last illness when religious persecution deprived her of the sacraments Mary Ward confided to Mary Poyntz: "I do not only want [lack] my daily communions, but also the satisfaction to feel I feel the want [lack] of that great benefit, as if I did not esteem it as I have done."[17] Mary Ward's continued fidelity to God's will despite this aridity was a concrete manifestation of the fundamental orientation of openness to God's will which she saw as integral to the estate of justice.

The love that seeks to be wholly God's and the freedom to refer all to God are central components of the estate of justice. These qualities led Mary Ward to compare this estate with the state of original justice. Her understanding of the latter can be ascertained from her retreat notes of April 1619 in which she described this state of original justice as one: "where sense obeyed reason and reason the divine will. Where there was neither darkness of understanding nor inclination to evil. Whose work was the will of their master, and whose satiation, that their God was pleased with them."[18] For Mary Ward, it is the right state of human beings before God, the harmony and equity of a well-ordered disposition, which constitutes justice or righteousness and it is this state which she saw as God's original gift to humanity.

That Mary Ward did not identify the estate of justice with the state of original justice, however, is clear. She prayed for as much of this original state as may be imparted, recognizing that the effect of original sin, namely, "darkness of understanding and a propensity to sin, will still remain (at least in some measure)." Conscious also that free will though weakened is not extinguished by original sin, she resolved "to will in all to have a will conformable" to the divine will.[19]

In the third comparison used to clarify the estate of justice Mary Ward moved from reflection on the original graced state of humanity to reflection on the source of the way of life of the Institute. She stated "that perhaps this course of ours would continue till the end of the world, because it came to that in which we first began." The phrase "to that in which we first began" has a two-fold reference. First, it looks to the original graced state of humanity. Second, the actual foundation of her new religious congregation was the outcome of her understanding in 1611 that she was to adopt the "matter and manner" of the Society of Jesus, the spiritual source of which she found in "the book of Blessed Father Ignatius, his Exercises." [20] For

Mary Ward the disposition of the estate of justice so essential for her members harmonizes with the central aims of the Exercises, namely, the inner freedom and well ordered disposition which enable the positive rejection of all that is not "more conducive" for the honor and glory of God and the spiritual welfare of souls.

Mary Ward's concepts of freedom and the virtue of sincerity/ verity, which she saw as integral to the way of life in the Institute, illuminate the relationship between the estate of justice on the one hand, and, on the other hand, the state of original justice and the spirituality she finds expressed in the Exercises. Her personal insights, too, enrich the themes expressed in the Exercises. They penetrate more deeply into the Exercises than did some of the Jesuit interpretations discussed earlier, which were influenced by the general tenor of the spirituality of the period.

Mary Ward's concept of freedom has a three-fold dimension: freedom from attachment to earthly values and things; freedom for any kind of good works; and freedom to refer all to God. As Olga Warnke points out, "this last freedom, so characteristic of Mary Ward, is that union of heart and will with God that makes the other two freedoms possible and authentic."[21] Mary Ward saw freedom, first, as a gift of God, second, as so integral to human beings that real freedom is a return of oneself and one's choices to God, and third, as both a disposition and a way of life. In her lived and formulated spirituality we cannot separate her notion of freedom from her love of God and her total commitment to seeking God's will. Freedom for her was a dimension of love, primarily God's redemptive love through Christ, which liberates human beings and enables them to respond in love to God and others and be open to all that is good and true.

The grace-given inner freedom which makes this response possible and of which Mary Ward wrote in 1615 became the subject of her subsequent reflections and writings. In July 1616, she elucidated the nature of the freedom to refer all to God. She described this freedom as such that "one is free from all and desires only one, which is to love God, and here one remains free and contented … being present to all, yet cleaving to nothing." It enables one to refer to God both what is naturally desired and that which one finds repugnant, "the mind equally satisfied whichsoever of these contraries should happen"; equally prepared "to do" or "not to do," confident that God will bring about what is in accordance with the divine will.[22]

Mary Ward's lived spirituality embodied the freedom of which she wrote. The ultimate test of her inner freedom and openness to God's will came prior to the suppression of the Institute and her confinement in prison. In 1619 faced not only with external opposition but also with a movement among some of the Liège members to change the direction of the Institute, she made the Exercises under John Gerard's direction. The honest notes she has left of her reflection on death reveal her struggle to come to terms with her own importance for the Institute and her reluctance to die before it was confirmed. She wrote:

> I humbled myself (though with some difficulty) and confessed the power of God, to do what he would have done by any (though perceived not this any other wise than that by faith I was bound to believe so). I saw how hardly and with much ado I was brought to do that little I have done (and) that God's working was the beginning, middle and sole cause why... . I turned to myself, offering with love to leave what I loved: very desirous to die ere this was done, that his working in it might the more appear... . I besought him, that this I now saw and did, might stead me when I lay a dying, because perchance these extremes would then make me unapt for all. This remains still as present and I find a great desire to die before, that God's glory and this deceit of my ability, may the better appear; but it seems my security, and best: to rest in God's will only, which I do, and will for ever.[23]

In the same spirit she wrote from prison in 1631: "If God would have me die, I would not live; it is but to pay the rent a little before the day. To live and suffer for God, or die and go to Him, are both singular graces, and such as I merit not."[24]

These instances of the freedom which Mary Ward regarded as the "felicity" of the estate of justice find expression in the Exercises in the disposition of the third class of persons and the third kind of humility (#167). It is the freedom to refer all to God which was most fully expressed by Christ.

For Mary Ward, referring all to God is akin to the finding of God in all things which underlies the Ignatian "Contemplation to Obtain Divine Love" (##230-237). "Refer" means to bring back, to return. To refer all to God culminates in the return of all we have been given, including our liberty and will, to the God who "works and labours" for us in all creation (##235-237).

Mary Ward used the word freedom only in reference to human beings. In speaking of God's grace as the source of human freedom she used the term "liberality." She saw the security of the Institute as lying in the "free recourse" of all its members to God.[25] Her own experience of God's liberality taught her that returning ourselves to God increases our knowledge of God's working within us, and enables us to find ourselves in God.

Mary Ward recorded many instances of God's liberality with graces in her life and her consequent growth in inner freedom. Her autobiography contains three significant mentions of freedom. Two refer to her vocation. Mary Ward described her discernment of God's will as a "happy begun freedom" and stated that God "freed" her by removing her father's and confessor's opposition to her decision to become a religious. Her third reference deals with the realization in 1600 that "love and freedom" give ascetical practices their validity.[26]

The three-fold freedom which Mary Ward formulated and lived is the fruition of the indifference spelled out in the Exercises. For Loyola "indifference" denotes distancing oneself for true vision, keeping oneself "in balance." Mary Ward expressed this as the "equanimity" which marks the harmonious state which she called the estate of justice. Indifference is not an end in itself but the means by which, freed from all inordinate attachments, we may seek and find God's will in the disposition of our lives for the end for which we were created (#1,#23). In common with Loyola, Mary Ward saw the right use of creatures within the context of God's goodness and sovereignty. She spoke of a "friendly separation from the things of this world" and a freedom "equally" to have or to lack them.[27] This involves affection for and acknowledgment of the goodness of creation, seeing God at work in history.

Removing disordered attachments does not leave a cold and cheerless void. Rather, love of God and of God's creation gives indifference its rationale. Such love was the motivating force in Mary Ward's life. Her actions and writings reveal her own personality and how affectivity played a key role in her spirituality. She addressed God as the "Friend of friends" and, in reference to human friendship, described herself as "so apt for friendship" and as having "ever loved more than ordinary."[28] In this context her use of the phrase "the long loneliness" to describe suffering takes on deeper meaning.[29] It refers both to her experience of God's apparent absence and to the opposition and rejection she faced from churchmen and from some of her own sisters. Recognizing that affectivity goes deeper than sensible feelings and cognitional satisfaction and must move the will, she saw it as evinced in the "great love and liberty of mind"[30] that flows out in love and service of others.

The Archives of the Institute contain Mary Ward's meditations in 1619 on the "Call of the Apostles." Her notes indicate that she was directed to meditate on the particular grace of a religious vocation and to pray for perseverance in this vocation for God's greater glory. Significantly, in her reflection Mary Ward returned to the disposition or estate she saw as essential to living out her vocation. She noted how the apostles freely placed their *affection* and consequently their *entire selves* at Christ's disposal. Then she distinguished having possessions from being possessed by them, seeing only the latter as militating against our love of God.[31]

Although Mary Ward and her Institute suffered the direst poverty, she did not see poverty as an end in itself but in terms of God's service. In 1636, she advised Winefrid Bedingfield in Munich: "Jesus forbid you should make such children as you teach pay one penny for windows, wood, or anything else. For God's sake, if you do that work of charity, do it like yourself, not mercenarily, else...follow my poor counsel and let it alone."[32] To her mind, the well ordered attitude to created things reveals itself in neither possessiveness nor neglect but in a loving surrender. Such freedom marks the sincerity/verity which attributes to God what is God's.

Precision and directness characterize Mary Ward's writing and thought. Hence, her references to sincerity require close attention. After pointing to interior freedom as an essential characteristic of the estate of justice she moved to justice, as constituting the state of a person enjoying this freedom ("a soul thus composed"). Next, likening this state to that of those in original justice, she referred in turn to "just persons, works of justice done in innocence, and that we be such as we appear and appear such as we are."

Mary Ward's next reference to justice also indicates that she sees justice as inseparable from sincerity. Although she has not previously specifically mentioned the virtue of sincerity, she now unites it with justice as a "*ground* for all those other virtues necessary to be exercised by those in the Institute." Their relationship is further emphasized by her next statement that: "being grounded in *this*," will en-

able the gaining at God's hands of "true wisdom and ability to perform all such other things as the perfection of this Institute exacteth."[33]
The virtue of sincerity, then, is not only a central component of the
estate of justice, but also manifests the right or well-ordered attitude
to God, to oneself, and to other human beings which constitutes
justice or righteousness.

Both naturally and as a virtue, sincerity is inseparable from verity
and means honesty of intention and freedom from hypocrisy, namely,
that we show ourselves as we are and that our works do not contra-
dict our thoughts.[34] Mary Ward used the words "verity," "true" and
"truth" on nine occasions in her autobiographical writings. Relating
verity to right judgement, she asked those who read her words "to
determine of all as the truth is"[35] and to distinguish God's goodness
from her own response. As a natural trait of her own character sincerity was signified by her dislike for all deceit in dealing with others,
with an especial fear of self-deceit. Nor could she feel any exaltation
in titles or offices or rely on the praises of others, seeing the latter as
only "guesses and conceits," and "without reality." Accustomed to
treat others with sincerity she found Mary Goudge's attempts to per-
suade her to remain with the Poor Clares "very unsuitable" to her
mind and way of acting.[36] Her disposition was such that she was
unable, without going against her nature, to act half-heartedly in
things of the soul. She urged her companions to love verity stating that
"all things are lies that are not as they are in deeds," and asking "who can
love a creature or a friend who is not as he seemeth to be?"[37]

Mary Ward's reflections and, above all, her practice endorse that
she saw the virtue of sincerity as evinced in love of and fidelity to the
truth. It is the grace-given desire to attribute to God what is God's
and "the single minded" living out of the way of life of the Institute,
that is, acting without self-interest and seeking only God's will.[38]

Seeing the verity of God as the source of human verity, Mary Ward
identified God's "words" as "works."[39] Acting from the same conviction, in her reply to her opponents who differentiated between the
fervor of men and women solely on the basis of gender, she equated
verity with "preventing" or grace-given truth.[40] Walter Principe, in
his examination of Mary Ward's spirituality, considers that in doing
so she found, "perhaps unwittingly," the original meaning of the
Hebrew word *emet*. *Emet*, translated in the Vulgate as *veritas*, is first
of all an attribute of God and denotes the truth and fidelity of God.[41]

Mary Ward's life provides instances of the sincerity which finds expression in fidelity and love of verity. Her love of and desire for truth is apparent in her Memorial to Urban VIII of February/March 1629 in which she enclosed a petition for the approbation of the Institute. Here she appealed to the Pope to establish the truth or falsity of the accusations made against its members by examining their case. In reference to the means by which she and her first companions sought to know God's will, she stated that "God is witness" that their only end and object in seeking their way of life has been God's will.[42] Joseph Grisar, commenting on this Memorial, sees it not merely as an historical document, but as also an uncommonly valuable testimony to human nobility, illuminating Mary Ward's character and thinking, namely her sense of justice and truth, obedience to the Pope, loyalty to her members, and a logical consistency of thought which points to unusual power of intellect and inner freedom.[43]

Despite this appeal, which does not appear to have been seriously considered by the cardinals in their deliberations about the Institute, opposition increased, culminating in accusations against Mary Ward's own fidelity and verity. On April 6, 1630, not believing that the order to close her house in St. Omer came from the Pope or represented the decision of the majority of the Cardinals, Mary Ward wrote to her members urging them to remain faithful to the Institute until the Pope himself informed them of its suppression.[44] Extracts taken from this letter by one of her opponents[45] were translated into Latin, and sent to the Cardinals of Propaganda and to the Roman Inquisition. After careful examination of these extracts Grisar concludes that if Mary Ward's letter is read without bias it corresponds completely to sound moral judgements. He goes further, stating that we must admire this letter as the testimony of one who not only defended the right for the sake of right, but saw therein the great work given to her by God, for which everything must be done and everything else put aside.[46]

Mary Ward's subsequent memorial to Urban VIII (November 28, 1630) attests to her fidelity to her vocation which she described as "entirely (as far as human judgement can arrive) ordained and commended by the express word of Him who will not deceive nor can be deceived." It also attests to her willingness to "desist," if the Pope gave her the least insinuation of his will.[47] Grisar assesses this memorial as "a moving proof of the human greatness of Mary Ward, a shining testimony of her loyalty to the Church and to its Head."[48] Given Mary Ward's love of directness, the lack of clear direction from the Pope compounded her difficulties. In fact, as far as can be ascertained from a study of the relevant documents this appeal was never answered and the Bull of Suppression had been signed, though not promulgated, prior to Mary Ward's memorial.

Olga Warnke points out: "the last fourteen years of Mary Ward's life have perhaps the most to say to us today. She remained true to her inner light and faithfully obedient to the Church."[49] During her imprisonment in 1631 Mary Ward faced two of the greatest tests of her fidelity and love of verity. Physically ill and confined in a filthy cell and thinking that her opponents would never permit her release, she felt that she had finally done all that was possible, "all labours now being taken out of her hands." Yet, just as in 1619 she had rejected as a "lie" any suggestion that she was essential to the Institute, so now she recognized that God's will required her to forward the truth by laboring "in defence of her own and hers their innocence."[50]

Mary Ward's resolve was put to the test a few days later when Dean Jakob Golla, who had been deputed by the Inquisition to arrest Mary Ward, refused to allow her to receive the last sacraments unless she signed a declaration renouncing her heresy. Seeing such a declaration as a betrayal of the "many innocent and deserving persons" who supported her, Mary Ward replied that she preferred "to cast her self on the mercy of Jesus Christ and die without the sacraments."[51] She then wrote to Urban VIII (March 27, 1631) confirming her innocence and obedience to Church authority.[52]

Mary Ward's letters from prison, written in lemon juice to avoid interception, have been preserved in the Institute's Archives in Munich. These letters contain words of encouragement to her members and suggestions of persons who could assist them. Confident in God's verity Mary Ward urged her companions to "be expedite and quietly industrious … in the business" and then to "commend the case to God, that He would vouchsafe to enlighten and forgive all, and use all they do to his honour and the good of the work … .Let us let God do what He will in His turn.[53]

In the years following the suppression of the Institute its members had no legal security and were greatly reduced in number. Until her death in 1645 Mary Ward, whose educational works had not been included in the Bull, continued in her fidelity to her vocation. Her letters express confidence in God's "unseen Goodness," concern for the spiritual and physical good of her companions, fidelity to her vocation and obedience to the Pope.[54] Her earliest biographer writes that her last words commended to her companions "the practice of God's vocation," "that it be constant, efficacious, and loving in all that belongs to the general and particular of the same." Mary Ward's final promise to them reflects her belief in God's continuing fidelity: "It matters not the who but the what. And when God will enable me to be in place I will serve you."[55]

Mary Ward's practice attests to her realization of the essential relationship of disposition to action, and that in any authentic spirituality'experience and response cannot be separated. She had no other ambition but "at her death to have been found faithful."[56] She saw Christ as the most perfect example of this fidelity. Her life bore witness to that of the God become human with whom she sought to be identified. Characteristically, she delayed her release from prison for a few days to spend Palm Sunday there. Her implicit Christology, an intrinsic element of her spirituality, unites prayer and response. Verity and fidelity, for Mary Ward, became concrete by following the "kenosis" of Jesus, who is the fullest expression of the divine-human encounter and the embodiment of God's fidelity and truth in history.

The truth of the Incarnation evokes a corresponding human response in fidelity and verity. The central components of the estate of justice, namely, justice, sincerity/ verity and freedom, correspond respectively to: the well ordered disposition of justice, namely, right relations with God, oneself, and human beings; the manifestation of this disposition in sincerity and verity, the faithful response to the liberality of God's graces; and the ensuing freedom, ultimately to refer all to God, and to find all in God.

Mary Ward's conviction that grace and human nature are in harmony was central to her understanding of the estate of justice. Her most explicit statement about grace refers to "fervour," the grace-given willingness to do good, "a prevenient grace of God, and a gift given gratis, which we could not merit."[57] As has been stated, this statement forms part of her explanation that the gift of verity, God's preventing truth entering human lives before any human meriting, is offered freely to both men and women. Their lack of "fervour" results from the neglect and refusal of this grace.

Referring to this statement, Walter Principe comments on Mary Ward's "remarkable grasp of the doctrine of grace."[58] Equally remarkable, given the absence of opportunities for women to receive theological training, and the separation of spiritual and dogmatic theology, is how Mary Ward recognized that spirituality must be based on sound theology.

Mary Ward's formulations of the role of grace in the spiritual and moral life flow from her considerations about the estate of justice and free-will. The frequent references to "prevenient grace" and to human concurrence found in her writings indicate her familiarity with the teachings of the Council of Trent and of theologians of her time.

Mary Ward first considered grace within the context of justification. She made it clear that by the estate of justice, she meant the restoration of human nature through grace to its original graced state insofar as this is possible. Her description of the effects of loss of original justice and her prayer that God restore to her as much of this state as is possible in this life indicate that she considered the original state of human beings to be a graced state. In this state grace enlightens the understanding and acts upon the will, liberating it and bringing it into harmony with God's will.

In like manner, Mary Ward saw God's gift of grace to fallen human nature as liberating and healing, bringing harmony of reason and affectivity. In tune with Trent, she described justification as the work of God but requiring human co-operation. This cooperation relates to our initial acceptance of justifying grace and to our seeking its restoration if lost by mortal sin, and its increase by continuing fidelity to God.

Mary Ward's concern with our co-operation, and, specifically, with the freedom of the human will, sprang from her love of God and desire that her disposition and actions completely conform to God's will. On August 20, 1628 she wrote of receiving a "great clear and quiet light or knowledge" of what God does in and by human beings and how they should respond. Although she stated that her insight was more distinct than she could express, she attempted to formulate the respective properties of God's action and human concurrence. She distinguished as properties of God's "immeasurable bounty and goodness": the supernatural destiny ordained for human beings, God's initial movement of the human being to desire to act in accordance with this destiny, the subsequent graces given, and the gift of free-will. Human beings concur with God by seeking to *know* the good that God desires and by choosing to *act* in conformity with this good.[59]

These conclusions are the fruit of Mary Ward's earlier attempts to grapple with how we co-operate with grace. For her, the first requisite and sign of our co-operation with grace is our response to God's initial motion. This response is shown in desire. The greater the desire, the more effectual will be the exercise and acts of free will which follow. The right use of free will in action is manifested first in our desiring the grace of willingness, the gift of a loving God, second in our esteeming this gift as God's love deserves, and third in acting accordingly. Mary Ward stressed that our willingness to choose the good God offers is necessary to bring this good to perfection. Sin, therefore, results from a lack of willingness. Its malice lies not only in our rejection of the good God offers, but also in the misuse and perversion of free-will.[60]

Mary Ward did not pretend to have fathomed the mystery of human freedom: that on the one hand, human co-operation with grace is entirely the fruit of God's grace and that for all action God's prior movement of the will is necessary, and on the other hand, that sin is entirely to be attributed to human beings. She referred to free-will as something in man "nearly his own, freely given him to use at his will, while he continued man."[61] It is interesting that Karl Rahner, likewise grappling with the relationship of grace and freedom, discusses our capacity to retain "something" wholly our own, and interprets this as the individual's moral responsibility.[62] Referring to the mystery that human beings must labor or not gain, but not gain through their labor, and recognizing that cooperation with grace is but the creature's loving response to God, Mary Ward records the "light and certainty" she received that she was "to labour thus some little time," but after that short space God would give what she now sought, "without my labour."[63]

From Mary Ward's love of God arises her love for God's gift of the freedom to co-operate with grace. Although she recognized the fragility of the human condition and described the human will as "exceeding stubborn and perverse," she rejoiced in the gift of free will which enabled her to "will to have a will" conformable to God's. This she saw as the beginning, (but only the beginning), of that perfection to which God brings those in this life who "do not hinder God and will apply themselves."[64] Linking perfection with verity, she emphasised the relationship of intellect and will, urging her companions to seek knowledge of verity in order to "love it and affect it."[65] True freedom comes when God enlightens our reason and liberates our free will.

Mary Ward's experience of God's verity and fidelity governs her understanding of how God moves human beings, endowed with reason and free will and redeemed by Christ, to co-operate with grace. From experience she understood that God does not force this co-operation, but, rather, takes compassion on human labour and proposes what is to be done, leaving human beings free to use these means or not.

Mary Ward's identification of God's "immeasurable goodness" with God's Being governs her understanding of the relationship between grace and human nature. God's gifts, commands, words and works are good because God is good. This understanding led her to see the action of grace as bringing harmony to human nature. Human beings, created in God's image, are the recipients of God's goodness, verity and fidelity, the fullest manifestation of which is their justification through the grace of Christ. Her statement that the rejection of God's grace results in "endless detriment" to both the individual and other human beings [66] endorses her conviction that acting in accordance with grace is in harmony with the true good of human beings.

Mary Ward's spirituality provides an equilibrium between love of God and love of human nature. During her era moral theology generally reflected a pessimistic view of human nature and spiritual writers urged hatred of self. Mary Ward saw natural gifts, including her own, as suffused with grace and meriting her love. She rejected as unlovable only the ingratitude and illconcurrence found in the excessive self-interest which aims to possess the gifts of God without regarding the Giver.

In this context, Mary Ward wrote: "If I shall see myself favoured by God, I will continually cry out, *Tu solus, tu solus, nihil sum*; this my God, is none of mine, I will not rob it to become great, take me, all that I am, with it, and let me still see what I am without thee."[67] Again, concerned that the good she saw in creatures and in her own natural gifts might lead her to neglect the absolute Good which they reflect and which is their source, she prayed for the grace to know what "to hate and love" in herself, "agreeable to equity and justice."[68] Looking at what she, and all humanity, are without God led her to see not a totally corrupted human nature, but one in need of and open to the elevating and healing grace which God desires to give. Such grace ennobles human nature. It makes possible the well ordered interior disposition such that one seeks to find God within all human gifts and loves, and to love them for God.

The optimism which sees grace as essentially harmonious with and bringing harmony to human nature underlies Mary Ward's conviction that through God's goodness and fidelity the estate of justice is possible in this life. Regard for this harmonious state and concern that "all are not thus freed" motivated Mary Ward to seek the personal good of others. Her way of seeking this good excluded the denigration of the "secular" world found in an anthropology which sees human nature as radically spoiled by original sin. Rather, she directed her apostolate to the service of all, sought to instruct young women as to the manner in which they could make a significant contribution in society, and placed great value on the acquisition of knowledge.

In 1633 Mary Ward described God's nature as "so truly good" as to serve those "busied in his service."[69] Writing to Winefrid Bedingfield in 1627 she praised the progress of her Latin scholars and encouraged Winefrid to continue to increase her own happiness and God's honour and service by advancing her pupils "apace in that learning."[70] Her concern that her works of education be available to the poor indicates that she saw the healing of social injustices as essential to works of justice.

Mary Ward indicated that her insights with respect to grace arose immediately within the context of her prayer and remotely from what she read and heard. Her own references and the content of her writings suggest several contemporary sources for her understanding of justification and her theology of grace.

Mary Ward's understanding of justice as the well-ordered relationship with God, oneself and others was firmly based in Scripture. Paul applies the term "righteousness" or "justice" first to God and only then to human beings. Justice is God's free gift through Jesus Christ (Rom. 5:15-19). The justice which human beings seek to bring about is not our own but God's and is expressed in right relations.

Reference has been made to the high regard in which Mary Ward held Scupoli's *The Spiritual Conflict* and to its influence on her spirituality. Through Southwell's *Short Rule of Good Life* she gained knowledge of the themes of the Exercises, and his positive anthropology is similar to her own. In addition, his work included a diagrammatic exposition of justification. While one can find phrases similar to those used by Scupoli and Southwell in her reflections on freedom, justice and verity, the phrase "prevenient grace" does not appear in either work. Rather, her use of this phrase and her emphasis on the need for human cooperation with grace are more reminiscent of the Council of Trent's teaching that justification is to be derived from the "prevenient grace of God" but that human beings through this grace can dispose and convert themselves to their own justification by freely consenting to and co-operating with that grace.[71]

An English translation of the decrees of the Council of Trent on original sin and on justification was provided in an appendix to Peter Canisius' *Summe of Christian Doctrine*, published between 1592 and 1596. This work was divided into two sections under the respective headings of wisdom and justice. The scriptural text used in this work to summarise the whole of christian doctrine: "My sonne, coveting Wisedome, conserve Justice, and God will give it unto thee,"[72] recalls Mary Ward's insights into the relationship of the estate of justice to the obtaining of "true wisdom" from God. More in tune with Mary Ward's understanding of justice is Francisco Arias' *Treatise on Spirituall Profit* which emphasises the role of reason, the virtues, and God's limitless grace, power and love. This work was printed in English at St. Omer in 1617.

Mary Ward's exposition of the state of original justice and her understanding of justice also has similarities to St. Thomas' description of the original rectitude of the first human beings and of justice as implying a general rectitude of order. He defines justification as "a kind of transformation from the state of injustice to the state of justice," that is, a right order in our actions and interior disposition. Mary Ward's description of the "delicacy" of the state of original justice echoes St. Thomas almost exactly.[73] Such a disposition is the fruit of habitual grace.

Mary Ward's understanding of the need of human beings for grace recalls St. Thomas' exposition of the disharmony caused by original sin.[74] Through Grace, the new law of Christ, spoiled human nature is both healed and elevated. Mary Ward believed with St. Thomas that God moves us to justice in the mode proper to each, according to our nature, as beings who can exercise free choice. Her description of the gift of the habitual willingness which liberates the will first to desire and esteem and then to choose and actively commit oneself to what God wills agrees with St. Thomas' delineation of the effects of grace.[75]

Closer to Mary Ward's time was Robert Bellarmine. He was well known in England among Catholics and Protestants alike. Robert Southwell and John Gerard were among Bellarmine's pupils and English clergy who studied controversial theology at Douay and in Rome were familiar with his writings. Gerard maintained contact with him and encouraged Mary Ward's members to place their confidence in Bellarmine regarding approbation of the Institute.[76] Mary Ward's writings contain many ideas which agree with his expositions of original justice and grace.

Bellarmine describes the first human being as endowed with original justice and grace, and free from the tendency to evil, weakness, ignorance and difficulty which human beings experience after the fall.[77] He asserts absolutely (*tamen absolute dici potest*) that while Baptism does not restore all that pertains to original justice, it restores that gift insofar as it converts the mind to God and makes it subject to God.[78] In treating grace, free will and the question of knowledge of moral truth, Bellarmine stresses that God, as universal mover, gives us the first motions for good.[79]

Mary Ward's interpretation of justice as primarily the interior disposition from which works of justice flow and her portrayal of Christ as the "exemplar" of the just person echoes Bellarmine's description of justice. Bellarmine sees *interna justitia* as comprising both habitual justice and actual justice, the performance of works of justice.[80] As support for his theological claims he cites Scripture, the decrees of the Council of Trent, the church fathers and St. Thomas. His commentary on the Psalms, the fruit of twelve years reflection and first published in 1611, focuses on Christ's justice and verity and on the justification of the impious through the grace of Christ.[81]

Mary Ward's interest in the relationship of grace and freewill is not surprising given the nature of the then current discussions with respect to grace. During the *De Auxiliis* debate Jesuits such as Suárez,

Lessius and Bellarmine had been concerned to explain how the will remained intact even under the impulsion of efficacious grace. This debate was silenced in 1611 by Paul V. Thomas Clancy argues that it had little influence on popular consciousness,[82] but Mary Ward was probably aware of it since she and her members attended Jesuit churches for instruction. Jesuits would have been familiar with Loyola's warning in the Exercises that grace should not be stressed at the expense of freedom (#369) and with the views of Bellarmine and Leonard Lessius who agreed with Bellarmine. Lessius supported Mary Ward's early plans and gave his *imprimatur* to Richard Burton's *Defensio* of the Institute. Her insights into grace and freedom may have been influenced by one of his works first published in English in 1614.[83]

Whether Mary Ward read the works of St. Thomas, Bellarmine and Lessius, or whether their teachings were brought to her by individual Jesuits is difficult to ascertain with certitude. Certainly, her Institute sought to provide "higher learning, moral and divine."[84] She herself read Latin and insisted that her students be fluent in it. This was the language of the Mass, of the Vulgate version of the Bible which was used by English Catholics prior to the Douay version, and of most of the theological writings of the time. Mary Ward was familiar with the psalms of the breviary and the Primer, and frequently cited Scripture in her writings.

Mary Ward's writings indicate how individual Jesuits helped her Institute and she exhorted her members not to abandon their love for the Society of Jesus despite persecution by some of its members.[85] It was through the courage of the early Jesuit missionaries that she first came into contact with Jesuit spirituality. As has been seen in earlier chapters, Mary Ward numbered Richard Holtby among her early confessors and was given the Exercises and assisted in her plans for the Institute by Roger Lee and John Gerard. In addition, William Baldwin, who initially recommended Roger Lee to her, was responsible for a manuscript work in English entitled *De Gratia*.

Mary Ward's brother George, whom his peers regarded as an "eminent theologian," taught theology in Liège. He is reported to have been in contact with her in England in 1618 and was in Ghent with Gerard in 1627. John Poyntz and Thomas Babthorpe, whose sisters were among Mary Ward's first companions, also lectured in theology at the Jesuit College in Liège.

Other Jesuits who supported Mary Ward and her companions and had studied St. Thomas' treatise on grace were Henry More, John Floyd, Richard Gibbons, Anthony Hoskins, Edward Coffin, Richard Burton and Thomas Fitzherbert.[86] These men combined their knowledge of theology and their missionary labors with the translation or compilation of devotional works. Mary Ward lived near the Jesuit printing press at St. Omer, and its director, John Wilson, gave her support. Despite her familiarity with Latin, she appreciated works of instruction and devotion in her native tongue as her request for them in 1639 indicates.[87] The number of original editions of devotional works at the Bar Convent York, founded in 1686 by Frances Bedingfield, endorses that Mary Ward passed on this appreciation to her early companions.

The primary source for Mary Ward's spirituality and its underlying theology and anthropology depended upon the inspirations and grace she received from God. Her contrast between the knowledge gained from reading and instruction and that which comes during prayer recalls Loyola's words that the Holy Spirit will teach one better than any human being what reason dictates to be for the greater glory of God.[88] In this context Rahner's conclusion to his analysis of grace and freedom is interesting. He writes that the best way to gain insights into the relationship of grace and human freedom is by reflection on the frame of mind of a person at prayer.[89]

The years 1607 to 1615 were crucial for the emergence of the definitive characteristics of Mary Ward's spirituality. This period culminates in the insights she received in 1615 into the nature of the inner disposition which unites activity with the pursuit of union with God. These insights gave a radically new orientation to her spirituality and found concrete expression in her response to the needs of the church and the society of her age.

Mary Ward's understanding of the estate of justice underlay her Christology, her understanding of personal goodness as the source of moral rectitude and works of justice and her concept of freedom as the interior disposition which directs subsequent decisions. Her conviction that grace and nature are in harmony gave rise to the positive anthropology that governed her concept of the human person, understanding of discernment, and recognition of the important role played by affectivity in moral decision making.

Notes

[1] This note, written while Mary Ward was living in Rome, is dated "St. Gregory's Day, 1636" which in those years fell on March 12, 1636. It is cited by Chambers, vol.II, 441-442; Orchard, 117, and Wetter, (IX): 21.

[2] The full text is given in Appendix A.

[3] *The Painted Life*, no. 27.

[4] "Retreat Notes," 1619, cited by Chambers, vol. I, 474.

[5] *AB*, cited by Chambers, vol. I, 403.

[6] Letter to Nuncio Antonio Albergati, 1621, cited by Orchard, 23.

[7] "Resolutions," 1612-1614, cited by Chambers, vol. I, 358.

[8] "Letter to Albergati"; *AB*, cited by Chambers, vol. I, 180; Orchard, 23-24; Peters, 93.

[9] *AB*, cited by Chambers, vol. I, 227-228; Orchard, 27; Peters, 108,112, note 5.

[10] "Letter to Albergati," cited by Peters, 115.

[11] *AB*, cited by Chambers, vol. I, 192.

[12] Compare with Mary Ward's Retreat Notes, Liège, October 1619 and reflections, 1619 and 1620, Wetter, (VIII): 20, (IX): 7, 16. See also: Chambers, vol. I, 470.

[13] From the "Various Papers," no. 37, held in Archives of the Institute of the Blessed Virgin Mary, Munich, Wetter, (IX): 15 ; excerpts also cited by Chambers, vol. I, 471; Peters, 255, 267, note 34.

[14] "Letters to Winifred Wigmore," (Perugia, October 10, 1624) and to Barbara Babthorpe (Munich, February 16, 1627), cited by Chambers, vol. II, 109, 224-225.

[15] Poyntz, *A Briefe Relation*, cited by Chambers, vol. II, 323. In the same passage Mary Poyntz refers to these two years as "the time when her business was in the height of treaty in Rome." Events of these years include Mary Ward's journey to Rome in February 1629 to submit to Urban VIII a further Petition regarding her Institute and the suppression of her houses in St. Omer, Liège, Cologne and Trier.

[16] *AB*. Her words read: "During these two years I suffered extreme aridity without any intermission, and without any cause, but I believed that I had wholly lost the spirit of devotion … through some unknown negligence of mine… . This thought caused me great grief and sometimes fear whether I should be saved or not, but this never with doubt or mistrust in the divine mercy, but only I feared myself, lest I should thus fall away forever. By an especial grace, this fear was nevertheless always accompanied by a firm resolution, followed by acts when the occasion occurred, that although I might never see God, yet I would serve him until death". See also Chambers, vol. I, 164.

[17]Poyntz. *A Briefe Relation*, cited by Chambers, vol. II, 495.

[18]"Retreat Notes," April 1619, Wetter, (VIII): 7, cited by Peters, 260, 268, note 55.

[19]Ibid, cited by Peters, 268, notes 57,58.

[20]Letter to Mutius Vitelleschi, Superior General of the Society of Jesus: "Reasons why we may not alter... ," January 8, 1622, cited by Chambers, vol. II, 16-17, Orchard, 70, Peters 349, note 56.

[21]Barbara Olga Warnke, I.B.V.M. *Mary Ward: And not by Halves*, Chancellor's Address, III, delivered at Regis College, Toronto, November 26, 1985, (Toronto: Regis College Press, 1985), 21.

[22]"Reflection," Spa, Liège, 1616, cited by Chambers, vol. I, 396.

[23]"Retreat Notes," April 1619, cited by Chambers, vol. I, 450-451; Peters, 260-261, 269, notes 59-68. Underlining is in the original.

[24]"Letters from Prison," February 18, 1631, lemon juice letters, no. 56:5, excerpts cited by Chambers, vol II, 359, Peters, 583, note 83. Mary Ward had written in similar fashion to Barbara Babthorpe on September 16, 1623, stating: "to live or die for God is equal gains, when His will is such". (cited by Chambers, vol. II, 98-99).

[25]*Painted Life*, 38.

[26]*AB*, cited by Chambers, vol. I, 38,55; Orchard, 9,10.

[27]"Retreat Notes," 1619, Wetter, (VIII): 18.

[28]*AB*; "Letters from Prison," February 18, 1631; "Letter to Winefrid Bedingfield," October 29, 1633, excerpts cited by Chambers, vol I, 19, 38; vol. II, 352-353, 420. "Retreat Notes," 1619, Wetter, (VIII): 14. See also Mary Ward's letters to Winifred Wigmore, October 25, 1623, and May 6, 1628, and to Frances Brooksby, November 26, 1633, letters nos. 10 & 49, cited by Chambers, vol II, 99-100, 253-254, 396.

[29]"Retreat Notes," April, 1618, Wetter, (VII): 24-25; "Letter to Winifred Wigmore," October 27, 1624, excerpts cited by Chambers, vol II, 138; Orchard, 73, 139, Peters, 418, note 632.

[30]"Letter to Frances Brooksby," May 15, 1624, excerpts cited by Orchard, 91.

[31]"Retreat Notes," 1619, from the Archives of the Institute of the Blessed Virgin Mary, Ascot, England, Wetter, (VIII): 18.

[32]"Letter to Winefrid Bedingfield," 1636, cited by Chambers, vol. II, 441.

[33]Emphasis added.

[34]In Mary Ward's era verity was used frequently in the sense of moral truth; agreement of the words with the thoughts. (Samuel Johnson, *A Dictionary of the English Language*, s.v. Sincerity, Verity.)

[35]*AB*, cited by Chambers, vol. I, 403.

[36]*AB*, cited by Chambers, vol. I, 131, 143, 145; Orchard, 20.

[37]From Mary Ward's addresses, December 1617 - January 1618, *Liber Ruber*, Wetter, (VI): 12; cited also by Chambers, vol. I, 410; Orchard, 57. Mary

Ward describes verity as total reliance on God, doing all for God and doing it well, and seeking to know God's will.

[38]Compare: Warnke, *Mary Ward: And not by Halves*, 19.

[39]"Letter to Albergati," cited by Orchard, 29.

[40]From Mary Ward's addresses to her companions, December 1617 and January 1618, *Liber Ruber*, Wetter, (VI): 12; Chambers, vol. I, 408-409; Orchard, 56-58; Peters, 267, 268, note 37.

[41]Walter Principe, Mary Ward: Changing Concepts of Holiness," *The Way* 53, Supplement (Summer 1985): 22-23.

[42]Mary Ward, "Memorial to Urban VIII," March 25, 1629, from the Vatican Archives and translated by Elizabeth Dunn, IBVM, excerpts quoted in full by Wetter, *Mary Ward's Prayer*, 52-53, and in part by Orchard, 78, Peters, 506,507.

[43]Grisar, 443.

[44]This original letter in English has not survived. That it ever existed is assumed only on the basis of the existence of the Latin excerpts, which contain no introduction or conclusion. They are quoted in full by Grisar, 612-615, (in Latin with a German translation), 612-615, and Peters, 797-798 (German), 525 (English). Orchard cites them in part 113-114 (date and place incorrect).

[45]Henrietta Peters suspects, although she states that she cannot prove this, that it was Robert Stafford, rector of the Jesuit house in Liège, who was responsible for translating the extracts into Latin and sending them to Cardinal Carafa. (Peters, 526).

[46]The German reads: "als das Zeugnis einer Seele, … die nicht nur das Recht um des Rechtes willen verteidigte, sondern darin die ihr und den Ihrigen von Gott gegebene große Aufgabe sah, für die alles eingesetzt werden mußte". (Grisar, 635).

[47]"Memorial to Urban VIII," November 28, 1630, cited by Chambers, vol. II, 330-331, Grisar, 739, and Peters, 563-564.

[48]The German reads as follows: "ein ergreifender Beweis der menschlichen Größe Maria Wards, ein leuchtendes Zeugnis ihrer Treue gegen die Kirche und deren Oberhaupt" (Grisar, 743).

[49]Warnke, *Mary Ward: And not by Halves*, 22.

[50]See Chambers, vol. II, 348-349.

[51]Ibid., 367.

[52]Letter to Pope Urban VIII, March 27, 1631, cited by Peters, 579, note 12.

[53]"Letters from Prison," February 17 and 20, 1631, cited by Chambers, vol. II, 353, 362; Orchard, 108, Peters, 574, note 69.

[54]"Letters to Winefrid Bedingfield," October 8, 1633, October 29, 1633, November, 9, 1634, excerpts cited by Orchard, 116-117; "Letter to Ur-

ban VIII," London, February 14, 1640, Biblioteca Apostolica Vaticana, lat. 8620, f. 65r, cited by Chambers, vol. II, 420, 426, 470.

[55]"Letter from Mary Poyntz to Barbara Babthorpe," January 31, 1645, cited by Orchard, 121, Peters, 611.

[56]Mary Ward's words before the commission of Cardinals 1629/30 cited by Chambers, vol. II, 294; Peters, 119, note 12.

[57]From Mary Ward's addresses, December 1617 to January 1618, *Liber Ruber*, cited by Chambers, vol.I, 408; Orchard, 56.

[58]Principe, "Mary Ward: Changing Concepts of Holiness," 20.

[59]"What I find and am drawn to practise," 1619, "Reflection," 1620, Wetter, (VIII): 14-15, 21; (IX): 9, 15, 20. See also Chambers, vol. I, 468-469; vol. II, 271. See also: Peters, 481, note 78. Emphasis added.

[60]Ibid.

[61]"Retreat Notes," April 1619, Wetter, (VIII): 14-15.

[62]*Sacramentum Mundi*, s.v. "Grace and Freedom," by Karl Rahner.

[63]"Reflection," 1620, Wetter, (IX): 16; "Reflection," written between April and October, 1619, Wetter, (VIII): 21. Underlining is part of the original text.

[64]"Letter to Roger Lee," November 1st, 1615; "Reflection," 1619, cited by Wetter, *Mary Ward's Prayer*, 32; (VIII): 7; "Reflection," 1620, Wetter (IX): 16.

[65]From Mary Ward's addresses cited by Chambers, vol.I, 413; Orchard, 59.

[66]"Reflections," June 1620 and August 20, 1628, cited by Chambers, vol. II, 272.

[67]Ibid., October 1619, Wetter, (IX): 6; see notes of April 1619, Wetter (VIII).

[68]"Retreat Notes," 1618, Wetter, (VIII): 6.

[69]Letter no. 91, cited by Peters, 589, note 14.

[70]"Letter to Winifred Wigmore," 1624, cited by Grisar, 138; Letters to Cardinal Borghese," February 29, 1625, to her companions, February, 1633, and to Winefrid Bedingfield, July 16, 1627, October 29, 1633, excerpts cited by Chambers, vol.II, 64-65, 155, 237-238, 409, 420.

[71]Council of Trent, session VI, ch. IV.

[72]St. Peter Canisius, *A Summe of Christian Doctrine... with an Appendix of the Fall of Man, & Justification, According to the Council of Trent...*, trans. in part by Henry Garnet, (printed secretly in England: 1592-1596), 449-485. The text cited is given as Eccli, 1.33. In the Revised English Version of the Bible, Sirach 1.26 reads:"If you desire wisdom, keep the commandments, and the Lord will supply it for you." The first part of the work, headed "Wisdom", treats the theological virtues, commandments of God and the Church, and the Sacraments. The second, entitled "Justice" takes up sin, good works, the cardinal virtues, gifts and fruits of the Holy Spirit, Beatitudes and the evangelical counsels.

[73]"where sense obeyed reason and reason the divine will" (Mary Ward); "what is highest in man is subject to God and the lower powers of one's soul are subject to what is highest, that is, reason" (St. Thomas, *Summa Theologiae*, 1a.82,1 and 4; 92,1 -3; 1a.2ae.113:1. ad.1).

[74]Ibid., 1a.2ae,109.

[75]Ibid., 1a.2ae. 111,3. See also: Jean-Marc Laporte, *Patience and Power: Grace for the First World* (New York, Mahwah: Paulist Press, 1988), 205. Laporte distinguishes first, *simplex volitio*, or in modern terms, wish or willingness. Such willingness is powerless without God's grace. The subsequent *infusio gratiae*, or energizing of the will, is followed either by the *intentio finis/electio*, the choosing and implementing of this willingness or the refusal to make such an election. In the person's task of intending, choosing and implementing the value willed, grace is both operative and co-operative.

[76]Grisar, 36.

[77]Bellarmine, "De Gratia Primi Hominis," book 1, ch.12, *Omnia Opera*, vol.5, 170. Bellarmine describes the first human being as *iustitia originale et habitu gratiae gratum facientis ornatus*.

[78]Bellarmine, "De Amissione Gratiae," Book 5, ch.20, *Omnia Opera*, vol.5, 453.

[79]Bellarmine, "De gratia et libero arbitrio," book 4, ch. 14, book 5, *Omnia Opera*, vol.6, 30-31, 36-106.

[80]Bellarmine, "De Justificatione," book 1, ch.1, *Omnia Opera*, vol.6, 150.

[81]Bellarmine, "Explanatio in Psalmos," in *Opera Omnia*, vol. 10. See especially: Psalms 1, 18(19), 44(45), 50(51), 51(52), 64(65), 71(72), 72(73).

[82]Clancy, *Introduction to Jesuit Life*, 151.

[83]Lessius deals with the invincible ignorance of infidels. He states that they will not be damned for the sin of infidelity but for "some other things, which they have done against the law of nature, the which by help of God they might have eschewed." He goes on to emphasise that no one can impute his damnation to God but to his own "negligence" and "wickedness, whereby he hath neglected God's holy inspirations …, and willingly and wittingly against his own conscience hath thrown himself headlong into sin." (Leonard Lessius: *A Controversy in which is Examined, Whether Every Man May Be Saved in His Owne Faith and Religion?* (St. Omer: English College Press, St. Omer, 1614): 13.)

[84]Excerpts from Andrew White's document of February 4, 1621 cited by Chambers, vol.II, 53-57.

[85]In her addresses to her companions, December 1617-January 1618, Mary Ward refers to the excellent guidance given by the Jesuits (cited by Chambers, vol.I, 411 and in *Mary Ward's Prayer*, lectures given by Immolata Wetter, IBMV, to members of the IBVM, 1974, [photocopied]: 90).

[86]Mary Ward explicitly recommends Burton's manner of celebrating Mass. *Liber Ruber*, 281, cited by Chambers, vol. I, 468; Peters, 214.

[87]Letter to Mary Ward's companions in Rome, cited by Chambers, vol. II, 466.

[88]De Guibert, *Jesuits*, 96.

[89]*Sacramentum Mundi*, s.v. "Grace and Freedom," by Karl Rahner.

Chapter 5

Mary Ward's Insights Relevant to Contemporary Moral Theology

There was a Father that lately came into England whom I heard say that he would not for a thousand of worlds be a woman, because he thought a woman could not apprehend God. I answered nothing, but only smiled, although I could have answered him, by the experience I have of the contrary. I could have been sorry for his want - I mean not want of judgement - not to condemn his judgement, for he is a man of very good judgement; his want is in experience.[1]

Mary Ward's comprehensive view of the human person, the *subject of moral action*,[2] graced with *freedom*, and called to exercise the *responsibility* which such freedom entails has much to offer to moral theology today. Her insights into these areas stand out more clearly when compared with the spirituality and moral theology of her age on the one hand and on the other hand with the changing emphases in recent works of moral theologians. The latter reflect the second Vatican Council's call for "special attention" to moral theology's scientific exposition and orientation.[3]

5.1 The Human Person as the Subject of Moral Action

The move to a focus on the human person was implicit in the general mentality of Renaissance humanism. This focus, albeit placed in a Christian and scriptural context and influenced by the spirituality and anthropology of Ignatius of Loyola, was reflected in the aims of the Jesuit *Ratio Studiorum* and in Mary Ward's educational methods and content. Post-Tridentine moral theology undoubtedly allowed for Christian moral life to be deeply personal and permeated with religious meaning. The bishops and theologians at the Council of Trent and later moral theologians affirmed the dignity of the human being whom God calls to a supernatural destiny. They stressed the correspondence between a good moral life with the needs of human nature.

Still, one can detect a somewhat static view of the human person. The Council of Trent, in its work of renewal, directed its attention to reforming human behavior. This, together with the challenge of the new moral questions arising from religious, political, social and economic changes, led moral theologians to focus on determining how human actions were or were not in conformity with moral norms. Trent gave less attention to the essential aspects of the person subject to these norms and to personal interior disposition as the source of morally right actions.

On the one hand, moral theologians implicitly affirmed the value of human activity. They attempted to deal with the situations Christians faced in daily life, and they provided clear explanations how Christians should act with moral responsibility in meeting these situations. On the other hand, theologians and canonists developed these explanations in the context of the law and its prescriptions. Francisco Ingoli's facile dismissal of what the times required in favor of established canon law is an extreme instance of a legalism which subordinates the personal growth and changing needs of human beings to unchanging laws.

In contrast, the Second Vatican Council endorsed a morality which took greater account of the human person by emphasizing that human activity must be judged insofar as it refers to the human person integrally considered.[4] It accepted that the human race has passed from a rather static concept of reality to a more dynamic, evolutionary one. By affirming the goodness of God's creation and humanity's dignity the Council sought to illuminate the mystery of the human person.[5]

As contemporary moral theologians recognize, taking the person as the central criterion for moral evaluation is problematic and requires an adequate concept of "person."[6] In addition, theologians can and often do reach irreconcilable conclusions which they claim to be based on an adequate consideration of the person.[7] James Gustafson, raising the question as to what constitutes the "normatively human," states that finding this is an ongoing process of discovery since human beings are constantly developing and changing. He suggests that to be human is to have a vocation; it is to become what we now are not and calls for a surpassing of what we are. In his view, apart from a *telos*, a vision of what humanity can and ought to do, we will flounder and decay.[8]

Mary Ward, I suggest, had such a vision. Her comprehensive concept of the human person flowed from her conviction of God's goodness and fidelity, epitomised by the grace offered to all through Christ, and from her experience of and response to God's love. At the same time, her human relationships and the knowledge she gained from instruction and reading enriched her perception of the dynamic possibilities of human beings graced by God. Governing these insights was her conviction of that "verity" by which she says she "must and ever will stand" namely, that "women may be perfect."[9]

One of Mary Ward's most comprehensive expositions of the essential dignity of the human person is found in her addresses to her companions in 1617 and 1618, which were occasioned by criticisms of them because they were women. Her defence of the graced dignity of women springs from her conviction of the universality of God's grace. In this context she proposed the following truths about the graced dignity of all human beings.

Created in the image and likeness of God, endowed with freedom, intellect, and affectivity, and destined by God for eternal life and the beatific vision, human beings are graced with the ability to apprehend God. Through Christ's passion, death and resurrection, God freely (gratis) offers the gift of moral integrity to all. Although the possibility remains that persons may deliberately reject God's gifts and thus their own human dignity, through God's "preventing truth" all are invited to be perfect. By responding to this call in freedom and responsibility, all, women and men, are capable of great things.[10]

In contrast to the explicit formulations of contemporary moral theology, Mary Ward emphazised affectivity as an important aspect of human persons. Her belief that genuine human love is a reflection of God's love for us led her to endorse the necessity and value of human relationships. She described the married state as the "free possession of worldly affections," and saw the gift of chastity as accompanied always by an infusion of love.[11]

Her spirituality and practice testify to her conviction that love of God and receptivity to God's love are inseparable from the love of and openness to other persons. Hence, she saw personal growth as realized through responsible relationships and the promotion of the good of others in society. Decrying the "penuriousness" of her era which considered that "women did not know how to do good except to themselves," she rejected any individualism in the seeking of personal perfection and did not place her own interests before the common good.

In like manner, Mary Ward's concept of justice emphasizes personal and relational harmony and works of justice. In tune with her understanding of God's works as good she sought to find God within these works. She resisted all compromise with a concept of enclosure which devalued the "secular" world and she urged that human beings must take responsibility for the maximum realization of the harmony of the *Regnum Dei.* Her vision of a new role in the church for women offered them freedom from the oppressive concept of women characteristic of her era. That many were so freed is confirmed by the survival of her Institute.

Again, Mary Ward's appreciation of God's goodness led her to stress that there is no disharmony between God's designs for human beings and the goods necessary for their temporal happiness. The "great things" which she envisaged as within the capabilities of women included the acquisition of knowledge. In general the education of women was neglected or, at best, given grudgingly. Richard Mulcaster, an educator of the time, for instance, did acknowledge that women had minds which ought not "in conscience" be "left lame," and should have schooling - provided young men did not suffer in consequence![12]

Mary Ward's aim to offer education to young women and especially to the poor ran counter to both English penal laws and the church's imposition of canonical enclosure on religious orders of women. Her educational system attests that she was aware of the intellectual advances of the period and desired to enable Catholic women, and thus the Church as a whole, to keep pace with these advances. Moreover, just as she urged her members to conduct the Spiritual Exercises, so she provided training for those teaching in her schools rather than relying on visiting male teachers as was the usual custom.[13]

In her emphasis on the importance of the acquisition of knowledge, Mary Ward did not identify knowledge with the mere acquisition of information and skills. Rather, she related the desire for knowledge to the desire for the truth intrinsic to human persons. Acknowledging that the "content and satisfaction" brought by knowledge "be exceeding great," she was convinced that, given their supernatural destiny, human beings are driven on in their desire for knowledge. To her mind, the purpose of human knowledge is knowledge and love of God, whose Verity is proclaimed in words and works, revealed and created. She spoke of such knowledge as both bringing personal happiness and enabling its recipients to profit themselves and others.

In this context, she warned her companions that seeking knowledge for its own sake, though "pleasing," is both "unprofitable and a lie." Rather, "to attain perfection, knowledge of verity is necessary, to love it and affect it."[14] Her use of "to affect" was synonymous with "to seek," "to be pleased with" and to "act upon."[15] In her view, the knowledge which has verity as its goal is intimately related to love and involves acceptance of the responsibility to show forth truth in thought and action.[16]   Mary Ward's reflections reveal the relationship she saw between knowledge - the commitment to seek the truth - and love. She frequently referred to knowledge as sight. Receptivity to knowledge was for her a grace-given freedom and an increase of love. Her account to Roger Lee of her insights into the "estate of justice" endorses this. She described her insights as occurring first in her *understanding*. Reflection upon her experience and understanding led her to the *judgement* that this first estate was the "fountain and best disposition" for a soul to be in. This judgment was accompanied by *love* for this estate and the *decision* to seek by God's grace to attain it, for herself and for the good of others.

Her spiritual notes also indicate her awareness that the process of human knowledge involves not only discursive reasoning but a loving receptivity. She wrote: "I reflect on my matter; I see without labour the substance of what discourse could show; lay what I am about before God, and spend the rest of my time in importuning him to know or have what that meditation exacts of me or leads me to." Elsewhere, she recorded "I am not moved so much to pray as to see."[17]

Although the immediate context for Mary Ward's exposition of her understanding of the human person was her defence of the capacities of women, she did not regard these capacities as exclusive to women. By rejecting the dualism implicit in the anthropology underlying much of the prevailing spirituality, and by decrying any dichotomy based solely on gender between the capacities for holiness of men and women, she endorsed the graced dignity of each human person. In doing so, her concept of the person extends beyond the cultural and ideological humanism of her age and is more comprehensive than her era's moral theology. At the same time, her creative vision of the human person anticipates Vatican II's understanding of the person as a moral subject: finite and aware of one's sinfulness, uniquely graced by God, social and part of the material world, called to work for its betterment and to seek the wisdom of the Holy Spirit in the search for the truth.

Central to Mary Ward's understanding of the person as a moral subject is her concept of freedom and its corollary, responsibility.

5.2: Mary Ward's Concept of Freedom

Mary Ward's formulated and lived spirituality indicate that she understood freedom as primarily an interior disposition and way of life. It is manifested in the loving self-commitment to God which directs the exercise of free will. Her clearest articulation of the relationship between the disposition of freedom and free will came during a retreat she made in 1619 under John Gerard's direction. She noted the "great desire" by which she was "drawn in almost every occasion and alteration" to "find a will to nothing but what God would and because God would." In her view this "giving of all," although "not ideal," renders "the exercise and acts of free will which should come from hence more frequent and more effectual."[18]

Mary Ward saw *free will* as central to the dignity of the human person, "something" essential to the nature of human beings "without which they would not remain human." It is the power by which one wills a particular good as a means to the end one desires. To her mind, God gives free will and all "other parts and powers of the body and soul," to human beings so that they may use them well to reach their supernatural end.[19]

Given that free will brings an associated responsibility, she saw sinful actions as resulting from the misuse of freedom such that the will becomes perverted from the end for which it was made.[20] Recognizing that moral goodness depends on and grows through free choices and commitments and, likewise, that the will can be diverted from the true good and thus choose what is not in conformity with God's will, she stressed that for freedom to be effective the will must be liberated by grace.

The *epitome* of such liberation is the three-fold freedom which is a central component of the well-ordered disposition that Mary Ward called the "estate of justice." It is manifested first and foremost in faithful receptivity to God, that is, willing "in all to have a will conformable" to God's and "never to proceed" in that which is "less pleasing."[21] This freedom brings our decisions, choices and actions into harmony with the deeper harmony of our personal orientation and

God's will. On the one hand, freedom and ongoing openness to God's will are fostered by, and actualised in, the exercise of free will. On the other hand, our consistent choice of the good depends on and is directed by the habitual willingness and faithful receptivity to God which grace makes possible.

In tune with her identification of Christ as the "perfect model" of the just person and the strong Scriptural basis of her spirituality, Mary Ward placed her consideration of freedom within the context of the freedom won for humanity by Christ, and to which she saw all are called. Hence, she regarded freedom as including not only loving fidelity to Christ within the concrete situations of daily life but also as freedom for the prior self-commitment from which this fidelity flows, that is, the desire to place our "entire affection" at Christ's disposal.[22]

In defining freedom as primarily the personal freedom for a radical, on-going commitment of oneself to the good God wills, and second as empowering the will effectively to choose the true good in particular situations, Mary Ward drew attention to the fact that specific actions may indicate a way of life freely chosen and an underlying commitment. Here, her concept of freedom is broader than that explicitly formulated by the moral theologians in her era and anticipates the thinking of many moral theologians today.

The moral theologians in Mary Ward's era emphasized that only acts which arise from free choice are truly human or moral acts and stressed the need for grace to render the exercise of free will effective. Their elaboration of freedom was, however, explicitly concerned with specific instances of the exercise of free will. Moreover, influenced by the legacy of nominalism, they tended to see human action as a series of discrete acts. Thus, in their considerations of freedom they did not pay explicit attention to the ongoing fundamental commitment of the moral agent which is reflected in and directs moral choices.

In contrast, Mary Ward's concept of freedom anticipates the modern development of the "theory of fundamental option." Behind this notion which, admittedly, is not uniformly conceived or received, lies a view of the moral life as a unified, dynamic process. Those who espouse the notion point to the significance of the ongoing orientation or disposition which lies beneath and is manifested in concrete acts. The theory is also viewed as providing a corrective to a "legalistic, act-centred image of the moral life, punctuated by frequently alternating choices for and against God."[23]

Given the different historical context, movements in philosophy, and the growth of the human sciences which influence expositions of this notion today, it would be anachronistic to claim that Mary Ward's understanding of freedom as a basic self-commitment and way of life reflects presuppositions identical to those underlying modern interpretations. Nevertheless, in modern expositions of the graced freedom which makes possible the radical self-commitment to God in love and is manifested but not fully contained in concrete acts of free choice, one can find emphases similar to hers. These include an awareness of the inseparability of freedom and grace and the identification of the commitment of oneself to God with love of God flowing into love of others.

While a brief reference does not do justice to Bernhard Häring's thought or to the presuppositions which underlie his conclusions, worthy of mention are his two three volume works, each of which places the study of human conduct firmly within the context of the New Law of Christ. His approach indicates that he sees consideration of freedom as inseparable from consideration of the graced freedom attained for humanity by Christ.[24] Both he and Piet Franzen, who laments that considerations of freedom often imply that grace and freedom are in opposition, open their discussion of grace and freedom by recalling St. Paul's message of the "new and true freedom" brought by God's grace.[25]

That Mary Ward placed her consideration of freedom within the context of grace is due to four-interrelated factors. First, convinced of the verity and fidelity of God she saw God's goodness present in and gracing all the gifts and capacities given to human beings. Second, her understanding that human co-operation with grace is itself the gift of God's grace led her to identify the freedom to make a radical self-commitment to God as graced freedom. Third, her own experience of the love and goodness of God governed her conviction that the source of freedom is love, the love of God for human beings which frees them to respond in love of God and others. Fourth, while she recognized that human beings are capable of making a total refusal of God's love, she did not refer to this capacity as freedom, but, rather, as the rejection of the true freedom offered by God and won for humanity by Christ.

Mary Ward's concept of freedom reflects her comprehensive view of the human being made in the image of God and called to a supernatural destiny by a loving God. Admittedly, the moral theologians of her era commenced their statements of general principles with an exposition of the supernatural destiny of human beings. Their portrayal of how human beings are to direct the whole orientation of their lives towards God as the ultimate end tended, however, to emphasize more avoiding what displeases God than seeking of God's will in all the events of life. Moreover, in presenting our last end as a most powerful motive for conversion, manualists such as Martin de Azpilcueta did not focus on beatitude but rather sought to elicit fear of eternal misery.

In addition, the moral theologians in Mary Ward's time gave less attention to the New Law of Christ and did not consider grace as part of moral theology. Grace was left to scholastic theology where St. Thomas' treatise was not taken as a unity, and to controversial theology, which centered on defending Catholic teachings. Thus, while these theologians did not deny the harmony of grace and human nature, they treated the question only incidentally.

Mary Ward's concept of freedom offers significant insights to moral theology today. Where the moral theologians in her time presented morality more in terms of actions which met the obligations of the law than as the response of the entire person to the grace-given invitation of God, she gave explicit attention to the graced freedom which makes possible the ongoing commitment to God which directs our concrete decisions and choices. Moreover, her focus on the personal goodness of the moral agent and on the need to consider freedom within the context of grace and of how Christ won freedom for humanity have come to be recognized today as proper concerns of moral theology.

5.3 The Mutual Relationship of Personal Moral Goodness and the Performance of Morally Right Actions

Mary Ward's writings and practice reflected her conviction that moral rectitude flows from the well ordered interior disposition she associated with the estate of justice and which she saw as possible through God's grace. Hence, her consideration of morality focused first on personal moral goodness (being good), and then on the performance of right actions (doing good). Her belief that personal goodness lies in an interior disposition of openness to God, and that personal goodness is essential for the consistent loving service to others

and the performance of actions which are morally right underlies her
words to Roger Lee in 1615: "I end with desires *to be good,* which I
see I am not, and without that, it seems impossible I should be able
to do good... . How much this indisposition for God's favour doth
hinder me in all, I can better perceive in myself, than show to those I
should. I humbly beseech you, obtain my *amendment* of God, and
help me *to be good,* how dear soever it cost."[26]

Mary Ward's most comprehensive description of the interior disposition corresponding with personal goodness (*to be good*), is contained in her description of the estate of justice. Elsewhere she described it as that "grace that so much graceth all God's gifts" and
"excludeth bad affection."[27] To her mind the graced disposition which
is manifested in a habitual willingness to love and fulfil God's will is
essential for the close following of Christ, for attunement with God's
will is inseparable from conformity to Christ. In her expressions of
the good she was drawn to practise she consistently commenced with
a reflection on her interior disposition and its harmony or disharmony with the values and person of Christ.[28]

Mary Ward saw personal goodness as a necessary prerequisite for
the performance of "all such good works as are in this world to be
done."[29] Her view that personal goodness is not an end in itself but is
directed to the love of God flowing into love and service of others led
her to use the phrase "to do good" in two distinct, but to her mind,
related senses. She related the phrase first to the cultivation of the
virtues and the practice of asceticism conducive to growth in personal goodness, and to the morally good actions which are the fruits
of personal goodness; second, to the service of others for which personal goodness is essential.

While Mary Ward used the term "virtue" with respect to the quality or state of inner goodness, manifested in living rightly, she saw
particular virtues as dispositions facilitating the consistent performance of the morally right actions concomitant with these virtues
and as goods in themselves. The virtues she mentioned most often
were chastity and humility. Her description of the former reflected
her belief in the harmonious relationship of grace and human nature; the latter was inseparable in her mind from the virtue of sincerity /verity.

Her description of the virtue of chastity flows from her conviction
that the inner disposition synonymous with personal goodness is

manifested by and reaches its felicity in the inner freedom from whatever holds us back from God, and for those actions which lead to God's love and service. Her words about the beauty and necessity of chastity are aimed at all whatever their state of life. She described chastity as a gift of God and always accompanied by an infusion of God's love which enriches human love. In contrast, she judged unchaste acts as the misuse of our God-given reason and freedom.[30]

Mary Ward understood humility as a manifestation of verity in action and of justice, the right relationship towards God, oneself and others. Among her many references to humility, the following texts from 1619 and 1627 illustrate both her understanding of this virtue and her motivation for desiring it:

> Of bodily strength, beauty, or other abilities: to be wished for God's better service, I will give him what I have. And what I want I will find in Him by humble resignation to want what by his providence is withdrawn.

> I would have you love God much, and remember to thank Him often for all benefits as well secret as known, and beg of His goodness increase of zeal and still more ability to do His Goodness greater service, Who deserves far otherwise from ours than poor we have afforded.[31]

The practice of virtues flows from and is for the sake of love, both God's love for humanity and the human response of love for God and others. Such charity leads us to seek to give more than the minimum required by law. As has been mentioned, Mary Ward made frequent references to and sought the love of friendship with God. She described this divine love as like a "fire, which will not let itself be shut up,"[32] and it was this love which motivated her teaching and practice. According to her first biographer, she gave it as a rule that "charity should precede and prudence follow" and that "we were bound to give our lives for our neighbours' souls, and our goods for their lives, and not our superfluities, but what may touch us." Rejecting a "prudence which prejudiced charity" she refused to have one of her debtors arrested because it would ruin his family.[33]

The use of the phrase "to do good" in the sense of the performance of *morally right actions* occurs frequently in her writings, and in each case it does so within the context of love of God flowing into love of others. Stressing that verity and fidelity lie in doing well all

that has to be done, she gave as the criterion for her choice and esteem of a particular action that God was pleased. Her instructions
and service to others indicate that she saw objectively good actions as
those which were in harmony with those revealed in Christ's life and
teaching, in the commandments, and in the church.

Mary Ward associated the rightness of human actions with the
"good" these actions achieve, and sought to act towards others in
such a way as to bring them good. Distinguishing the "true good"
from all seeming goods, she exhorted her companions never to desire
the least thing that is contrary to God and their conscience, under
the pretext and in the hope of gaining a great good.[34] Among the
"simple and certain" goods of this life she mentioned specifically freedom from excessive self-interest and openness to God's will.[35] These
tend to result in harmony between the personal goodness concomitant with fidelity to conscience and the performance of actions which
are morally good.

Mary Ward understood that fidelity to the consistent performance
of morally right actions is the mark of personal goodness. Hence she
saw asceticism, that is, the exercises necessary for maintaining fidelity to God's grace, as an essential feature of morality. Again, her motivation was love of God flowing into love of neighbor. Such motivation not only means the avoidance of an individualistic attitude of
seeking perfection for one's own sake, but also gives validity to the
exercises necessary to acquire virtue and to eradicate the lack of verity and justice associated with sin. Mary Ward urged her companions
to act solely from love, because God had called them to a vocation of
love.[36] She stated her own approach clearly: "After businesses, I go to
find myself in God, without any will or private interest, and with a
will only to have His will, which I cease not till I find."[37]

Mary Ward's *Regulae Domesticae*, presented in June 1622 to Cardinal Bandini, charged by the Congregation of Bishops and Regulars
to deal with the Institute, included the hours allotted to formal prayer.
These agreed with the prevailing Jesuit system,[38] and included one
hour's meditation, daily Mass, the canonical hours, Litanies, and twice
daily Examen of conscience. Other documents indicate attendance
at sermons, daily spiritual reading and twice yearly General Confession. That Mary Ward did not see these practices as ends in themselves, but in terms of love and service of God, is seen in both her
spiritual notes and her concerns for her members' health. In 1634

when her members suffered severe poverty and a plague was ravaging Munich, she urged them to prefer their safety and that of those for whom they were responsible "before all things that obligeth not in conscience," such as "the hearing of sermons and frequent confession."[39]

The clearest indication of Mary Ward's understanding of asceticism comes from her reflections of 1618 and 1625, when she understood that the best satisfaction for sin lies in joyful receptivity to the passion of her own life in tune with the Passion of Christ. That Christ's Passion concludes with the Resurrection enabled her to see the meaning of human suffering and asceticism. Hence, although she practised external penances she saw the most important form of penance ("above all"), the bearing "well" of all difficulties as occur in the doing of God's will.[40]

In Mary Ward's view personal goodness is most clearly revealed in an enduring orientation of openness and fidelity to God's will. This grace-given disposition which is manifested in doing good is concomitant with the "liberty of mind"[41] and inner freedom such that, motivated solely by the one desire to love God, we refer all actions and choices to God. In contrast, sin, the lack of moral integrity, is the antithesis of this disposition and a refusal to be open to God's grace.

5.4: Sin and Conversion

Mary Ward's written reflections on sin are the outcome of her considerations of the material given to her during her retreats. As was said earlier, retreat givers varied in the validity of their interpretation and presentation of the First Week of the Exercises. In tune with the moral theology and spirituality of their time, they tended to stress close examination and enumeration of personal sins and focused on the punishments and evils which come from sin. The material given to Mary Ward reflects this emphasis and the precise instructions given.[42]

The difficulty Mary Ward experienced with any approach which focused on sin and on the sinner as an enemy of God without placing such considerations within the context of God's love and desire for the good of the sinner is apparent in her reflections. One of these, which takes the form of a dialogue between herself and her soul, is refreshing, indeed entertaining, although possibly not intended to be that way. Having been directed to consider the evils that come from sin, Mary Ward found her soul "not settle to it in good earnest." Moving specifically to the point that sin made her the enemy of God, she asked her soul of "what importance, or how she conceived of that." She received no response, her soul being, in her words, "without motion, most certainly asleep, her eyes shut and seeing no more than to perceive clearly that she did not see what imported her to see and was to be seen."[43]

As a result of this experience, Mary Ward returned to an approach more congenial to her nature, focusing primarily not on the evils that would come to herself or on enumerating her sins, but on the response she could make to the loving and good God. In this context she reasoned with herself thus: "Come near to God, it is no wonder if keeping thus aloof, thou wantest both love and contrition."[44]

Mary Ward's love of God and her appreciation that God is the author of all good are evident in her insights into the nature of mortal sin as the total and deliberate rejection by a free and rational human being of the good offered by God. Her exposition of this understanding in two reflections, April and October, 1619 is one of the clearest indicators of the relevance of her thought for moral theology today and repays careful examination.

The subjects of Mary Ward's two reflections are: "of the impediments to perfection," and "many are called" (Matt. 22:14) respectively. Her first consideration proceeded as follows. First, she asked herself why, given her desire to love God fully and her aptness for friendship, she was so wanting in the efforts of friendship towards God. Second, she saw clearly that the very motion to ask this question came from God and not from herself. Third, distinguishing the original or first cause of all such motions as incite to goodness from concurrence with or execution of these motions, she perceived that human beings have some little part in this concurrence, although she was not clear how much.[45]

Fourth, relating the above insights to the subject of the damnation of infidels, Mary Ward concluded the sole cause of damnation is human beings' refusal of the motions for good given to them by God. She arrived at this conclusion by realizing that human beings can have no part in the original or first cause of any good and that God would not damn them without any fault on their part. Fifth, in seeking to determine what enables us to refuse God's grace, she identified our capacity for free choice. Sin occurs when the will, which exercises this freedom of choice, becomes "perverted," and turns from God and from the end to which it was made. Sixth, likening this rejection to pride, Mary Ward prayed that her readers would, in humility, come to know the importance of not neglecting the good motions given by God.

In her second consideration a year later, Mary Ward returned to her central point, that damnation comes from a turning away from God, and a "deliberate election" of what does not belong to "nor could have little or much connection" with God.[46] At the end of this reflection she turned to consideration of the estate of justice. The additional insights she received throw into harsher light the contrast between the full malice of sin, the immediate rejection of God and deliberate election of other than God, and the well ordered disposition she identified with personal goodness.

In an age when the focus on mortal sin implied that the faithful frequently sinned mortally Mary Ward's insights bring out more fully the malice of sin, as the perversion of the good given by God and an abuse of humanity's God-given freedom. She saw clearly that on the one hand, any so-called freedom which leads to a rejection of God is not true freedom, and on the other hand, that God's gifts and graces to human beings can be discerned by the true freedom they bring. She equated sin with interior disorder and a lack of willingness, the antithesis of "true greatness of mind."[47] In like manner, she saw venial sins as disposing the soul to "greater disorders," and questioned whether her own imperfections indicated the basic attitude or refusal of fidelity she identified with a state of grave sin.[48]

Mary Ward's reflections reveal that her consideration of sin and of herself as a sinner was always within the context of God's love for her and her desire to respond to this grace. In this context, the full gravity of mortal sin and of the disposition which gives rise to such sin appears in its full malice as the rejection of the love given by the God of goodness. It is in this context also that she saw conversion primarily in terms of a change in interior disposition, a turning and returning to full commitment to God's will. Her motivation for conversion was a "longing desire in every action that God be pleased in that particular."[49]

Love of God and of God's will is inseparable from love of neighbor, the desire for one's neighbor's good. Aware that the desire to do good does not necessarily result in the objectively good being accomplished, for we may be mistaken in our judgements, Mary Ward emphasized the importance of knowledge of the good and sought to communicate it to others. At the same time she stressed that personal goodness is essential if our service to others is to be conducive to their good. In her instructions to her companions she cited the teaching and example of Christ ("Eternal Truth") as endorsing the value of keeping and teaching the commandments.[50]

The inseparability Mary Ward saw between the cultivation of personal moral goodness and the doing of good to others reflects her conviction that true freedom consists of both referring all to God ("cleaving to nothing") and finding God in all ("being present to all"). Interestingly, one finds similar themes in the discussion of many moral theologians today regarding the nature of the human person's fundamental commitment to God. Joseph Fuchs, for instance, cites love of others as the true moral commitment of the basic freedom of the person.[51] Bernard Lonergan, treating of the human person's radical self-commitment, sees religious conversion, the commitment to love God and others, the source of which is God's love for humanity, as generally preceding moral conversion, the consistent option for the truly good.[52]

Evidence of the specific good Mary Ward sought for others is to be found in her works in London in 1609, 1618 and from 1639, her plans for the Institute, the practical implementation of these undertaken by her members, and in both the letters of commendation she received and her opponents' accusations. In 1621, Andrew White, S.J., one time professor of divinity in Liège, called attention to the value of the involvement of the Institute in bringing others to conversion and teaching higher learning, "moral and divine."[53] In the same year, the Infanta Clara Isabella, daughter of Philip II of Spain, desirous that the Institute's moral instruction of women continue, sent personal letters on its behalf to the Pope, Cardinal Bellarmine and Mutius Vitelleschi.[54] In 1622, Matthew Kellison, president of Douay College, referred to the Institute's moral instruction.[55] At that time its members were working in St. Omer, Liège, London, Suffolk, Cologne and Trier.

5.5 Mary Ward's Insights into Moral Instruction and Guidance
Mary Ward's crucial insight into the relationship of being good to doing good rested upon her conviction of the basic goodness of hu-

man nature as created and graced by God, absolute Goodness. This insight led her to take as the starting point for moral guidance, not the human being as a sinner, but the human being both in need of and potentially open to the grace which the God of fidelity and love desires to give. She stressed the positive aspects of moral integrity, her motivation for doing good to others arising "rather forth of love, and a desire that all should be good, than to keep them from sinning."[56]

Recognising the positive aspects of human desires for the good and of the role of the affections in moving the will, Mary Ward recommended that conversion should spring from love of God, not fear. Conversion is best achieved by offering the better, that is, by changing the object of desire, rather than seeking to destroy the nature of desire as, for instance, by inducing self-hatred.[57]

Mary Ward's personal practice was evidence of this. She identified commitment to Christ with the placing of our affections at Christ's disposal; recognizing her capacity for receiving and giving affection, she sought to discover the obstacles to her affection for God. Hence, she attributed her misuse of grace and natural gifts to a desire for self-esteem, and she resolved to choose the better by acting so that through these gifts God would lead others to goodness.[58]

Mary Ward's recognition of the positive role played by desire and affectivity reflects her comprehensive view of the human person. This contrasted with the prevailing formulations of moral theology and ascetical literature which generally considered the passions solely as obstacles to moral rectitude. Associated with this pessimistic view was an anthropology which by urging us to suppress our lower nature, often strayed into an unconscious dualism which saw matter as evil and the spirit as good. No evidence of this dualism exists in Mary Ward's writings. Rather her writings suggest that instead of disharmony within human beings and a disorder in the so called "lower nature," she stressed the lack of moral rectitude which can arise from pride of intellect and reason. Emphasising that morally right actions arise from the interior disposition of openness to God's grace, she pointed to our need for a "ready mind and courageous heart."[59]

The moral theology and to a lesser extent the spirituality of her era emphasized the distinction between command and counsel. Mary Ward, however, saw Christ as calling all to perfection. At the same time, she recognized that human beings grow in moral goodness and freedom by continual fidelity to God's offer of grace. Hence, she looked to the factors which impede freedom and stressed the need for the transformation of disordered desires. In so doing, she expressed concerns which today's writings on moral issues take up. Only recently have theologians, influenced by a more comprehensive view of the person and by the growing rapprochement between moral theology and spirituality, come to consider the importance of affectivity for the moral life.[60]

Mary Ward's approach to the making of moral decisions and to moral guidance focused on the human person, created in the image of the God of absolute "Goodness, Verity and Fidelity," endowed with freedom, and called to commitment to the person of Christ, "the most perfect model of all virtue."[61] For her the practical living out of this commitment was discipleship.

5.6: Morality as Discipleship

Because Mary Ward related "being good" and "doing good," she understood discipleship as firstly desiring Christ's disposition of openness to and love of God's will and secondly performing actions which flow from this disposition. Reflecting on the following of Christ she wrote:

> This seemed to be the way: that they should first know it, after desire, and endeavour for it a little, and that God would do the rest. I purposed to gain it myself, then teach it by example, and tell it to such as know it not otherwise; me thought I should do much good by this. Jesus grant it, I will do my best.[62]

Mary Ward's motivation for "being good" was love, love of God flowing into love of neighbor. As her words above indicate, she sought to practise discipleship and to communicate her insights to others by personal example and by instruction.

Mary Ward's innovative insights for moral theology do not lie in her identification of morality as discipleship. Since apostolic times the close following of Christ has consistently been seen as the truly Christian response to God's universal invitation to perfection. Rather, the significance of Mary Ward's practice and instruction lies in the relationship she saw between freedom and discipleship. For her the following of Christ manifests the graced freedom she saw as essential to the estate of justice. Her insights into this relationship anticipate and illuminate changing emphases in moral theology and in understandings of morality which emerged prior to and following the Second Vatican Council.

Associated with these changes is a perception that moral theology cannot be exclusively concerned with commandments and sins but must be linked with spiritual theology and centred on the vocation of human beings, seen in the light of Scripture and the saving mystery of Christ. Bernhard Häring criticized the moral theology of the manuals of Mary Ward's era for being barren of mentions of Christ and bearing little resemblance to his teaching.[63] He echoes earlier theologians who called for a christo-centric moral theology which makes Christ the model for a more personalist approach. Arthur Vermeersch, for instance, citing Pius XI, spoke of moral theology as the school of Christian love. He claimed that its role was to supernaturalize the aspirations of human beings and bring about love of the good, not the abstract good but Christ's personal love revealed in the suffering of the Cross.[64]

A christo-centric view of morality raises the question of how we should understand imitation of Christ. While explicit treatment of morality as discipleship is absent from the works of moral theology of Mary Ward's era, devotional works emphasized the following of Christ as central to the Christian life, and pointed out how Christ showed us how to live this life.

Various writers assigned different emphases to the nature of this imitation in practice. As has been noted, many devotional works proposed a monastic model of spirituality, and in contrast to the lived spirituality of the recusants, encouraged an individualistic type of spirituality. At the same time, in an age of religious persecution, the model of the suffering Christ sustained those who sacrificed their lives, reputation and possessions for their faith. While the martyrs' witness strongly influenced Mary Ward's spiritual formation, her subsequent reflections brought further insights into martyrdom so that she realized that the validity of suffering lies in its accordance with God's will.

Theologians today are likewise concerned with how the imitation of Christ has concrete relevance to moral theology.[65] In Häring's view, taking Christ as our norm for perfection does not mean simply copying a pattern. Only by incorporation as living members of Christ's mystical body can we imitate him.[66] Joseph Fuchs, insisting that Christian life is misconceived unless it is seen as an imitation of Christ, also cautions that imitating Christ does not imply simple repetition. Rather, Christians must relate their individuality and situation to those of Christ and strive to conform their conduct with that of Christ. Love of Christ becomes the source of all individual moral actions and decisions.[67]

As has been emphasized, Mary Ward considered moral goodness and rectitude as inseparable from love. Hence, for her, morality is essentially a fundamental and free commitment to Christ and to the love and service of others for the sake of Christ. Her insights into Christ as epitome of the just person led her to see the following of Christ essentially as imitating his disposition of total commitment to God's will. This commitment, epitomised by the three-fold freedom she envisaged, flows into works of justice and involves serving and suffering with Christ.

Mutually enriching is a comparison of Mary Ward's understanding of discipleship as the actualization of the threefold freedom of the estate of justice with Karl Rahner's thesis that "following Jesus has its ultimate truth and reality and universality in the following of the crucified."[68] Rahner tries to avoid the two extremes of interpreting the call to follow Christ as a literal reproduction of his life and the turning of this call into abstract moral principles that would reduce Jesus' life and death to merely illustrating a moral precept or ideal which could exist independently of him. Rahner focuses on the common feature which transcends all individual manifestations of imitating Christ in our own historical situations, namely the opportunity offered by Christ of dying with him.[69]

Rahner proposes that the uniqueness of Jesus' death lies in his decision to surrender himself freely and totally to God in faith, hope and love. This decision was not made at the moment of Jesus' death but reflected a fundamental "yes" to God throughout his life. It involves the transcendence of individual objects by freely renouncing them.[70] Mary Ward speaks of this fundamental "yes" in terms of the "freedom to refer all to God," that is, "being present to all but cleaving to nothing."[71] For Mary Ward as for Rahner the Resurrection which completes and makes effective Jesus' death provides the guarantee that true freedom lies in surrendering all we are and desire to the God of love.

While Rahner points to the similarities which must exist between our dying and that of Christ, he also stresses the unique difference in that Christ was sinless, his death redeeming sinful humanity.[72] Robert Doran, likewise, proposes readiness in freedom to enter into the paschal mystery of Christ as the one valid authentication of ecclesial ministry. Only by such discipleship can the church in its ministry collaborate with God in meeting the mystery of evil and the existence of sin with God's own solution.[73] Interestingly, both Mary Ward and Doran cite similar instances of discipleship, referring to the apostles' freedom and to their joy in being chosen to suffer in defence of Jesus' name.[74]

In Mary Ward's life we can see the lived response to Jesus' call to discipleship as recorded in the Gospel. She anticipated Vatican II's directive that the task of moral theology is to "show the nobility of the Christian vocation" and to "bring forth fruit in charity for the life of the world."[75] Her practice was in tune with the authentic ministry to which Doran refers and to the radical character of Christian morality which Fuchs describes as the loving personal decision and responsibility to imitate Christ in working for the Christian structuring of our world.[76]

The contemplation which gave rise to Mary Ward's insights into discipleship cannot be separated from her lived response, the fruit of her contemplation. Her willingness to enter into the Paschal mystery of Christ is seen in her acceptance of the "long loneliness" - the deprivation of human support and of tangible signs of God's presence - and in her prayer that at the time of death she would remain steadfast in her willingness "to leave what she loved," namely to die before the confirmation of the Institute if God so wished.[77]

Mary Ward sought to bring about a fundamental change in society and the Church. In doing so her life bore witness to that of the God become human with whom she sought to be identified. In 1625 while praying for the Institute in St. Mark's church in Rome she recalled Christ's question to his apostles: "Can you drink the chalice, that I must drink?" In response she offered herself to bear with joy the great difficulties, troubles, and persecutions she saw she would encounter in fulfilling God's will.[78] Her final plan for the Institute stated that its members must stand "under the banner or sign of the Cross to serve the Lord."[79] The joy and hope with which she herself carried out this directive was such that she was able to write even while in prison that God "gives no more than is ladylike and most easy to be borne."[80]

Because she saw Christ as the perfect model of the just person, Mary Ward's concrete formulation of morality as imitation of Christ is found in her exposition of the estate of justice. Christ is the perfect example of the well-ordered estate of justice. He is the "true wisdom" which the perfection of this estate brings and from which comes the strength for and knowledge of the good works to be done in this world. The personal goodness which seeks harmony with Christ's disposition adds a radically new dimension to human morality. The motivation of love for the person of Christ reflects this dimension. This love is inseparable from and reflected in the love of others. Such love in its rejection of possessiveness and arrogant self-interest ennobles human love.

Notes

[1] From Mary Ward's addresses, December 1617 to January 1618, *Liber Ruber*, 229-230, cited by Chambers, vol I, 410-411; Peters, 268, note 41.

[2] The phrase: "the human person as the subject of moral action" is being used here in a broad sense. It includes not only the notion of the moral agent as free and responsible, but the broader aspects suggested by the phrase "the human person integrally and adequately considered" used by the members of the second Vatican Council (see below, note 14). In his article: "Personalist Morals," (*Louvain Studies* 3 (1970-71): 6-15) Louis Janssens treats in detail those aspects of the human person which he considers are comprised in this phrase.

[3] Documents of Vatican II, "Decree on Priestly Formation", #16.

[4] *Gaudium et Spes*, #51. The official commentary on section 51 explains: (i) that, in its expression that "the moral procedure of any act... must be determined by objective standards which are based on the nature of the person and his acts," a general principle is formulated, one which is applicable not only to marriage and sexuality but also to the entire domain of human activity, and (ii) that it is affirmed through the choice of the expression that "human activity must be judged in so far as it refers to the human person integrally and adequately considered."
(*Schema constitutionis pastoralis de Ecclesia in mundi huius temporis, Expensio modorum partis secundae*, Typ. pol. Vat. (1965), 37-38, cited by Louis Janssens, "Artificial Insemination: Ethical Considerations," *Louvain Studies* 8 (1980): 4).

[5] *Gaudium et Spes*, #3, #5, #10, #12, #51.

[6] See, for instance: Bruno Schüller, "Autonomous Ethics Revisited," and Franz Böckle, "Nature as the Basis of Morality," in *Personalist Morals*, ed., Joseph A. Selling, (Leuven: Leuven University Press, 1988), 55.

[7]Compare: Lisa Sowle Cahill, "Catholic Sexual Ethics and the Dignity of the Person: A Double Message." *Theological Studies* (50): 1989.

[8]James M. Gustafson, "What is Normatively Human?" *The American Ecclesiastical Review* 165 (1971): 207.

[9]Mary Ward's addresses, cited by Chambers, vol. I, 414; Orchard, 58.

[10]Ibid., cited by Chambers, vol. I, 409-414.

[11]*AB*; "Reflection," October 12, 1619, Wetter, (IX): 13, also cited by Chambers, vol. I, 46, 473.

[12]Compare: Norman, "A Woman for All Seasons: Mary Ward (1585-1645), Renaissance Pioneer of Women's Education," reprinted from: *Paedogogica Historica; International Journal of the History of Education,* ed., K. De Clerck, XXIII/1 (1983): 130-131. Catholic women in England were permitted only the form of education acceptable to the state authorities. Divergence was considered as treason, punishable with death or life imprisonment. Government surveillance was strict. Even in such relatively safe European countries as Bavaria, Flanders and Rome, English informers eagerly traded incriminating evidence with the English Government. In England twenty three Catholics who continued to teach local children in Catholic homes were martyred. As a result, many young women who wished a Catholic education were sent abroad to foreign enclosed monastic orders and were enclosed within the convent for the duration of their schooling. In addition, canonical enclosure limited the opportunities of women to run day schools for the local poor. Compare: Ibid., 128-129.

[13]Excerpts from a questionnaire presented to Mary Ward in 1619 by one of the Jesuits in Liège, original preserved in the Royal Archives in Brussels and cited by Wetter (VIII): 2; "Letter to Winifred Wigmore," April 22, 1627, cited by Orchard, 94.

[14]Mary Ward's addresses, cited by Chambers, vol. 1, 413. See also: Peters, 268, note 42.

[15]Samuel Johnson, *A Dictionary of the English Language,* s.v. "To Affect".

[16]Mary Ward's addresses, cited by Chambers, vol. 1, 413.

[17]"Reflections," 1619, 1620, cited by Wetter (IX): 7, Chambers, vol. I, 470; Peters, 255, 267, note 34.

[18]"Reflections," 1619, Wetter, (VIII): 21.

[19]Ibid., Wetter, (VIII): 15.

[20]Ibid., 1619, Wetter, (VIII): 15; (IX): 8; Chambers, vol. I, 470.

[21]Ibid., April 1619, Wetter, (VIII): 7; cited by Peters, 268, note 58.

[22]*Painted Life,* no.27; "Retreat Notes," 1619, Wetter, (VIII): 18.

[23] *New Dictionary of Theology,* s.v. "Fundamental Option," by Brian V. Johnstone, CSSR.

[24]Häring, *Law of Christ,* vol.1, 402-403, 428-429; *Free and Faithful in Christ: Moral Theology for Clergy and Laity,* vol. 1. *General Moral Theology,* A

Crossroad Book, (New York: The Seabury Press, 1978), ch.4; see also, 60, 68, 73-74, 124-125 and *New Catholic Encyclopedia*, s.v. "Spiritual Freedom" by Bernhard Häring. In addition, although Fuchs takes as his starting point the modern concept of "basic freedom" and sees Christian freedom, the freedom of the spiritual person in the Pauline sense, as basic freedom exercised in grace under the guidance of the Holy Spirit, whereas Mary Ward commences with the graced freedom won by Christ for humanity, his understanding of the fundamental commitment to God in terms of love of God, flowing into love of others, bears similarities to hers. (Josef Fuchs, *Human Values and Christian Morality*, (Dublin: Gill and Macmillan, 1970), 93-96, 108). McCormick, likewise concerned with basic or fundamental freedom, refers to the recurrent description of the self-disposition concomitant with this freedom as self-disposition under the "divine empowerment" of "God's enabling love". (Richard A. McCormick, *The Critical Calling:Reflections on Moral Dilemmas Since Vatican II* (Washington, D.C.: Georgetown University Press, 1989), 174.)

[25]Piet Fransen, S.J., "Grace and Freedom," in *Freedom and Man*, ed., John Courtney Murray, (New York: P.J. Kennedy & Sons, 1965), 31.

[26]See Appendix A.

[27]*AB*, cited by Chambers, vol I, 44.

[28]"Resolutions," 1612-1614, "Reflections," 1619, Wetter, (VII): 8-11; (VIII): 20-22; (IX): 3, 5, 6. See also: Chambers, vol I, 357-362;

[29]"Retreat Notes," 1619, Wetter, (VI): 14.

[30]"Reflection," October 12, 1619, Wetter, (IX): 13-14; Chambers, vol. I, 473.

[31]"Reflection," October 10, 1619, cited by Wetter (IX): 9; "Letter to Frances Brooksby," October, 1627, Wetter, *Mary Ward's Prayer*, 44. Emphasis added.

[32]"Allocutions," collated by Lohner, cited by Chambers, vol. I, 466.

[33]Poyntz, *A Briefe Relation*, 76, cited also by Chambers, vol. II, 194-195.

[34]"Allocutions," cited by Chambers, vol. I, 466.

[35]"Retreat Notes," 1619, cited by Wetter, (VIII): 20-21, Chambers vol. I, 469.

[36]Addresses, cited by Chambers, vol. I, 465.

[37]"Retreat Notes," 1619, Wetter, (VIII): 21, cited by Chambers, vol I, 468.

[38]Grisar, 100-101.

[39]"Letters to Winefrid Bedingfield," 1634, cited by Chambers, vol.I, 426-427.

[40]"Reflections," October 10, 1619, Wetter, (IX): 9-11; cited by Chambers, vol I, 418.

[41]"Letter to Frances Brooksby," May 15, 1624, excerpts cited by Orchard, 91; "Reflections," Spa, Liège, 1616, Wetter, (VI): 8.

[42]Even if one allows for the fact that not all her spiritual notes have survived and none of her retreat notes after 1620 are still in existence, only the retreat notes of 1619 deal with material from other than the first week. The exactitude of the retreat giver's directions can be inferred from Mary Ward's remarks in her reflections of 1618 and 1619. These indicate her concern about remaining in prayer for a quarter of an hour after the time specified and neglecting to enumerate all her sins as the meditation instructed.

[43]"Retreat Notes," April, 1618, Wetter, (VII): 21.

[44]Ibid., 19.

[45]Ibid., April 1619, Wetter, (VIII): 14-15.

[46]Ibid., October 1619, Wetter, (IX): 8.

[47]Ibid., 1616, 1618, Wetter, (VII): 13, 15, 19. See also Peters, 284, 293, note 45.

[48]Ibid., April, 1618, cited by Chambers, vol. I, 418 and Wetter, (VII): 17-18.

[49]"Reflections," October, 1619, Wetter, (IX): 10.

[50]From Mary Ward's addresses cited by Chambers, vol. I, 466.

[51]Fuchs, *Human Values and Christian Morality*, 95.

[52]Bernard J.F. Lonergan, S.J., *Method in Theology* (Toronto: University of Toronto Press, 1990), 240-243; *Understanding and Being*, eds, Elizabeth A. and Mark D. Morelli, (Toronto: University of Toronto Press, 1990), 228; *Insight: A Study of Human Understanding* (New York: Harper & Row, 1978), 598, 610-611, 623. In *Method in Theology* Lonergan uses the term "moral conversion" to denote the concept of "habitual willingness" developed in *Insight*.

[53]Andrew White's document of February 4, 1621, cited by Chambers, vol. II, 53-57.

[54]Grisar, 35-38; Peters, 298, 299.

[55]Burton and Williams, eds., *Douay College Diaries: Third Douay Diary*, 397, 398.

[56]"Reflections," October 10, 1619, Wetter, (IX): 12.

[57]*AB*, cited by Chambers, vol. I, 166.

[58]*AB*, cited by Chambers, vol. I, 44; "Retreat Notes," 1619, Wetter, (VIII): 14.

[59]"Resolutions," 1612-1614 cited by Chambers, vol. I, 360.

[60]Theologians who deem it necessary to pay greater attention to affectivity both as giving a more holistic view of the human person and for its relevance to the moral life include: Häring, Laporte, Lonergan, Doran, and Gustafson. See, for instance, the following: Häring, *Free and Faithful in Christ*, 71; Laporte, *Patience and Power*, 205-214: Bernard J.F. Lonergan, S.J., "Natural Right and Historical Mindedness," in *A Third*

Collection : Papers by Bernard J.F. Lonergan, S.J., ed., Frederick F. Crowe, (New York: Paulist, 1985), 173; *Method in Theology*, 30-31, 289; Robert M. Doran, *Theology and the Dialectics of History*. (Toronto: University of Toronto Press, 1990), 85-89, 214-215; James M. Gustafson, "Moral Discernment in the Christian Life," in *Introduction to Christian Ethics: A Reader*, eds., Ronald P. Hamel and Kenneth R. Himes, O.F.M., (New York: Paulist, 1989).

[61] *Painted Life*, #27. See also: Chambers, vol. I, 434.

[62] "Retreat Notes," 1619, Wetter, (VIII): 11.

[63] *Sacramentum Mundi*, s.v. "Moral Theology" by Bernhard Häring.

[64] Arthur Vermeersch, S.J. "Soixante ans de théologie morale," *Nouvelle Revue Théologique*, 56 (1929). 880, cited by John C. Ford and Gerald Kelly, *Contemporary Moral Theology*, (Westminster, Maryland: The Newman Press, 1964), 64-65.

[65] Mary Ward made no dichotomy between "human" morality and "Christian" morality. The tendency to polarization which, if Vincent McNamara's survey is accurate, characterizes much of the debate on the relationship between the two is quite contrary to her thinking, and to that of her age. Compare: *New Dictionary of Theology*, s.v. "Moral Life, Christian," by Vincent McNamara.

[66] Häring, *Law of Christ*, vol. I, 234 - 235.

[67] Fuchs, *Human Values and Christian Morality*, 6-12.

[68] Rahner, "Following the Crucified," *Theological Investigations*, 18: 161-165.

[69] Ibid., 159-161.

[70] Ibid., 162-163.

[71] "Reflections," Spa, Liège, 1616, Wetter, (VI): 8.

[72] Rahner, "Following the Crucified," 166.

[73] Doran, *Theology and the Dialectics of History*, 110, 111.

[74] "Retreat Notes," 1619, Wetter, (VIII): 18; *Painted Life*, 42; Doran, 111.

[75] Documents of Vatican II, "Decree on Priestly Formation," #16.

[76] Fuchs, *Human Values and Christian Morality*, 74-75.

[77] "Retreat Notes," April, 1618, April 1619, Wetter, (VII) and (VIII); "Letter to Winifred Wigmore," August 27, 1624. See Chambers vol.I, 452; vol.II, 138.

[78] *Painted Life*, 42; cited by Chambers, vol. II, 196.

[79] "The Third Plan of the Institute," Wetter, (IV): 15. See also "Second Plan," cited by Chambers, vol. I, 376.

[80] "Letters from Prison," February 13, 1633, cited by Chambers, vol.II, 356.

Chapter 6

Moral Knowledge: The Love of Verity

I have never done or said anything, either great or small, against his Holiness ... or the authority of Holy Church. But on the contrary, my feeble powers and labours have been for twenty six years, entirely and as far as was possible to me, employed for the honour and service of both, as I hope, by the mercy of God, and the benignity of His Holiness, will be manifested in due time and place.[1]

Or if a greater punishment be judged necessary than publicly to be declared a heretic, a schismatic, an obstinate rebel against Holy Church, to be taken and imprisoned as such, to have been at the gates of death through the inconveniences endured for nine weeks, to have been deprived of the Holy Sacraments ... to be held up to obloquy in all places... if more is needed than the sufferings of all in our company, ridiculed by the heretics at the present time for having left their country and parents, despised by Catholics, held as disgraced by their nearest relations, their annual revenues unjustly taken from them, so that in four of our Colleges ours are obliged to beg their bread, ... if all this is too little, I offer my poor and short life, in addition to these other satisfactions, when and where it may be thought meet. But hoping by the mercy of God, and by your benignity, that all will go better ... .[2]

The above excerpts are taken from two of Mary Ward's letters to Urban VIII. The first, she wrote the day before her release from the Anger prison; the second, she wrote a week later in response to the Pope's command that she come to Rome. They not only reveal her loyalty to the church and her concern for her companions, but also her optimism that the valuable work she was doing in God's name would be recognized.

Mary Ward's fidelity to discerning God's will manifests the central components of her formulated spirituality and its underlying theology and anthropology. Her teaching and practice are grounded in her unwavering confidence in the fidelity and verity of God whose grace harmonizes human nature.

Human decisions not only involve reason, but also reflect feelings, perceptions and values. Hence, both subjective and objective criteria are relevant to the validity of personal discernment. These criteria

172 Love–The Driving Force

include experiences of interior peace and desire to refer all to God manifested in loving service of God and neighbor, willingness to follow Christ, and subordination to the Holy Spirit operating in the Church.

Discernment, therefore, requires cultivation of a sensitive attentiveness to various interior and exterior movements which influence our judgments and decisions. It plays an essential complementary role in assisting us to apply general teachings and norms to specific circumstances and is of particular importance when we are unable to infer what we are to do solely through normative principles.

The introduction to Mary Ward's autobiographical writings provides the key to understanding her definition and practice of discernment. Her words echo her earlier prayer that all the Institute's members would seek the "estate of justice": "Verity will free them from errors, rectify their judgements, perfect their knowledge, endow them with true wisdom, make them able to discern things as they are in themselves, the difference between trifles and matters of importance, what is to be done or not to be done in all."[3] For Mary Ward, discernment is not so much an event as a state of spirit, an attentiveness to the graces given by God within the context of everyday life. It concerns the degree of harmony or disharmony that exists between our decisions, actions and thoughts and the well-ordered attitude towards God, ourselves, and others which constitutes righteousness or justice.

In a letter to Roger Lee (November 1615) Mary Ward referred to discernment. Her purpose was to seek Lee's confirmation that God wished her to embrace what she had perceived as good, namely, her enlightenment as to the estate of justice. She wrote: "I seem to love it, and yet am afflicted in it because I cannot choose but retain it, and yet dare not embrace it for truly good till it be approved."[4]

Mary Ward saw discernment as directed first to the general orientation of one's life and from there to specific decisions. Her own general orientation consisted of a great desire to follow Christ. In 1618, while considering the desired attitude towards created things from the first Principle and Foundation of the Spiritual Exercises, she reflected: "I was glad when I saw that, that way Christ took in the use of all created things was the perfectest. To proceed as Christ did was the portion of grace I only desired for my part."[5]

In these texts, one finds the principles underlying Mary Ward's understanding of discernment, and those she practised and taught to her companions. First, while discernment concerns the sincere, free and loving human response to God, it receives its verity and assurance from God's verity and fidelity which "cannot and will not deceive." Second, the aim of discernment is to distinguish the true good, the doing of God's will, from all illusionary forms of good. Third, the true good is in conformity with the teachings and example of Christ who expresses the most perfect choice of the true good. Fourth, Mary Ward realized that reflection on experience does not contain the whole of the experience, and that the judgements which follow are not necessarily granted directly by God. Aware, also, that both reason and affectivity can be disordered she saw discernment as requiring a harmony of will, understanding, and affectivity with the will of God. Fifth, discernment is related to action, "what is to be done or not to be done in all."[6]

Significantly, one of the first events recorded in her autobiography reveals Mary Ward's sensitivity to her experience of God's grace. At the age of thirty-three, she recalls the anxiety and discomfort she experienced as a child when in the company of her aunt, Alice Wright, whom she loved very much. This aunt confided in her regarding actions which Mary Ward says she knew even then "not to be well."[7] While Mary Ward only hints at Alice Wright's rash liaisons prior to and after her marriage to William Readshaw, contemporary documents indicate that the Readshaws experienced marital troubles and that Alice had later been charged with adultery.[8]

Mary Ward's memory of her aunt's behavior contrasts with recollections of conversations with Margaret Garrett, a servant of the Babthorpes. Through this woman Mary Ward gained a great love and appreciation for the virtue of chastity, which she ranks as one of her greatest graces. Her different responses to these two influences reveal her early realization that the forces for evil cause inner disharmony, whereas those for good bring interior content and peace.

Mary Ward's discernment of her spiritual experiences shows this same sensitivity. Her love was first for God's will in general, and then for the particulars God made known to her. In like manner, her initial attraction was to "religious life in general."[9] When George Keynes, however, assured her that God willed her to be a lay sister with the Poor Clares, Mary Ward followed his counsel. She described the "aversion and grief" she experienced in this mode of life as such that "death by any kind of torment ... appeared most sweet." Nevertheless, she remained in that convent for almost a year "until God should by some other means give more certain signs" of what she was to do.[10]

In 1624-1626 when reflecting on the aridity and feelings of abandonment by God that she had experienced, Mary Ward discerned its cause as her inability to follow Keynes' direction of her conscience. His direction was "entirely by fear," whereas, for Mary Ward "to labour through love, even death, appeared to be easy but fear … made but little impression."[11] In later years she warned her companions against yielding to temptations that God had abandoned them.[12]

Mary Ward's accounts of how she had been led to the knowledge of her vocation reveal that by being receptive to God's love she had the capacity to receive God's light as certain. At the same time, her accounts indicate a willingness to await God's revelation. Between May 1607 and May 1608 she sought to discern "more certain signs from God" about whether she was to leave the Flemish Poor Clares. She recalled that God did not "command" or "force" but "compassionating her labours" proposed the "means" and left her the liberty to use them or not.[13] These "means" included both the "rule of reason" and "some divine ordering still more marked."[14] In 1608 and 1609, confident that all things are wrought by God for our good, and discerning that she had acted "disinterestedly," Mary Ward followed the only guidance offered, that of her novice-mistress.[15]

Mary Ward's choice of action when obedience to her confessor appeared to be in conflict with her own experience clearly shows that her conviction of God's verity and fidelity determined her practice of discernment. As has been seen, the period's moral theology and spirituality, including the *Directory* of 1599, laid great stress on obedience to one's confessor or "ghostly father." When Richard Holtby opposed her leaving England to enter religious life Mary Ward neither dared do what he declared was unlawful nor embrace what he proposed as her greater good. In this conflict, she prayed that God's will would be done and attempted to be open to whatever God wished.[16]

In May 1609, Mary Ward confided to Roger Lee, on whose counsel she then depended, the enlightenment she had received from God that she was not to be a Poor Clare. Lee's initial disapproval, and her fear of "being deceived and of believing that to be good which was not so,"[17] led Mary Ward to delay her departure from the convent for six or seven months. In addition, at Lee's request and against her own desire, she vowed to become a Carmelite if he so commanded. Later confirmation from God that she was not to be a member of a monastic order conflicted with this vow. Mary Ward records: "To resist that which now operated in me, I could not, and to have a will in opposition to the vow, I ought not. In this conflict, giving myself to prayer, I protested to God, so liberal, that I had not and would not admit on this occasion any other will than his."[18] Realizing that in "these two contraries," God could not be "against himself," she manifested her desire to do God's will through prayer and performing external penance.

Mary Ward's belief that God willed her to establish an order of religious women, adopting the "matter and manner" of the Society of Jesus, raised significant questions for the moral theologians and canonists. Neither moral theology nor canon law allowed for such a religious order. In fact, Bishop Blaise asked Lessius and Suárez, two of the most eminent moral theologians of the time, about its legality and holiness.

The conflict between Mary Ward's discernment of God's will and Church laws for religious life raise questions which continue to be relevant to moral theology. Karl Rahner, proposing the need for what he terms a "formal existential ethics," claims that "there is an individual ethical reality of a positive kind which is untranslatable into a material universal ethics."[19] As instances of this, he cites Ignatius' delineation of "three times when a correct and good choice of a way of life may be made." The first two imply the existence of a specific and binding call by God to an individual, discernment of which is not covered by the application of general material norms.

Loyola first instances occasions "when God our Lord so moves and attracts the will that a devout soul, without hesitation or the possibility of hesitation, follows what has been manifested to it." The second "time" has a similar implication: "when enough light and understanding are derived through experience of desolations and consolations and discernment of diverse spirits."[20] His description of these "times," the fruit of his own mystical experiences, bears strong similarities to Mary Ward's description of her key experiences of 1609, 1611 and 1615. These accounts and her Memorial to Urban VIII in 1630 indicate that Mary Ward saw her mission to found the Institute as "ordained and commended" to her by God's "express word."[21] At the same time she followed Loyola's advice in the Exercises that all matters about which a choice is to be made must be lawful within the church (#170). Her Memorial states clearly that she did not in any way pretend to prefer her lights before the authority of the church, nor her interior assurance before the Pope's judgement and authority.

The influence of the period's moral theology and spirituality, together with the Church's opposition to her plans, is evident in Mary Ward's retreat notes of 1618. Having resolved "to embrace with great affection" whatever might make her "like unto Christ in life and manners," she felt "trouble and unquiet after," fearing that this imitation of Christ might conflict with her "election and chosen course of life."[22] She discerned that this disquiet and fear did not come from God because it hindered the effect of her prayer for grace to follow Christ's example. That she resolved this conflict is apparent in the "solid contentment" she experienced as a result of subsequent discernment. Experiencing a presentiment that "some great trouble" would occur with regard to the confirmation of the Institute, she felt both an increased love for it and a great desire to serve and suffer with Christ.[23]

The difficulties Mary Ward experienced in 1618 arose from her knowledge of the era's moral theology and devotional literature. Moral theology by concentrating on explaining the obligations of the commandments, divine and human, made no explicit reference to discipleship. Devotional works stressed close imitation of the suffering Christ but also tended to propose a monastic model of spirituality and the performance of a multiplicity of prayers and ascetical practices. In addition, canon law and the prevailing anthropology regarding woman's nature insisted on enclosure for women religious.

In contrast, Mary Ward, while recognising the valid contribution made towards the conversion of England by monastic women, sought to perform "works of Christian charity" that "could not be undertaken in monastic convents." This, she saw as the kind of life which Christ taught his disciples.[24] The peace of mind she received from this discernment is seen in her 1619 reflection on "Christ compared with an earthly king" when she was filled with gratitude for "such an estate" in which she might so "nearly" [closely] follow Christ.[25] Again, in 1625 she offered herself to bear with joy the great difficulties, troubles, and persecutions she saw she would encounter in the establishment of the Institute.[26]

While Mary Ward's practice of discernment arose immediately from attentiveness to the Holy Spirit and self-knowledge, the repeated allusions to Scripture in her writings suggest that her source was primarily scriptural. In addition, she reveals a familiarity with Loyola's

Rules for the Discernment of Spirits as well as Southwell's *Short Rule of Christian Life* and Scupoli's *Spiritual Combat*. Roger Lee's instructions to her members in 1614 presume a knowledge on their part of the Ignatian "Rules for the Discernment of Spirits"; Mary Ward refers to having used them since 1609.[27] Moreover, she and her members attended Jesuit churches for confession and instruction. At the same time she brought her own insights to these rules.

Loyola offers two sets of rules for discernment, these being in tune with the aims and subject matter of the first and second weeks of the Exercises. The rules for the "first week" deal with the choice between good and evil for the person striving to overcome sin. The rules for the "second week" guide those committed to greater generosity in the service of God. Here, distinction is made between the actual good and what is presumed good, but is really illusory. Both sets of rules deal with the interior and exterior forces that affect personal choice. As with other authors, Loyola believes interior impulses come from good and evil spirits or from human nature itself.

Commenting on these rules, Joseph de Guibert sees them as applying in three ways: first to such extraordinary favors of God as revelations and visions; second, to internal enlightenment or impulses which arise in the mind, but because of their unusual clarity of thought or vehemence of impulse, lead their recipient to be conscious of an external force; and third, to experiences of general states of consolation or desolation which can be an indication of God's will. He describes "consolation" as comprising experiences such as: an intense love for God, love of others for God's sake, an interior joy which attracts one to spiritual things and causes one to be at peace and rest with God, and an increase of faith, hope and charity. Desolation includes all that is contrary to consolation and is marked by the absence of inner peace and feelings of sadness, tepidity and being separated from God. Since evil can be disguised as good, De Guibert emphasizes Loyola's advice that it is essential to observe the "whole course" of our thoughts, ensuring that this course terminates in what is truly good.[28]

Mary Ward's practice and teaching of discernment correspond in great part with Loyola's rules. In her instructions to her companions, she decried gloom and sadness in the service of God, stating that "a troubled dejected spirit will never love God perfectly, nor do much for God's honour," and that "virtue is not gotten by sleeping or crying, that is, slothfulness or anxiety."[29] By contrast, Mary Ward associated true consolation with the "content" and "mirth" which come from the grace-given "free and open access to God"[30] and the referring of all to God. In this context she advised her companions: "In our calling, a cheerful mind, a good understanding, and a great desire after virtue are necessary, but of all three a cheerful mind is the most so."[31]

Mary Ward's discernment was grounded in her conviction of the verity and fidelity of God, her commitment to God's will, and her obedience to the Holy Spirit as revealed within the mystical body of Christ, the Church. Convinced that no conflict can exist between God's will and the natural and supernatural fulfilment of human nature, Mary Ward recognized that God's love for human beings is the source of and provides the liberty for their response in love. In this context, she discerned the inner harmony and peace, the gifts of the Holy Spirit, which are the signs of the faithful living out of this love. The freedom to refer all to God, expressed in readiness to "effect" whatever God wills, and to decline whatever is contrary, brings an inner harmony such that, in all that is not sin: "to be pleased with it, is to please God by it."[32]

A necessary implication of any emphasis on the person as the center of free and responsible decisions is the recognition of the binding force of conscience and the freedom of conscience. John Mahoney, in his study of the making of moral theology, emphasizes conscience as one of the terms and concepts whose durability has influenced moral theology's development.[33] Surveys of the meanings given to conscience throughout history, however, suggest that the term has had a "complex, ambiguous history."[34] Indeed, Häring goes so far as to claim that "a history of moral theology could well be written in the main perspective of how conscience was understood and presented."[35]

In chapter 3, attention was drawn to certain aspects of the understanding of conscience in Mary Ward's era. It was noted that during this period moral theology emerged as an independent discipline within the context of the seminary. There, by focusing on training confessors, it came to be identified with the study and solving of cases of conscience. Exponents of moral theology devoted lengthy considerations to conscience and, in particular, to the question of the doubtful conscience. Their focus was primarily on the judgement of conscience. Conscience was defined as a dictate of reason and its operation was seen as primarily deductive, the application of universal principles to particular situations.[36] Less attention was given to the basic sense of responsibility which characterizes persons, and to their specific perception of values.

The years 1556-1666 which witnessed the heightened development of casuistry also saw the adoption of probabilism, the system which proposed methods to move from doubt to practical certitude. During these years, clergy studying for the English mission were taught how to deal with the dilemmas of conscience they would confront. Underlying these concerns was the belief in the binding force of conscience and its inviolability. The heroism of the English recusants and martyrs testifies to the positive nature of the casuists' emphasis on the inviolability of conscience and the associated responsibility to follow one's conscience.

In theory the casuists' expositions of the resolution of cases of conscience encouraged penitents to rely almost entirely on expert opinions rather than on personal discernment. The casuists stressed that for conscientious judgements to be objectively right, knowledge of objective norms and particular circumstances was necessary. They gave little or no attention, however, to the role of affectivity in contributing to this knowledge. Moreover, with the association of morality and the law, freedom of conscience tended to be viewed in terms of freedom from the law. Hence, explicit attention was not given to the development of the inner freedom which seeks to discern whether one's values and perceptions are in harmony with the true good.

Reflected in this approach are the ambiguities in the period's anthropology. On the one hand, the power of human reason to arrive at moral knowledge was strongly endorsed. On the other hand, there was a strong focus on fallen human nature and thus on the human being as a sinner. Both moral and spiritual works divorced the keeping of the moral norms essential for salvation from aspects of the Christian life which belong to the pursuit of perfection. Consequently, the obligations of conscience were viewed differently in each area.[37]

While Mary Ward emphasized the inviolability of conscience and the responsibility to obey it, she considered conscience more broadly than contemporary manualists. Recognizing the moral consciousness or basic sense of responsibility which characterizes human persons, she exhorted her companions never to desire the least thing that is contrary to God and their conscience.[38] At the same time, Mary Ward's desire that her members "determine all as the truth is"[39] and her own practice of seeking advice indicate that she considered not only the actual judgement of conscience, but also the importance of the formation of conscience.

In Mary Ward's view the sources of moral knowledge that inform the conscience include reason and affectivity. Among the means by which she was led to her own judgements she includes the "rule of reason" and a "feeling affection" for what had to be done, her "least endeavours" being rewarded by "increase of knowledge and love."[40] As has been noted, in her time the term "affectivity" included love, kindness, good-will, passion, and, more technically, "appetite."[41] Her Scriptural understanding of discernment and her own experience enabled Mary Ward to recognise that the signs of the work of the Spirit in our lives life can be found in the joy and interior peace that touch feelings, intellect and will. In her mind, the transforming freedom of God's love ennobles human love, such that one refers both the naturally desired and naturally declined to God, finding God in both.

Mary Ward's understanding of the freedom of conscience is in terms of freedom to do the will of God. In upholding this freedom she stressed the necessity of fidelity to one's conscience. Her own growth in spiritual maturity and freedom together with the freeing direction of John Gerard, are evident in her words to her companions in December 1617 and January 1618 that ultimately verity is "only God," not "an entire dependence" on a spiritual guide or on any other creature.[42] She cites freedom of conscience in choice of vocation as one of the reasons for being unable to change the essentials of the Institute.[43] She also encouraged others to exercise freedom of conscience. This is particularly apparent in her dealings with Sister Praxedes, one of her members in Liège.[44]

The Douay casuists' single reference to discernment suggests that the English missionaries were familiar with the Ignatian rules of discernment. The moral theology of the time, however, generally left treatment of discernment to devotional literature. The latter attempted to steer a path between maintaining the need for docility to the Spirit and a fear that such emphasis might either lead to false mysticism and quietism, or be interpreted as replacing the need for guidance from church authorities.

Recent commentators on past moral theology's treatment of conscience, many of them unreasonably harsh in their judgements,[45] refer to the exclusion of the Holy Spirit's gifts from moral theology's content. They attribute this exclusion to the separation of moral theology from spiritual theology. Emphasizing that discernment has a valid place in moral theology, many theologians see its role as particularly important in the formation of conscience and in guiding the judgement of conscience. Underlying their claims, and in tune with Vatican II's broader view of the person, is the return to a comprehensive understanding of conscience. More explicit attention is given to conscience's evaluative and normative functions and to its relationship to the person's basic orientation.

Bernhard Häring, Karl Rahner, Joseph Fuchs, James Gustafson, and Charles Curran emphasize that moral theology as a scientific discipline must give attention to the practice of discernment.[46] They stress that discernment has a specific role to play in moral decision-making. Discernment assists us to discover God's unique call to us and to apply general and abstract norms within our own specific situations.

Mary Ward referred to God's gift of true wisdom which is fostered by the practice of verity and sincerity and faithful attentiveness to the signs of the Holy Spirit in our lives. Her understanding of this wisdom has overtones of the virtue of prudence - the knowledge which enables us to distinguish rightly what helps and what hinders us in tending to God.[47] Mary Ward's insights anticipate the thinking of those moral theologians today who emphasize the relationship of prudence and discernment, and focus on feelings and affectivity as sources of morally correct knowledge.

Häring, for instance, citing St. Thomas' thesis that the efficacy of the New Law is based on the grace of the Holy Spirit, claims that a truly traditional Christian morality must place its chief emphasis not on casuistry but on the signs by which we can discern the Spirit. He sees the gifts of the Holy Spirit as completing and perfecting prudence and states: "We arrive at perfect prudence only through docility to the guidance of the Holy Spirit and through such prudence we become foresighted and discerning."[48]

Gustafson, too, compares moral discernment to the virtue of prudence and sees it as involving reason, sensibilities, and the will. As a virtue it is a lasting disposition of the self which does not exist independently of the law and is open to the concrete situation. It is informed by love, trust, hope and other gifts of the Spirit. Noting that the capacity for moral discernment is common to all persons, Gustafson emphasizes the impact of the Christian faith on Christians' self-understanding, desires and values (and therefore on their interpretations of their historical situation), and on the direction it gives to moral ends. He sees the process of interpretation that is part of moral discernment as an expression of Christians' fundamental commitment to God and respect for moral principles and moral rules.[49]

While Mary Ward's insights into discernment's role in guiding conscience are reflected by many theologians in recent years, the significant questions that her discernment of her vocation raised for the moral theology of her time remain largely unanswered and need to be addressed by contemporary moral theology. Those questions concern the matter of God's unique commands to individuals, the Church's relationship with those who receive such commands, and the historical nature of material moral norms and ecclesiastical laws.

That Mary Ward believed that God had directed her to model her Institute on the Society of Jesus is seen in her autobiography and letters to Urban VIII. This conviction and her fidelity to the will of the God whom she believed could not and would not deceive allowed her while imprisoned to overcome the temptation to yield to the opposition which had weakened her physical strength. In like manner, after the Institute's suppression she continued to use every means at her disposal to establish the truth of "the great work given her by God," for which "all else" must be "put aside."[50] Her last wish was that her companions cherish their vocation.

At the same time, the conflict of conscience Mary Ward experienced because of the Church's opposition is indicated clearly. She *could not* resist what God willed, and at the same time felt that she *ought not* act in a manner contrary to those to whom she owed obedience. While Mary Ward remained faithful to her discernment of God's will and her conviction that the Holy Spirit speaks through the mystical Body of Christ, her conflict indicates the inadequacy of the established canon law incorporated into her era's moral theology. In spite of the practice of many bishops and the appeals of Cardinal Pazmany and of Father Kutscher who declared enclosure to be contrary to freedom of conscience,[51] the canon law was maintained. Urban VIII after 1632 treated Mary Ward and her companions with kindness, and admitted that there had been much malice in the accusations against them. At the same time, however, he upheld rigidly the Council of Trent's decrees regarding enclosure.[52]

Grisar, after studying the relevant documents, including many held only by the Vatican archives, emphasizes that despite the rejection and seemingly hopeless extinction of the Institute in 1630-1631, any suggestion that Mary Ward's conviction was a delusion would be premature.[53] Rather, the later approval of her Institute and its enriched development indicate that ecclesiastical laws can be adapted, and point to the need for the recognition of the historicity of such laws and, indeed, of the interpretations made of material moral norms.

In this context, Mary Ward's experience suggests that Karl Rahner's proposal for a "formal existential ethics" merits attention.[54] His discussion points to the need for moral theology to provide a formal treatment of the question of God's individual call to persons. This call does not conflict with or discount the obligation of fidelity to moral norms but requires a particular concrete realization of one's love for God and desire to follow Christ. Here the person's unique relationship with God is involved, and God's will can be discerned only by attentiveness to the signs of the Holy Spirit in a freedom rooted in love. Moreover, such an ethics recognizes that God's individual invitations may anticipate what is positively approved and laid down by the official church authority.[55]

Mary Ward was born into an era characterized by religious conflict. Many of her relatives and acquaintances suffered severe penalties for their faith, and she herself knew the fear and uncertainty that accompanies religious persecution. Ironically, however, her greatest suffering came from the very church which she endeavored to serve so faithfully. Her conviction that in the apparent "contraries" of God's directive to her and the Church's opposition "God could not be against himself" has a great deal to say to the church today. It was this conviction which enabled her to remain loyal to both, and to state confidently in 1645: "It matters not the who but the what. And when God will enable me to be in place I will serve you."[56]

Notes

[1] "Letter to Urban VIII," Munich, March 27, 1631, cited by Chambers, vol. II, 367-368; Peters, 579.

[2] Letter to Urban VIII," Munich, April 10, 1631, cited by Chambers, vol. II, 381-382; also cited in part by Orchard, 112.

[3] *AB*, Wetter (I), 4. See also: Chambers, vol I, 403.

[4] See Appendix A.

[5] "Retreat Notes," April 1618, Wetter, (VII): 16, cited in part by Peters, 285, 293, note 44.

[6] *AB*, Wetter (I), 4.

[7] *AB*, cited by Chambers, vol I. 17-18. See also Peters, 36. Chambers mistakenly names this woman as Martha Wright.

[8] Aveling, *Northern Catholics*, 186. See also Peters, 51, note 40.

[9] *AB*, cited by Chambers, vol. I, 47.

[10] *AB*, cited by Chambers, vol. I, 123, 133; Orchard, 17.

[11] *AB*, cited by Chambers, vol. I, 165.

[12] Marcus Fridl, *Englische Tugend-schul Mariae*, vol.2, (Augsburg, 1732): 474-49, cited by Wetter, *Mary Ward's Prayer*, 99-100.

[13] *AB*, cited by Chambers, vol. I, 142; Orchard, 19. Mary Ward's words are: "The manner of God employed on this occasion was not to command me, or divinely to force me, but as if compassionating my labours (to)... propose the means to solace me, leaving me the liberty to use them or not."

[14] Ibid.

[15] *AB*, cited by Chambers, vol. I, 145; Orchard, 20. See also: Poyntz, *A Briefe Relation*.

[16] She states: "I prayed much ... forcing myself as best I could to put my mind into a state of indifference and myself totally in the hands of God, entreating him, almost night and day, to do his holy will on this occasion, and not to permit anything in me or in any other person, to prevent the same; which truly he disposed for the best and by means customary to his Goodness, when he wills to bestow a favour".(*AB*, cited by Chambers, vol. I, 90; Orchard, 13).

[17] "Letter to Albergati," see Orchard, 24, 25.

[18] *AB*, cited by Chambers, vol. I, 228, and in part by Orchard, 28.

[19] Karl Rahner, "On the Question of a Formal Existential Ethics," *Theological Investigations*, 2: 229.

[20] *Spiritual Exercises*, #175, #176. Many English translations of the *Spiritual Exercises*, including that of Louis Puhl, S.J., have "much" time, rather than "enough" time. In a course given at Regis College, Toronto, Fall, 1991, Valentìn Ramallo S.J. stated that the latter translation is correct.

[21] "Memorial to Pope Urban VIII," November 28, 1630, cited by Chambers, vol II, 330-331.

[22] "Retreat Notes," April 1618, Wetter, (VII); cited by Peters, 237, 244.

[23] Ibid. See Chambers, vol. II, 418 - 419; Peters, 237, 238, 244, notes 52-57.

[24] *Ratio Instituti*, second plan for the Institute, 1616, quoted in full by Chambers, vol. I, 376.

[25] "Retreat Notes," April, 1619, Wetter, (VIII): 11.

[26] *Painted Life*, 42.

[27] "Reasons why we may not alter," letter to Mutius Vitelleschi, January 8, 1622, cited by Chambers, vol. II, 16-17, Peters, 349, note 56. Acknowledging the need for vocations to receive confirmation, Mary Ward states

that she and her companions used prayer, the best advice they could find, and the trials prescribed in the Exercises.

[28]Compare: Joseph de Guibert, *Theology of the Spiritual Life*, trans., Paul Barrett, O.F.M. Cap., (New York: Sheed and Ward, 1953), 132-136 and *Spiritual Exercises*, ##316-317, #333.

[29]From Mary Ward's addresses cited by Chambers, vol. I, 465; Fridl, vol. 2, 15, cited by Wetter, *Mary Ward's Prayer*, 94.

[30]Compare: Mary Ward, "Retreat Notes," 1619, Wetter, (IX): 3, 22; letter, Mary Ward, possibly to Barbara Babthorpe, October 29, 1622, cited by Chambers, vol. II, 69; *Painted Life*, no. 41, cited by Peters, 418, note 63.

[31]From Mary Ward's addresses cited by Chambers, vol. I, 468.

[32]"Retreat Notes," 1619, Wetter, (VIII): 13, cited by Chambers, vol. I, 460.

[33]Mahoney, *The Making of Moral Theology*, xi.

[34]*New Dictionary of Theology*, s.v. "Conscience" by Seán Fagan; compare also: *New Catholic Encyclopedia*, s.v. "Conscience" by C. Williams.

[35]Bernhard Häring, *Free and Faithful in Christ*, vol. I, 229.

[36]Laymann and Busenbaum respectively define conscience as follows: "Conscientia est iudicium rationis practicae circa particularia per ratiocinationem deductum ex principiis universalibus contentis in Synteresi,"and "Conscientia est dictamen rationis." Paulo Laymann, *Theologiae Moralis in V Lib Partibus*, vol., 1I, (Venice, 1651, 1744), book 1, tract 1, cap. II; Hermani Busenbaum , *Medulla Theologiae Moralis*, Tomus Primus, (Tornaci: J. Castermann, 1848), book 1, tract 1, cap 1, *De Regula Interna Conscientia*.

[37]Compare: Häring, *Free and Faithful in Christ*, vol. I, 252; *New Catholic Encyclopedia*, s.v. "Conscience," by C. Williams.

[38]From Mary Ward's addresses cited by Chambers, vol. I, 466.

[39]*AB*, cited by Chambers, vol. I, 403.

[40]*AB*, cited by Chambers, vol. I, 132; "Reflections," 1620, Wetter, (IX): 15.

[41]Samuel Johnson, *A Dictionary of the English Language*, s.v. Affect, Affection.

[42]From Mary Ward's addresses cited by Chambers, vol.I, 410.

[43]"Reasons why we may not alter," letter to Mutius Vitelleschi, January 8, 1622, cited by Chambers, vol. II, 16-17, Peters, 349, note 56.

[44]When Sister Praxedes did not accept the way of life Mary Ward proposed for the Institute, Mary Ward suggested to John Gerard that Sister Praxedes present to him the enlightenment she claimed to have regarding the Institute. ("Letter to John Gerard," April 1619, given in full by Wetter, (V): 6-7; Chambers, vol, I, 452-453; Peters, 264, 270, notes 80, 81).

[45]See C. Williams' assessment of the treatises of the seventeenth century, *New Catholic Encyclopedia*, s.v. "Conscience."

[46]See for instance: Charles E. Curran, *Themes in Fundamental Moral Theology* (Notre Dame: University of Notre Dame Press, 1977), 214-216;

Fuchs, *Human Values and Christian Morality*, 32; *Christian Morality: The Word Become Flesh*, trans. Brian McNeil, (Dublin: Gill and MacMillan; Washington D.C.: Georgetown University Press, 1987), ch. VII; Gustafson, "Moral Discernment in the Christian Life," 596-597; Häring, *Law of Christ*, vol. I, 109; Karl Rahner, *The Dynamic Element in the Church* (Freiburg: Herder; Montreal: Palm Publishers, 1964).

[47] Compare: *Summa Theologiae*, 2a.2ae. 47, 1.

[48] Häring, *Law of Christ*, vol. I, 109, in reference to *Summa Theologiae*, 1a.2ae, 106, 1, and vol III, 298.

[49] Gustafson, "Moral Discernment in the Christian Life," 583-597.

[50] Compare: Grisar, 635.

[51] Grisar, 535.

[52] An account of Mary Ward's audience with Urban VIII in 1632 is given by Chambers, vol. II, 405. Grisar cites instances of his support of enclosure, including withholding permission for his widowed sister-in-law to live with her nieces because they were members of an enclosed order. Grisar, 154-156.

[53] Grisar, 744.

[54] Rahner, "A Formal Existential Ethics", 218-234. Compare: Rahner, *The Dynamic Element in the Church*, 70.

[55] Many current moral theologians distinguish ethics as essential and existential emphasizing that the latter complements the former. While it is beyond the scope of this work to discuss the various nuances they give to these terms, in general, essential ethics denotes those norms which are regarded as applicable to all and where one's behavior is but an instance of a general essential moral norm, while existential ethics refers to the experience of an absolute ethical demand addressed to the individual. Compare: McCormick, *Critical Calling*, 194. Although existential ethics has been accused of promoting subjectivism (*New Catholic Encyclopedia*, s.v. "Existential Ethics," by J. V. McGlynn), the distinction between existential and essential ethics is valuable in drawing attention to the individual invitation of God which is contained within all moral norms, and the importance of discerning and elaborating the signs which individuals use in arriving at their decisions and in determining whether their actions are appropriate. Casuistry certainly aids one to determine how universal norms are to be applied to particular acts but it must be complemented by personal attentiveness to the forces which enhance or militate against personal fidelity.

[56] "Letter from Mary Poyntz to Barbara Babthorpe in Rome," January 31, 1645, cited by Orchard, 120.

Chapter 7

Conclusion

For matters pertaining to morals I could never find satisfaction in the answers of those whom I knew were not well acquainted with the subject treated of; much less should I have felt it in matters spiritual under the same circumstances, because these are in themselves far more important and more likely than others to be prejudiced by ignorance. And more so, so greatly have I from the first loved integrity (proportionate to the occasions) that unless I had gone against my nature it would have been impossible for me to act halfheartedly in things of the soul, where all is intended and should be full and entire.[1]

On December 13, 1545, forty years prior to Mary Ward's birth, the Council of Trent convened. Among its aims were the increase and exaltation of the faith and christian religion, the extirpation of heresy, peace and union within the church and the reformation of clergy and christian people.[2] In December 1564, during the Council's last session, Girolamo Ragazoni, Bishop of Venice, summed up its outcomes. He referred specifically to its doctrinal decrees concerning original sin, justification and the sacraments, its reforming decrees and its restoration of ecclesiastical discipline.[3]

Almost four centuries later, October 20, 1962, the members of the Second Vatican Council with the endorsement of Pope John XXIII stated the Council's purpose. The Council members proposed to respond more faithfully to the Gospel and to present God's truth in a way which would reveal "the lovable features of Jesus Christ" whose love impels the love and service of others. The Council's primary focus was on spiritual renewal. Such renewal, they hoped, would result in "a happy impulse on behalf of human values such as scientific discoveries, technological advances, and a wider diffusion of knowledge." Emphasis was placed on the necessity for openness to whatever concerns the dignity of the human being and contributes to a genuine community of peoples.[4]

Each of these Councils acted as catalysts for significant stages in the making of moral theology. While the Council of Trent determined moral theology's emergence as an independent discipline different from other branches of theology, Vatican II gave strong impetus to moral theology's evolution by recognizing its relationship to dogmatic and spiritual theology. Just as the Council of Trent's seminary legislation was in large measure responsible for the orientation and content of subsequent moral theology, so too Vatican II's call for a renewed moral theology was made within its considerations of priestly formation.

The Council of Trent inherited the legacy of the cultural, philosophical, social, economic movements from the late Middle Ages and Renaissance. These resulted in a new humanism with the shift of focus from God to humanity in the interpretation of the world, and the breakdown of Christian unity. The sixteenth and seventeenth centuries marked a watershed in the development of human knowledge and consciousness. This era saw great achievements in art, literature, political theory, economics, and natural philosophy. At the same time, the period was characterized by a lack of educational opportunities for women, general illiteracy among the poor, and the extremes of superstition - the belief in witchcraft reached its peak between 1590 and 1630.

Mary Ward's era witnessed the rivalries of the Renaissance princes, rise of nation states, growing power of the merchants, and the opening up of new lands to Europeans. The twentieth century has experienced two world wars, numerous national conflicts, effects of the dialectical materialism of communism, and the heightened growth of imperialistic capitalism. Technological and scientific achievements and the discovery of previously unknown areas of the universe exist side by side with the impoverishment of large sections of the world and an increasing awareness of the threat posed to the earth by the misuse of its resources. The second Vatican Council inherited the effects of existentialism and phenomenology in philosophy, developments in theological anthropology, a more fully developed historical methodology, and a greater understanding of the human person through the human sciences. Conciliatory moves among Christians have coincided with both a decline in religious commitment and the development of radical fundamentalist sects.

Moral theology is not only affected by its contemporary situation but must seek insights into this situation. At the same time no new development emerges in a vacuum but is influenced by and reflects its tradition. Joseph Selling, pointing to the radical nature of the

revolution which he considers to have taken place in the discipline of
moral theology because of Vatican II, stresses that this revolution is
not to be equated with an overthrow of the tradition. Rather, it requires going back to the sources of the tradition and an identification of its core questions and insights.[5]

In chapter three aspects of the tradition were examined, namely,
the orientation and content of moral theology during its initial stages
of development as a distinct discipline. With the separation of moral
theology and spirituality, matters pertaining to morals came to be
addressed in two different forms: manuals which conveyed moral
theology in the strict sense, and ascetical works which dealt with the
practice of the Christian life. Both types of work were practical in
orientation, little explicit attention being given to the principles of
dogmatic or spiritual theology.

Mary Ward's observations reflected her conviction of the harmonious relationship that she believed should exist between spirituality
and moral theology. This conviction grounded her lived and formulated spirituality, her concept of morality, and her insights into the
communication of moral principles. Mary Ward's understanding of
moral rectitude as having its source in the well-ordered disposition
of the morally good person forms the link between moral and spiritual theology. Her notions of the "estate of justice", freedom, discipleship, discernment, conscience, sin, and conversion reflect her
belief that the analysis of the moral act cannot validly be divorced
from consideration of the moral agent. Central to moral theology's
task, therefore, is consideration of the development of the qualities
of personal goodness which constitute the interior disposition from
which moral rectitude flows. A rigid separation between moral and
spiritual theology lessens the effectiveness of moral theology's communication of the central constituents of moral conduct.

Despite some opposition to the compartmentalization of moral
theology and spirituality which had existed since the counter-
Reformation, a rigid separation between the two disciplines was maintained until well on into the twentieth century. Joseph de Guibert
notes the commonly held view that moral theology's content properly comprises treatment of the commandments and virtues only insofar as they are obligatory, while consideration of the counsels and
the perfection of the Christian life belongs to spiritual theology. This
view is reflected in the works of such theologians as Henry Davis and

Adolphe Tanqueray who wrote in the 1940s in the areas of moral theology and spiritual theology respectively.[6] Accompanying this view was an implicit acceptance of mediocrity as the prevailing state of the majority of ordinary Christians.

Mary Ward's comprehensive view that all are graced by God and offered the freedom won for humanity by Christ was determinative of her view of morality as discipleship and of her approach to moral guidance. Her understanding of the way spiritual theology can enrich moral theology goes beyond that explicitly formulated in her era. Her views anticipate the moves of Vatican II and of recent theologians for a greater rapprochement between these two branches of theology. These moves have emphasized the need for moral theology to have a Christocentric approach and give priority to considering the new law of Christ and the primacy of charity in the moral life. They call for moral theology to treat grace in a systematic way, to center attention on the human agent, and to emphasize the role of the virtues and asceticism in the Christian life.

In their more personalist approach, theologians have portrayed morality in terms of discipleship. This is defined as human persons' faithful and loving response, through Christ's grace, to the God of love and fidelity.[7] In addition, many theologians writing in the fields of both moral and spiritual theology, lament the past divorce of both disciplines from dogmatic theology and stress the need for both to have a sound theological basis.[8]

The second Vatican Council presented a similar view of morality in terms of personal vocation. It directed that moral theology "should show the nobility of the Christian vocation of the faithful, and their obligation to bring forth fruit in charity for the life of the world." Emphasizing the implications of this understanding of morality for moral theology's scientific content and orientation, the Council stated that, in common with other theological disciplines, moral theology should be renewed by "livelier contact with the mystery of Christ and the history of salvation."[9] These directives have resulted in significant differences between the content and orientation of moral theology today and the moral theology of Mary Ward's era.

In the light of moral theology's history and recent developments, the definition of moral theology given in the *Oxford Dictionary of the Christian Church* may appear deceptively simple. In arriving at an adequate definition a fundamental question needs to be addressed, namely, "What constitutes the moral person?" In defence of the moral theology of Mary Ward's time, it may be said that this question was at least implicit. It was more explicitly addressed in the period's spiritual writings. In their treatment of the elements of the Christian moral life one finds a two-fold emphasis: the keeping of the commandments and the response to Jesus' specific call to intimate discipleship. The manuals of moral theology concentrated on the former and did so in the context of the legalism of their age. While obedience to the commandments both demands and is conducive to personal holiness, such an emphasis is in danger of neglecting the importance of morality as a primarily personal response.

That the moral theology of Mary Ward's era responded to the needs of the times and assisted Catholics faced with the dilemmas posed by the division of Christianity is undeniable. From the late-seventeenth century, however, moral theology's history is a less dynamic one. Concern with the problem of "probabilism" led to an abstract kind of casuistry which endured well on into the twentieth century. Richard McCormick is only one of many who cite instances of the type of minutiae which often dominated moral theologians' discussions.[10]

Moral theology today has been influenced by developments in theological anthropology and the human sciences. These have led to a greater understanding of the human person. As a result, morality has come to be viewed increasingly in terms of personal goodness, where moral virtues are seen as indications of the maturity and growing interior freedom of the morally good person. Moral theology's task then is to demonstrate clearly the constituents of the moral life of human beings called by Christ to perfection. Within this perspective moral conduct emerges as profoundly reasonable and in harmony with human nature. It is a response to God's loving invitation revealed to us in history through Christ who in his human life exemplified the fullness of this moral conduct.

Mary Ward's lived and formulated spirituality reveals the enrichment to moral theology which can result from its closer relationship with spiritual theology. The theology and anthropology underlying her spirituality are significant not only in the area of personal moral formation, but also in informing the "principles" for morally significant actions. Bridging both disciplines is her exposition of the well-ordered interior disposition which is the source of morally right actions. In her view morality is above all a personal response manifested in the deep commitment to God from which specific moral acts flow. This self-commitment presupposes freedom, the basis of which is love. Both spiritual and moral theology find their highest common denominator and perfection in Charity, the love of God for God's sake and love of neighbor for God.

For Mary Ward the means chosen to express this love flowed from an original experience of God's grace and from fidelity to discerning the movements of the Holy Spirit within her. Her discernment brought knowledge of her inner orientation and led to action. In looking first to interior disposition and second to the actions which flow from this disposition, Mary Ward envisaged a harmony between persons and their behavior, namely the sincerity/ verity by which "we be such as we appear and appear such as we are."[11] Such harmony of will, intellect and affectivity, flows from co-operation with the grace given by the God of verity and goodness and from fidelity to discerning the signs of the Holy Spirit.

In other words, Mary Ward's comprehensive understanding of the dignity of human persons is inseparable from her conviction that they must take responsibility for the actualization of this dignity. This actualization is exemplified in the well-ordered disposition of justice and the works of justice it engenders. Mary Ward's creative vision of a world-wide apostolic Institute of religious women saw the purpose of such works of justice as bringing into greater harmony the prevailing situation of this world and the *Regnum Dei*, wrought through Christ.

One of theology's major tasks is to communicate the truths of God's love and desires for humanity. Mary Ward's approach to moral instruction shows how these truths can be communicated effectively. She affirmed strongly that morality is not imposed from outside human persons but is in harmony with their deepest desires. Her conviction of God's goodness and verity underlay her understanding of grace as God's gift of love which "graceth all God's gifts" and her insights into the graced dignity of all human persons, women and men, lay and religious. Seeing Christ as the epitome of the estate of justice Mary Ward identified moral goodness with the following of Christ in love and service of others.

Mary Ward was born nearly twenty years after the Council of Trent dissolved and over three hundred years prior to the second Vatican Council. Her insights into the fundamental principles underlying moral theology, however, are in tune with and relevant to the re-orientation of moral theology envisaged by Vatican II and the ap-proaches taken by many moral theologians within the last thirty years. The Council of Trent coincided with the Renaissance and the recov-ery and appreciation of the riches of the classical age. Vatican II in-herited a greater interest in history and in the historicity of the human person. While this means a significantly different approach to moral theology, its continued development depends not only on insights into the contemporary situation but a mining of past tradi-tions.

As Lonergan warns in a comparable context, extremes will appear on the right and left. In his view, what is important "is a centre, big enough to be at home in the old and the new, painstaking enough to work out one by one the transitions to be made, strong enough to refuse half measures and to insist on complete solutions even though it has to wait."[12]

Mary Ward's spirituality and practice are instances of such a "cen-tre." Her innovative vision of the service to the Church which could be made by an apostolic congregation of religious women was re-jected by the Church. In recent times, however, she has been praised by such diverse personages as Pius XII who endorsed her with Saint Vincent de Paul as a model for the laity and Mother Teresa of India who referred to her as bringing a new dimension to human persons especially to women. In her love and uncompromising fidelity to the will of God, and her loyalty to the Church, Mary Ward provides a means of communicating to everyone the central tenets of her expo-sition of the well-ordered relationship with God, oneself and others - the moral goodness which is the source of moral rectitude. Mary Ward's last extant spiritual note, written in her own hand and penned in 1636, five years after the suppression of her Institute, reflects her conviction that the God of love makes possible both the knowledge and living out of this estate:

O how well ordered are thy deeds, my Lord God!
Then thou saidst that justice was the best disposition;
Now thou showest how such justice is to be gotten.[13]

Notes

[1] *AB*, cited by Chambers, vol I, 132.

[2] *Canons and Decrees of the Council of Trent*, Session 1, December 13, 1545, repeated in the Bull concerning the confirmation of the Council, December 1563.

[3] Ibid., Oration of Bishop Girolamo Ragazoni of Venice delivered in the final session of the Council, December 3rd and 4th, 1563, conducted under the Supreme Pontiff, Pius IV.

[4] *Documents of Vatican II*, "Message to Humanity," #4-#6.

[5] Joseph A. Selling, ed., "Evolution and Continuity in Conjugal Morality," in *Personalist Morals* (Louvain: University Press, 1988), 248.

[6] Adolphe Tanqueray, S.S., D.D., *The Spiritual Life; A Treatise on Ascetical and Mystical Theology*, translated by Hermann Branderis, S.S., A.M., second edition, (Westminster, Maryland: The Newman Bookshop, 1948); Henry Davis, S.J. *Moral and Pastoral Theology*, four volumes, sixth edition, (London and New York: Sheed and Ward, 1949).

[7] Fritz Tillman, *Die Idee der Nachfolge Christi*, volume 2 of *Handbuch der katholischen Sittenlehre*, (Dusseldorf: L. Swann, 1934), 5, cited by John A. Gallagher, *Time Past, Time Present: An Historical Study of Catholic Moral Theology* (New York and New Jersey: Paulist Press, 1990),163; Häring, *Law of Christ*, vol.1, 35, 42, 47, 399.

[8] Fuchs, *Human Values and Christian Morality*, 32, 38; Denis Hawkins, *Christian Ethics* (New York: Hawthorn Books 1963), 69.

[9] *Documents of Vatican II*, "Decree on Priestly Formation," # 16.

[10] Richard A. McCormick, "Moral Theology 1940-1989: An Overview," *Theological Studies* 50 (1989): 4, 5.

[11] Letter to Roger Lee, November 1st, 1615. See Appendix A.

[12] Bernard J.F. Lonergan, S.J. "Dimensions of Meaning," in *Collection: Papers by Bernard Lonergan, S.J.*, ed., F. E. Crowe, (Montreal: Palm Publishers, 1967), 267.

[13] See earlier: chapter 4, note 1.

Appendix

Text of Mary Ward's Description of the "Estate of Justice" as Contained in her Letter to Father Roger Lee, S.J. November 1, 1615.

Dearest Father,

I would exceeding gladly both for my better satisfaction and greater security acquaint you with what hath occurred in these two days, especially that which yesterday I wrote to your Reverence about, and going now to set it down, the better I discern it, the less able I find myself to declare it. I seem to love it, and yet am afflicted in it because I cannot choose but retain it, and yet dare not embrace it for truly good till it be approved.

It seems a certain clear and perfect estate to be had in this life, and such a one as is altogether needful for those that should well discharge the duties of this Institute. I never read of any I can compare in likeness to it, yet it is not like the state of saints, whose holiness chiefly appears in that union with God which maketh them out of themselves. I perceived then an apparent difference, and yet felt myself drawn to love and desire this estate more than all those favours. The felicity of this estate (for as much as I can express) was a singular freedom from all that could make one adhere to earthly things, with an entire application and apt disposition to all good works. Something happened also discovering the freedom that such a soul should have had to refer all to God, but I think that was after, or upon some other occasion; howsoever that such a thing there was I am very certain.

I seemed in my understanding to see a soul thus composed, but far more fair than I can express it. It then occurred, and still continues in my mind, that those in Paradise, before the first fall, were in this estate. It seemed to me then, and that hope remains still, that our Lord let me see it to invite me that way and because he would give me grace in time to arrive to such an estate, at least in some degree.

That word justice and those that in former times were called just persons, works of justice, done in innocence, and that we be such as we appear and appear such as we are, those things often since occurred to my mind with a liking of them. And that you may know all and judge according (though several times since I began to write, I have found an extraordinary horror in myself, and with all a fear that you would see it all to be nought, and be much afflicted at it); but howsoever, blessed be our Lord, who hath provided me of such as can tell me what is good.

I have moreover, thought upon this occasion, that perhaps this course of ours would continue till the end of the world, because it came to that in which we first began.

Once I found a questioning in myself why this state of justice, and virtue of sincerity should appear unto me so especially requisite as a ground of all those other virtues necessary to be exercised by those of this Institute, and it occurred that the Fathers of the Society, being men, wise and learned, they might by those their natural parts, perform the functions of this Institute without so special concurrence of God's grace, as might require their continual vigilance and care, in the practice of those above-said virtues, and therefore if anything should be in danger to decay amongst them, it might be this, as also that we, wanting that learning, judgement, and other parts that men have, yet being grounded in this, we should gain at God's hands true wisdom, and ability to perform all such other things as the perfection of this Institute exacteth of us.

After both that day and the next, as my meditations further discovered the condition of this Institute, methought I better understood those particulars, one by one, practically, not confusedly, than before I had done; they led me severally to that first estate as the fountain, and best disposition for a soul to be in, that would perform all this well, and from thence I could without labour return to them again and discern with great clearness and solid tranquillity the excellence and convenience of them.

So as a great part of these two days hath been exceeding pleasing, and I hope profitable, for I end with desires to be good, which I see I am not, and without that, it seems impossible I should be able to do good, at least according to the estate of life whereunto I think I am called, for my will is so exceeding stubborn and perverse, as that it will not let me possess any good with certainty or without fear to lose it again. And how much this indisposition for God's favour doth hinder me in all I can better perceive in myself than show to those I should. I humbly beseech you, obtain my amendment of God, and help me to be good, how dear soever it cost. Bestow on us all your blessing.

Your ever unworthy
M.W.

Upon All Saints Day 1615
which was on a Sunday.

Bibliography:

Primary Sources
(A) Mary Ward's Writings

(i) *Copies of Mary Ward's Writings contained in the Archives of the Institute of the Blessed Virgin Mary at Munich, Germany.*

(These five have been copied, edited and annotated by Immolata Wetter in the Letters of Instruction I-IX. Excerpts from this material can be found in secondary works on Mary Ward.)

Autobiographical Fragments covering the period up to 1595 written from 1617.

Autobiography, 1600-1609, fragments in English and a longer section in Italian (in Elizabeth Cotton's handwriting) written between 1624 and 1626.

Letters to Roger Lee (November 1, 1615); Fr. Tomson, (John Gerard), c. 1619 and to Antonio Albergati, Nuncio in Cologne, c. 1621.

Various Papers from the period 1612-1636.

"The Third Plan of the Institute," presented to the Congregation of Bishops and Regulars, February-March 1622, manuscript, Vatican Library, Capp.47, ff. 57-62.

(Not in Letters of Instruction I-IX.)

"Mary Ward's Prayer." Lectures using material from Mary Ward's letters and retreat reflections, and given by Immolata Wetter I.B.V.M. to Members of the Institute of the Blessed Virgin Mary in 1974.

(ii) *Published Collections*

The Mind and Maxims of Mary Ward. Edited by the Institute of the Blessed Virgin Mary. London: Burns Oates & Washbourne Ltd 1959.

Orchard, N. Emmanuel IBVM, ed., *Till God Will: Mary Ward Through Her Writings.* London: Darton, Longman & Todd, 1985.

Parker, Pauline. *The Spirit of Mary Ward: Her Character and Spirituality.* Bristol, England: Thomas More Books, 1963.

Secondary Sources
(B) Biographies of Mary Ward

(i) *Manuscripts*:

Poyntz, Mary. *A Briefe Relation: Of the holy life and happy Death of our Dearest Mother, of holy Memmory. Mrs Mary Ward.* circa 1647-1657. Typescript of the "Manchester" manuscript of the English life of Mary Ward believed to have been written shortly after her death.

Pageti, Vincentio. *Breve Racconto della vita di Donna Maria della Guardia,* 1662. Pageti was Secretary of Cardinal Borghese and Apostolic Notary. (Archives of the Institute, Munich).

Bissel, Domenico, Canon Regular of the Holy Cross in Augsburg. Sketch of Mary Ward's Life written in 1674. (Archives of the Institute, Munich).

Lohner, Tobias S.J. *Gottseeliges Leben und fürtreffliche Tugendten Donna Maria della Guardia, Hochlöblichen Stüfferin der Engelländischen Gesellschaft,* 1689. (Archives of the Institute of the blessed Virgin Mary, Altötting, Germany.)

Genmaltes Leben–The Painted Life. The originals of the fifty very large oil paintings dating back to a few years after Mary Ward's death. (Convent of the Institute of the Blessed Virgin Mary, Augsburg).

(ii) *Published Biographies*

Chambers, Mary Catherine Elizabeth. *The Life of Mary Ward.* Edited by Henry James Coleridge. Volumes I and II. London: Burns and Oates, 1882, 1885.

Fridl, Marco. *Englische Tugend-Schul,* 2 volumes. Augsburg, 1732.

Grisar, Joseph S.J. *Mary Wards Institut vor Römischen Kongregationen 1616-1630.* Miscellanea Historiae Pontificiae. Volume 37. Rome: Pontifical Gregorian University, 1966.

Khamm, Corbinianus, O.S.B. *Relatio de origine et propagatione Instituti Mariae nuncupati Virginum Anglarum.* Monachii, 1717.

Leitner, J. *Die Geschichte der Englischen Fraulein und ihrer Institut.* Regensburg: 1869.

McGovern, Kathleen, I.B.V.M. "Mary Ward and the Institute of the Blessed Virgin Mary." Part 1 of *Something More Than Ordinary: The Early History of Mary Ward's Institute in North America.* Richmond Hill, Ontario, Canada: The A Team, 1989.

Mary Oliver, IBVM. *Mary Ward, 1585-1645.* NY: Sheed & Ward, 1959.

O'Connor, Margarita I.B.V.M. *That Incomparable Woman.* Montreal: Palm Publishers, 1962.

Peters, Henrietta. *Mary Ward: ihre Persönlichkeit und ihr Institut.* Innsbruck, Vienna: Tyrolia, 1991. English Translation by Helen Butterworth. *Mary Ward: A World in Contemplation.* Leominster, Herefordshire: Gracewing, Fowler Wright Books, 1994.

(iii) *Other Works and Journal Articles on Mary Ward's Thought*

Brennan, Margaret. "Women and Theology." *The Way* 53, Supplement (Summer 1985): 93-103.

Brodrick, James S.J. "Mary Ward." Reprinted from *The Tablet*, London, January 27, 1945.

Broderick, William S.J. "One Mission: Many Ministries." *The Way* 53, Supplement (Summer 1985): 34-46.

Byrne, Lavinia. "Mary Ward's Vision of the Apostolic Religious Life." *The Way* 53, Supplement (Summer 1985): 73-84.

Chase, Martin. "When God is Sought Sincerely." *The Way* 53, Supplement (Summer 1985): 119-128.

Fitzgibbon, Basil. "Mary Ward," *The Month* no. VIII (1952): 356-357.

Hallensleben, Barbara. *Theologie der Sendung: Die Ursprünge bei Ignatius von Loyola und Mary Ward.* Frankfurt am Main: Josef Knecht, 1994.

Hicks, Leo S.J. "Mary Ward's Great Enterprise." *The Month*, Volume CLI: (February 1928): 137-146; (April 1928): 317-326; Volume CLII: (July 1928): 40-53; (September, 1928): 231-238; Volume CLIII: (January 1929): 40-48; (March 1929): 223-236.

Norman, Marion. I.B.V.M. "A Woman for All Seasons: Mary Ward (1585-1645), Renaissance Pioneer of Women's Education." Reprinted from: *Paedogigica Historica; International Journal of the History of Education.* XXIII/1. Ghent: 1983.

Principe, Walter H. "Changing Concepts of Holiness." *The Way* 53, Supplement (Summer 1985): 14-33.

Warnke, Barbara Olga.I.B.V.M. "Mary Ward: And not by Halves." Chancellor's Address, Regis College, Toronto, 1985. Toronto: Regis College Press, 1985.

Wetter, Immolata I.B.V.M. "Mary Ward's Apostolic Vocation." *The Way.* Reprinted from Supplement 17 (Autumn 1972).

(iv) *Recusant Literature*

Allen, William. Cardinal. *A Briefe historie of the glorious martyrdom of xii. reverend priests.* Pr. (Rheims, Jean Foigny), 1582. *CRC* 55 (1970).

___. *An Apologie and True Declaration of the Institution and Endeavours of the Two English Colleges, the one in Rome, the other now resident in Rhemes.* Imprint false; Pr. (Rheims, Jean Foigny), 1581. *CRC* 67 (1971).

Alonso de Madrid. *A Breefe Methode or Way Teaching All Sortes of Christian People, How to Serve God in a Moste Perfect Manner.* Translated by I.M. n.p.d. Pr. (secretly in England) (1602-1615).

B., I. *A Treatise with a Kalendar, and the Proofes thereof, concerning the Holy-daies and Fasting-daies in England.* Pr. secretly in England, 1598. *CRC* 109 (1972).

Bagshaw, Christopher. *A Sparing Discoverie of our English Jesuits and of Fa. Parsons proceeding under pretence of promoting the Catholike faith in England: For a caveat to all true Catholikes our very loving brethren and friends, how they embrace such very uncatholike, though Jesuiticall deseignments.* Dedication: W.W. (William Watson). Pr.(London: J, Roberts), 1601. *CRC* 39 (1970).

Bellarmine, Cardinal Robert. *A Most Learned and Pious Treatise, full of Divine and Humane Philosophy, framing a Ladder, wherby our Mindes may ascend to God by the Steppes of his Creatures.* Translated into English by T.B. Gent. Doway: 1616. Tr, (Francis Young). Imprint false. Pr. (secretly in England), 1615. *CRC* 22 (1970).

___. *An Ample Declaration of the Christian Doctrine for the use of those who teach children, and other unlearned persons; Composed in forme of a Dialogue, betweene the Master and Scholar.* Translated into English by Richard Hadock. Roan: n.d. (1602-1605). Imprint false; pr. (secretly in England.) *CRC* 341 (1977).

A Briefe Collection Concerning the Love of God towards Mankinde, & how for divers causes we are justlie bounde to love and serve him. With preparation to Prayer and certaine necessarie prayers and thankesgeving to God for his benefites, daylie to be used. Also a devote Meditation to procure Contrition and excite Devotion With other vertuous prayers. Doway:Laurence Kellam, 1603. *CRC* 170 (1973).

Bristow, Richard. *A briefe treatise of diverse and sure wayes to finde out the truth in this... time of heresie: conteyning sundry worthy motives unto the Catholike faith.* Antwerp: apud Johannem Foulerum, 1574. *CRC* 209 (1974).

Bucke, John, Compiler, *Instructions for the use of the beades, conteining many matters of meditacion or mentall prayer, with diverse good advises of ghostly counsayle. Where unto is added a figure or forme of the beades portrued in a Table. For the benefit of the unlearned.* Dedicated to Anne Lady Hungaforde, sister to the Duchesse of Ferria. Louvain: (Jan Maes), 1589.

C., N., Compiler, *The Pigeons Flight from out of Noes Arke, over the floud, into the Arke again (Gen.8.8). Resembling well the fall of Hereticks,*

Schismaticks, &c. out of Holie Church, their continuance with-out, and returne againe. 1602-1605. Pr. secretly in England. *CRC* 352 (1977).

Canisius, Peter Saint. *A Summe of Christian doctrine composed in Latin ... with an Appendix of the fall of Man and Justification, according to the Doctrine of the Council of Trent. Newlie translated into English. To which is adjoined the explication of certain Questions not handled at large in the Booke as shall appeare in the table.* Translated (in part by Henry Garnet, with appendices), Pr. (secretly in England), (1592-1596) *CRC* 35 (1971).

Certayne devout Meditations Very necessary for Christian men devoutly to meditate upon Morninge and Eveninge every day in the weeke: Concerning Christ his lyfe and Passion and the fruites thereof. Duaci, apud Joannem Bogardi, 1576. Imprint false: (London: William Carter). *CRC* 5 (1969).

Clare. *The Rule of the holy virgin S. Clare, Togeather with the admirable life, of S. Catherine of Bologna.* Translated by Sister Catherine of St. Magdalen (Elizabeth Evelinge), or Sister Magdalen of St. Augustine (Catherine Bentley) from a work by Dionisio Paleotti. Pr. (S. Omer: English College Press), 1621. *CRC* 274 (1975).

D., T.H. *Nine rockes to be avoided, of those who sayle towards the port of perfection.* Pr. secretly in England, 1600.

F.G., translator. *A Manual of Prayer newly gathered out of many and divers famous authors as well auncient as of the tyme present.* 2 parts. Rouen: Fr. Persons' Press, 1583. *CRC* 372 (1978).

Garnet, Henry. *A Treatise of Christian Renunciation. Compiled of excellent sentences & as it were diverse homelies of ancient fathers.* With *The declaration of the fathers of the Council of Trent."* Pr.(secretly in England), 1593. *CRC* 47 (1970).

___. *The Societie of the Rosary. Wherein is conteined the beginning, increase, & profit of the same.* Pr. (secretly in England): (1593-1594).

Lanspergius, John. *An Epistle or exhortation of Jesus Christ to the soule, that is devoutly affected towarde him.* Translated by Philip Howard, Earl of Arundel, probably in conjunction with John Gerard, S.J.). Pr. Secretly in England), (1592-1593). *CRC* 56 (1970).

Lessius, Leonardus. *A Controversy, in which is examined, whether every man may be saved in his owne faith and religion?."* (S. Omer: English College Press), 1614. *CRC* 106 (1972).

Loarte, Gaspare S.J. *The Exercise of a Christian Life... with certaine verie devout Exercises & Praiers added thereunto, more than were in the first Edition.* Translator's dedicatory epistle signed: James Sancer (pseudonym of Stephen Brinkley). Pr.(London, William Carter), 1579. *CRC* 44 (1970).

___. *Instructions and advertisements, how to meditate the misteries of the Rosarie of the most holy virgin Mary.* Newly translated into English by John Fen. Secretly printed in London by William Carter, (1579).

Luis De Granada. *A Memoriall of a Christian Life. Wherein are treated all such thinges, as apperteyne unto a Christian to doe.* Translated by Richard Hopkins. Rouen: George L'Oyselet, 1586. *CRC* 272 (1975).

___. *Of Prayer and Meditation. Wherein are Conteined Fowertien Devoute Meditations for the morninges and eveninges. And in them is treyted of the consideration of the principall holie Mysteries of our faithe.* Translated by Richard Hopkins. Paris: Thomas Brumeau, 1582. *CRC* 64 (1971).

___. *A Spiritual Doctrine Conteining a Rule to live wel, with divers Praiers and Meditations.* Abridged. Translated by Richard Gibbons. Louvain: Lawrence Kellam, 1599. *CRC* 204 (1974).

A Manuall, or Meditation, and most necessary Prayers: with a Memoriall of Instructions right requisite. Also a Summary of Catholike Religion; and an absolute order of Confession with directions for receiving: and other necessary things, for all well disposed persons. Doway: I.R. (1580-1581)). Imprint false (secretly at the "Greenstreet House" Press). *CRC* 5 (1969).

M., I. *A breefe Directory, and playne way howe to say the Rosary of our Blessed Lady: with meditations for such as are not exercised therein, Wherein are adjoined the prayers of S. Bryget, with others.* Bruges, Flandrorum. Excudebat Hu. Holost, 1576. Imprint false. Pr. (London: William Carter and John Lion). *CRC* 5 (1969).

More, Thomas. *A Dialogue of Comfort against tribulation, made by the right vertuous, wise and learned man, Sir Thomas More.* Made by an Hungarian in Latin, and translated out of Latin into French, & out of French into English. Now newly set foorth, with many places restored and corrected by conference of sundrie copies. Dedicated to Ladie Jane, Duchesse of Feria. Antwerp: Johannem Foulerum, 1573. *CRC* 25 (1970).

Mush, John. *A Dialogue betwixt a Secular priest and A Lay Gentleman. Concerning some points objected by the Jesuiticall faction against such secular priests, as have shewed their dislike of M. Blackwell and the Jesuits proceedings.* Printed at Rhemes, 1601. Dedication W.W. (William Watson). Imprint false. Pr. (London, A. Islip). *CRC* 39 (1970).

The New Testament of Jesus Christ. Translated faithfully into English, out of the authentical Latin, according to the best corrected copies of the same, diligently conferred with the Greeke and other editions in divers languages; With Arguments of bookes and chapters, ANNOTATIONS, and other necessarie helpes, for the better understanding of the text, and specially for the discoverie of the CORRUPTIONS of divers late translations, and for cleering the CONTROVERSIES in religion, of these daies. Rhemes: John Fogny, 1582. *CRC* 267 (1975).

Persons, Robert S.J. *A Brief Discours Contayning Certayne Reasons why Catholics Refuse to go to Church.* (London: Greenstreet House, 1580). *CRC* 84 (1972).

___. *The Christian Directory guiding men to eternall salvation. ....the first Booke consisting of two partes, whereof the former layeth downe the motives to resolution; and the other removeth the impediments; both of them having byn lately reviewed, corrected, and not a little altered by the author himselfe.* Pr.(S. Omer, Francois Bellet), 1607. *CRC* 41 (1970).

Pinelli, Luca S.J. *Briefe Meditations of the Most Holy Sacrament and of preparation, for Receiving the same. And of some other thinges apertaining to the greatnes and devotion of so worthy a Misterie.* A translation. Pr. (secretly in England), (1595-1600). *CRC* 289 (1976).

The Primer, or office of the blessed Virgin Marie, in Latin and English: according to the reformed Latin and with lyke graces privileged. Edited by R.V. (Richard Verstegan). Antwerp: Arnold Conings, 1599. *CRC* 262 (1975).

Rodriguez, Alfonso. *A Short and Sure Way to Heaven and present happiness. Taught in a treatise of our conformity with the will of God....* Translated out of the Spanish. Pr. (St. Omer: Widow of Charles Boscard), 1630. *CRC* 225 (1975).

Scupoli, Lorenzo. *The Spiritual Conflict. Written in Italian by a devout servant of God: and lately translated into English.* Translated by (John Gerard). (Another edition). Douai: Charles Boscard, 1603-1610). *CRC* 8 (1972).

Southwell, R.S. *A Short Rule of Good Life. To direct the devout christian in a reguler and orderly course.* Pr. (secretly in England), (1596-97), *CRC* 78 (1971).

Suso, Henry. *Certain Swete prayers of the Glorious name of Jesus, commonly called Jesus Matins, with the howers therto belonging.* Translated from the Latin. Pr. (London: William Carter), (1575-78). *CRC* 5 (1969).

Teresa, Saint. *The lyf of the mother Teresa of Jesus Foundresse of the monasteries of the descalced or bare-footed Carmelite nunnes and fryers of the First Rule. Translated by W.M. of the Society of Jesus. Very profitable for all vertuous and devout people, and for all those that are desirous to be such, or at least do not obstinately deprive themselves of so great a benefit.* Antwerp: Henrie Iaye, 1611. *CRC* 212 (1974).

Thomas, a Kempis. *The following of Christ, translated out of Latin into Englishe, newlie corrected and amended. Whereunto is added the golden epistle of sainct Bernarde. And now lastlie the rules of a christian lyfe, made by John Picus the elder earle of Mirandula.* An edition of (William Whytford's) translation. Pr. (Rouen, George L'Oyselet), 1585. CRC 353, (1977).

A Treatise of mental prayer in which is briefly declared the manner how to exercise the inward Actes of Vertues" by Fr. Ant. de Molina Carthusian.

Whereunto is adjoined a very profitable Treatise of Exhortation to Spiritual Profit written by F. Francis Arias of the Society of Jesus. Together with a Dialogue of Contrition and Attrition. All translated out of Spanish into English by a Father of the Society of Jesus, the first treatise by (John Sweetman); the other two treatises by (Thomas Everard). Dedicatory epistle signed by I.W. (John Wilson) (St. Omer: English College Press), 1617. *CRC* 15 (1970).

Vaux, Lawrence. *A Catechisme, or a Christian doctrine, necessarie for children and the ignorant people... Whereunto is adjoined a briefe forme of Confession.* Pr. (Secretly in England), 1599. *CRC* 2 (1969).

Weston, Edward. *The triall of Christian truth by the rules of the vertues, namely these principall faith, hope, charitie and religion... The second parte, entreating of hope.* Pr. Douay:(widow of Laurence Kellam), 1615. *CRC* 366 (1977).

Worthington, Thomas. *A Relation of Sixtene Martyrs: Glorified in England in Twelve Monethes. With a Declaration That English Catholiques suffer for the Catholic Religion and that the Seminarie priests agree with the Jesuites. In answer to our Adversaries calumniations touching these two points.* Doway: widow of James Boscard, 1601. *CRC* 350 (1977).

_____. *The Rosary of Our Ladie. Otherwise called our ladies psalter. With other godlie exercises mentioned in the Preface.* Antwerpiae: apud Joannem Keerbergium, 1600. *CRC* 339 (1977).

(v) *Further References*

Allison, A.F. and D.M. Rogers. *A Catalogue of Catholic Books in English Printed Abroad or Secretly in England 1558-1640.* London: Wm. Dawson and Sons Ltd, 1968 (reprinted with permission of the Catholic Record Society).

_____. *The Contemporary Printed Literature of the English Counter-Reformation between 1558 and 1640.* Volume 1: Works in Languages other than English. The London: Scolar Press, 1989.

Allison, A.F. "New Light on the Early History of the *Breve Compendio.* The Background to the English Translation of 1612." *Recusant History.* 4 no.1 (January 1957): 1-17.

_____."The Later Life and Writings of Joseph Creswell, S.J. (1556-1623)." *Recusant History* 15 no.2 (1979), 79-145.

_____."The Writings of Father Henry Garnet, S.J. (1555-1606)." *Recusant History* 1 no.1 (1951), 7-21.

Anstruther, Godfrey. *The Seminary Priests; a Dictionary of the Secular Clergy of England and Wales 1558-1850,* Volume I: Elizabethan 1558-1603. Gateshead, England; Northumberland Press Ltd., 1968; Volume 2: Early

Stuarts 1603-1659. Great Wakering, Essex, England; Mayhew-McCrimmon, 1975.

Aquaviva, Claudio. "Directoria Exercitiorum Spiritualium (1540-1599)." Edited by Ignatius Iparraguirre, S.J. Monumenta Ignatiana, Series Secunda; Exercitia Spiritualia Sancti Ignatii de Loyola et Eorum Directoria, nova editio, Tomus II, Directoria (1540-1599). *Monumenta Historica Societatis Jesu*, Volumen 76. Rome. 1955.

___. "The Directory." In *The Spiritual Exercises of Saint Ignatius translated from the Spanish with a Commentary and a translation of the Directorium in Exercitia*. Translated by W.H. Longridge. London: A.R. Mowbray & Co. Limited, 1955.

Aveling, J.C.H. *Catholic Recusancy in York 1558-1791*, CRS, London: 1970.

___. *The Handle and the Axe: The Catholic Recusants in England from Reformation to Emancipation*. London: Blond and Briggs, 1976.

___. *The Jesuits*. New York: Stein and Day, Publishers, 1982.

___. *Northern Catholics: The Catholic Recusants of North Riding of Yorkshire 1558-1790*. London: Geoffrey Chapman, 1966.

Azor, John. *Institutionum Moralium*. Pars Prima. Brixiae: Apud Io. Baptistam, & Antonium Bozzolas, Pars Secunda, Mediolani: Apud Haer. Pacifici Pontii, et Ioan. Baptistam, 1617.

Azpilcueta, Martin. *Enchiridion sive Manuale Confessariorum et Poenitentium*. Agrippinae: Cartusiae Buxianae, 1579.

___. *Manuale Confessariorum et Poenitentium Complectens pene resolutiones omnium dubiorum, quae communiter in sacris confessionibus occurrere solent*. Venice, 1604.

___. "Commentarius in cap. humanae aures xxii. De veritate responsi, Partim Verbo Expresso, partim mente concepto redditi." *Operum Martini ab Azpilcueta Doct. Navarri*. Tomus Secundus, Romae: Iacobi Tornerii. 1560. 453-465.

Bacht, Heinrich. "Early Monastic Elements in Ignatian Spirituality: Toward Clarifying Some Fundamental Concepts of the Exercises." In *Ignatius of Loyola His Personality and Spiritual Heritage 1556-1856*. Edited by Friedrich Wulf. St. Louis: The Institute of Jesuit Sources, 1977.

Bangert, William V. *A. History of the Society of Jesus*. St. Louis: Institute of Jesuit Sources, 1962.

Barry, Colman J., ed. *Readings in Church History*. Vol.2, *The Reformation and the Absolute States 1517-1789*. Maryland: The Newman Press, Westminster, 1965.

Basset, Bernard. *The English Jesuits*. London: Burns & Oates, 1967.

Bellarmine, Cardinal Robert. *Opera Omnia*, volumes, 5, 6, 11, s.v. "De Gratia Primi Hominis," " De Amissione Gratiae," "De Gratia et Libero

Arbitrio," "De Justificatione," "Explanatione in Psalmos." Venetian Edition Revised and Edited by Justinus Fèvre. Paris: 1873.

___. "A Treatise on Civil Government, 1586-1590." From *De Laicis* (The Treaty on Civil Government). New York: Fordham University Press, 1928: 10-18). Excerpt quoted in *Readings in Church History.* Volume 2, *The Reformation and the Absolute States 1517-1789.* Edited by Colman L. Barry O.S.B. Maryland: The Newman Press, Westminster, 1965.

___. "De Matrimonio Mulieris Catholicae cum Viro Haeretico. *Auctarium Bellarminianum: Supplèment aux Oevres du Cardinal Bellarmin.*" Edited by R.P. Xavier-Marie le Bachelet, S.J. (Paris: 1913): 541-543.

Bellenger, Dominic Aidan., ed. *English and Welsh Priests 1558-1800: A Working List.* Bath, England: Downside Abbey, 1984.

Blom, J.M. *The Post-Tridentine English Primer.* CRS, London: 1982.

Böckle, Franz. "Nature as the Basis of Morality." In *Personalist Morals.* Edited by Joseph A. Selling. Louvain University Press, 1988.

Bossy, John. "Moral Arithmetic: Seven Sins into Ten Commandments." In *Conscience and Casuistry in Early Modern Europe.* Edited by Edmund Leites. Cambridge University Press, 1988.

___. "The Character of Elizabethan Catholicism." *Past and Present,* 21, (April 1962). 39-59.

___. The English Catholic Community, 1570-1850. London: Darton, Longman & Todd, 1975.

Bouvier, P. "Authentic Interpretation of the Foundation." Copy of a paper presented in Paris, January 1, 1992.

Bowler, Dom Hugh., ed. *Recusant Roll, No.2 (1593-1594); No 3.(1594-1594) and No. 4 (1595-1596); Abstracts in English with an Explanatory Introduction.* CRS (Record Series) Volume 57, 1965, Volume 61, London: 1970.

Brodrick, James. *Robert Bellarmine: Saint and Scholar.* Westminster: The Newman Press,1961.

Buckley, Michael J. *Seventeenth -Century French Spirituality: Three Figures.* In *Christian Spirituality: Post-Reformation and Modern.* Edited by Louis Dupré and Don E. Saliers. New York: Crossroad, 1989.

Burton, Edmund H. and J.H. Pollen, eds. *Lives of the English Martyrs: Second Series, The Martyrs Declared Venerable.* Vol.I, *1584-1588.* New York: Longmans, Green & Co. 1914.

Burton E. H. and T.L. Williams, eds. *The Douay College Diaries, Third, Fourth and Fifth, 1598-1654 with the Rheims Report 1579-80.* Volume I. *The Third Douay Diary.* Volume II. *Fourth and Fifth Diaries with the Rhiems Report, 1579-1580.* Volumes XI & XII, CRS, London: 1911, 1912.

Busenbaum, Hermanni S.J. *Medulla Theologiae Moralis*, Tomus Primus. Tornaci: e typographia J. Castermann, 1848.

Cahill, Lisa Sowle. "Catholic Sexual Ethics and the Dignity of the Person: A Double Message." *Theological Studies* 50, (1989): 120-150.

Cain, James R. "Cloister and the Apostolates of Religious Women." *Review for Religious*, 27, (1968).

Calthrop, M.M.C., ed. *Recusant Roll No. 1 1592-1593*. CRS, Volume XVIII, London: 1916.

Camm, Dom Bede, O.S.B. "Jesuits and Benedictines at Valladolid, 1599-1604." *The Month*, XCII (July - December, 1898): 364-377.

Campbell, Kenneth L. *The Intellectual Struggle of the English Papists in the Seventeenth Century: The Catholic Dilemma*. Lewiston/Queenston: The Edwin Mellen Press, 1986.

The Canons and Decrees of the Sacred and Oecumenical Council of Trent celebrated under the Sovereign Pontiffs, Paul III, Julius III and Pius IV to which are prefixed essays on the External and Internal History of the Council. Translated by J. Waterworth. London: Burns & Oates, 1848.

The Canons and Decrees of the Council of Trent: Original Text with English Translation. Translated by Rev. H.J. Schroeder, O.P. London; St. Louis: B. Herder Book Co., 1950.

Caraman, Philip, ed. *John Gerard: An Autobiography of an Elizabethan*. London: Longmans, Green & Co. Ltd., 1951.

___ ed. *The Years of Siege: Catholic Life from James I to Cromwell*. London: Longmans, Green & Co. Ltd., 1966.

Catechism of the Council Trent. Translated by Very Rev. J. Donovan, D.D. Dublin: James Duffy and Co., Ltd., 1829.

Certeau, Michel de. "La Réforme de l'Intérieur au Temps d'Aquaviva. *Les Jésuites: Spiritualité et Activités Jalons d'une Histoire*. Reprint of "Jésuites." *Dictionnaire de Spiritualité*. VIII cols., 958-1065. Rome, 1974.

Chadwick, Hubert. *St. Omers to Stonyhurst: A history of Two Centuries*. London: Burns & Oates, 1961.

Clancy, Thomas H. *An Introduction to Jesuit Life: The Constitutions and History through 435 Years*. St. Louis: The Institute of Jesuit Sources, 1976.

___. "English Catholics and the Papal Deposing Power 1570-1640." Parts 1,2,3. *Recusant History* 6 no.3 (October 1961): 114-140; 6 no. 5 (April 1962): 205-227; 7 no. 1 (January 1963): 2-10.

___. *English Catholic Books 1641 -1700: A Bibliography*. Chicago: University of Loyola Press, 1974.

___. *Papist Pamphleteers: The Allen -Persons Party and the Political Thought of the Counter-Reformation in England 1572-1615*. Chicago: University of Loyola Press, 1964.

___. "Papist-Protestant- Puritan: English Religious Taxonomy 1556-1665." *Recusant History.* 13 no.4 (January 1976): 227-54.

___. "Spiritual Publications of the Jesuits, 1615-1640," *Recusant History,* 19 no.4 (October 1989): 426-446.

Cognet, Louis. *Post-Reformation Spirituality.* Translated by P. Hepburne Scott. New York: Hawthorn Books, 1959.

Conciliorum Oecumenicorum Decreta. Centro di Documentazione Istituto per le Scienze Religiose. Herder, 1962.

Conn, Walter E. "Moral Development: Is Conversion Necessary?" In *Creativity and Method: Essays in Honour of Bernard Lonergan, S.J.* Edited by Matthew Lamb. Milwaukee: Marquette University Press, 1981.

Copleston, Frederick, *A History of Philosophy,* Volume III, *Ockham to Suarez.* Westminster, MD: The Newman Press, 1953.

Courtney, Francis. "English Jesuit Colleges in the Low Countries (1593-1794)." *The Heythrop Journal* IV (July 1963): 254-263.

Crane, David. "English Translations of the *Imitatio Christi* in the Sixteenth and Seventeenth Centuries." *Recusant History* 13 no. 2 (October 1975): 79-100.

Crehan, Joseph. "Father Persons, S.J." in *English Spiritual Writers.* Edited by Charles Davis. N.Y. Sheed and Ward, 1961.

Crichton, J.D. "The Manual of 1614." *Recusant History* 17 no. 2 (October 1984): 158-172.

Curran, Charles E. *Themes in Fundamental Moral Theology.* Notre Dame: University of Notre Dame Press, 1977.

Dainville, François de, *Les Jésuites et l'Éducation de la Société Française: La Naissance de l'Humanisme Moderne.* Volume 1. Paris: Beauchesne et ses fils, 1940.

Davis, Henry. *Moral and Pastoral Theology.* Four Volumes. Sixth edition, London and New York: Sheed and Ward, 1949.

Decreta, Canones, Censurae et Praecepta Congregationum Generalium Societatis Jesu, cum Formulis, et Quorumdam Officiorum Regulis. Tomus Secundus, complectens Decreta VII ad XXI Congr. Incl. Avenione, ex typographia Francisci Seguin, 1830.

Delumeau, Jean. *Sin and Fear: The Emergence of a Western Guilt Culture 13th-18th Centuries.* Translated by Eric Nicholson. New York: St. Martin's Press, 1990.

Denziger, Henricus and Adolphus Schonmetzer. *Enchiridion Symbolorum: Definitionum et Declarationum de Rebus Fidei et Morum.* Herder: 1963.

Devereux, James A. "The Collects of the First Book of Common Prayer as Works of Translation." Reprinted from *Studies in Philology.* LXVI 5 (October 1969): 719-738.

___. "The Primers and the Prayer Book Collects." Reprinted from *The Huntington Library Quarterly.* XXXII,1 (November 1986): 29-44.

Devlin, Christopher. *The Life of Robert Southwell, Poet and Martyr.* London: Sidgwick & Jackson, 1967.

Donohue, James A. *Tridentine Seminary Legislation: Its Sources and Its Formation.* Volume IX. Louvain: University Publications, 1957.

Doran, Robert M. *Theology and the Dialectics of History.* Toronto: University of Toronto Press, 1990.

Driscoll, J.P. "The Supposed Sources of Persons's `Christian Directory'." *Recusant History.* 5 no. 6, October, 1960, 236-245.

Dupré, Louis. "Jansenism and Quietism." In *Christian Spirituality: Post-Reformation and Modern,*. Edited by Louis Dupré and Don E. Saliers . New York: Crossroad, 1989.

Durrant, C.S. *A Link between Flemish Mystics and English Martyrs.* London: Burns, Oates and Washbourne Ltd., MCMXXV.

Edwards, David L. *Christian England.* Volume 2: *From the Reformation to the 18th Century.* Grand Rapids: William B. Eerdmans, 1984.

Edwards, Francis, ed. *The Elizabethan Jesuits: Historia Missionis Anglicanae Societatis Jesu (1660) of Henry More.* Phillimore: 1981.

___. *The Jesuits in England from 1580 to the Present Day.* London: Burns & Oates, 1985.

Eisenbichler, Konrad, Gay MacDonald and Robert Sweetman, compilers. *Bibles, Theological Treatises, and Other Religious Literature 1491-1700.* Toronto: Victoria University - Centre for Reformation and Renaissance Studies, 1981.

Erasmus of Rotterdam. *Enchiridion Militis Christiani.* (The Handbook of the Christian Soldier) London: Methuen & Co. 1905.

Evennett, H. Outram. *The Spirit of the Counter-Reformation.* Edited by John Bossy. Cambridge at the University Press, 1968.

Farrell, Allan P. *The Jesuit Code of Liberal Education: Development and Scope of the Ratio Studiorum.* Milwaukee: Bruce Publishing Company, 1938.

Fitzpatrick, Edward A. *St. Ignatius and the Ratio Studiorum.* New York, London: McGraw-Hill Book Company, Inc. 1933.

Foley, Henry, S.J., ed. *Records of the English Province of the Society of Jesus.* 7 Volumes. London: Burns and Oates: 1877-1883. Volume II. The Manresa Press, 1875.

Ford, John C. and Gerald Kelly. *Contemporary Moral Theology.* Westminster, Maryland: The Newman Press, 1964.

Franzen, Piet. "Grace and Freedom." In *Freedom and Man.* Edited by John Courtney Murray. New York: P.J. Kennedy & Sons, 1965.

Frances de Sales. *Introduction to the Devout life.* Translated by John K. Ryan. New York: Doubleday & Company, Image Books, 1950.

Fuchs, Josef. *Christian Morality: The Word Becomes Flesh.* Translated by Brian McNeil. Dublin: Gill and Macmillan; Washington: Georgetown University Press, 1987.

___. *Human Values and Christian Morality.* Dublin: Gill and Macmillan, 1970.

Gallagher, John A. *Time Past, Time Present: An Historical Study of Catholic Moral Theology.* New York and New Jersey: Paulist Press, 1990.

Ganss, George E. *Saint Ignatius' Idea of a Jesuit University: A Study in the History of Catholic Education, including Part Four of the "Constitutions" of the Society of Jesus.* Milwaukee: Marquette University Press, 1954.

___. "The Authentic Spiritual Exercises of St. Ignatius: Some Facts of History and Terminololgy Basic to Their Functional Efficacy Today." *Studies in the Spirituality of the Jesuits* St. Louis, Missouri: Institute of Jesuit Sources, 1969. 1-35.

Gillow, Joseph. *A Literary and Biographical History or Biographical Dictionary of the English Catholics from the Breach with Rome, in 1534, to the Present Time.* Volume III. London: Burns & Oates, 1887.

Guibert, Joseph de. *The Jesuits: Their Spiritual Doctrine and Practice.* Translated by William J. Young, S.J., and edited by George E. Ganss. St. Louis: The Institute of Jesuit Sources, 1986.

___. *The Theology of the Spiritual Life.* Translated by Paul Barrett, O.F.M. Cap. New York: Sheed and Ward, 1953.

Guilday, Peter. *The English Catholic Refugees on the Continent 1558-1795.* New York: Longmans, Green, and Co., 1914.

Gustafson, James M. "The Focus and Its Limitations: Reflections on Catholic Moral Theology." In *Moral Theology: Challenges for the Future.* Essays in Honour of Richard A. McCormick. Edited by Charles E. Curran. New York: Paulist Press, 1990.

___."Moral Discernment in the Christian Life." In *Introduction to Christian Ethics: A Reader.* Edited by Ronald P. Hamel and Kenneth R. Himes, OFM. New York: Paulist Press, 1989.

___. "What is Normatively Human?" *The American Ecclesiastical Review* 165, (1971): 192-207.

Haas, Adolph. "The Mysticism of St. Ignatius according to his Spiritual Diary." In *Ignatius of Loyola: His Personality and Spiritual Heritage 1556-1856.* Edited by Friedrich Wulf. St. Louis: Institute of Jesuit Sources, 1977.

Hamilton, Dom Adam, ed. *The Chronicle of the English Canonesses Regular of the Lateran, at St Monica's in Louvain.* Volume I *1548 to 1625.* Volume II *1625-1644* London and Edinburgh: Sands & Co. 1904, 1906.

Happold, H.C. *Mysticism: A Study and an Anthology.* Penguin Books, rev.ed., 1970.

Häring, Bernhard. *Free and Faithful in Chirst: Moral Theology for Clergy and Laity*. Volume 1. *General Moral Theology*. New York: The Seabury Press, 1978.

___. *The Law of Christ: Moral Theology for Priests and Laity*. Translated by Edwin G. Kaiser. Volume I. Westminster, Maryland: Newman Press, 1961.

Havran, Martin J. "The British Isles." In *Catholicism in Early Modern History: A Guide to Research*. Edited by John O'Malley, S.J. Volume 2. *Reformation Guides to Research*. St. Louis, Missouri: Center for Reformation Research, 1988.

Hawkins, Denis. *Christian Ethics*. New York: Hawthorn Books 1963.

Henson, Canon Edwin, ed. *The English College at Madrid 1611-1767*. CRS, Volume XXIX, London: 1929.

___ ed. *Registers of The English College at Vallodolid 1589-1862*. CRS, Volume XXX, London: 1930.

Hicke, Leo, ed. *Letters and Memorials of Father Robert Persons, S.J.* Volume I (to 1588). *CRS* Volume XXXIX. London, 1942.

Histoire du Collège de Douay à laquelle on a joint La Politique des Jésuites Anglois. Ouvrages traduites de la Langue Anglaise. A Londres. M.DCC.LXII.

Holmes, Peter J. *Elizabethan Casuistry*. CRS, London: 1981.

___. *Resistance and Compromise: The Political Thought of Elizabethan Catholics*. New York: Cambridge University Press, 1982.

Holt, Geoffrey, ed. *St. Omers and Bruges Colleges, 1593-1773: A Biographical Dictionary*. CRS (Record Series), Volume 69, London: 1979.

Hunnybun W.M. and J. Gillow, eds. *Registers of the English Poor Clares at Gravelines, including those who founded filiations at Aire, Dunkirk and Rouen 1608-1837*. CRS, Miscellanea IX, Volume XIV, London: 1914.

Hunt, Noreen. "Enclosure." *Cistercian Studies* 21 (1986): 51-63; 22 (1987): 126-151.

Iparraguirre, Ignacio. "Élaboration de la Spiritualité de la Compagnie (1556-1606)." *Les Jésuites: Spiritualité et Activités Jalons d'une Histoire*. Monograph produced in liaison with *Dictionnaire de Spiritualité*, "Jésuites." Volume VIII cols., 958-1065. Paris: Editions Beauchesne; Rome: 1974.

Janssens, G.A.M. and F.H.A.M. Aarts, eds. *Studies in Seventeenth Century English Literature, History and Bibliography: Festschrift for Professor T.A. Birrell on the Occasion of his Sixtieth Birthday*. Amsterdam: 1984.

Janssens, Louis. "Artificial Insemination: Ethical Considerations." *Louvain Studies* 8, (1980-1981): 3-30.

Jonsen, Albert R. and Stephen Toulmin. *The Abuse of Casuistry: A History of Moral Reasoning*. Berkeley, Los Angeles, London: University of California Press, Ltd. 1988.

Johnson, Samuel. *A Dictionary of the English Language*, s.v. Sincerity, Verity.

Justice, Cornelius. "Evolution of the Teaching on Commitment by Monastic Vow from New Testament Times to the Ninth Century." *Cistercian Studies* 12 (1977): 18-40.

Kelly, Wilfrid, et al., eds. *Annales Collegii I:Liber Ruber Venerabilis Collegii Anglorum de Urbe*. CRS, Vol. XXXVII, London: 1940.

Kenny, A., ed. *The Responsa Scholarum of the English College Rome I*. CRS, Volume LIV. London: 1962.

King, Margaret L. *Women of the Renaissance*. Chicago: University of Chicago Press, 1991.

Kinsella, Nivardus. "Commitment by Vow in the 20th Century From the Code of Canon Law to Vatican II and After." *Cistercian Studies* 12 (1977): 67-81.

Kirk, Kenneth E. *Conscience and Its Problems: An Introduction to Casuistry*. London, New York, Toronto: Longmans, Green & Co. 1948.

Knowles, David. *The English Mystical Tradition*. New York: Harper, 1961.

Knox, Thomas Francis. Editor. *Records of the English Catholics under the Penal Laws*. Volume I, *The First and Second Diaries of the English College, Douay and an Appendix of Unpublished Documents*. Volume II, *The Letters and Memorials of William Cardinal Allen (1532-1594)*. London: David Nutt, 1878, 1882. Volume II, republished, New Jersey: The Gregg Press, 1965.

Lainati, Chiara Augusta, OSC, Mary Kathleen McGarry, OSC, and Margot H. King, "The Enclosure of Saint Clare." *Vox Benedictina*. 7 (July 1990): 253-280.

Laporte, Jean-Marc. *Patience and Power–Grace for the First World*. New York: Paulist Press, 1988.

Laymann, Paulo. *Theologiae Moralis in V Lib Partibus*, Tomus Primus. Venetiis: Apud Guerilios. 1651. Second Edition, 1744.

Lonergan, Bernard J.F. "Dimensions of Meaning." In *Collection: Papers by Bernard J.F.Lonergan, S.J.* Edited by Frederick E. Crowe. Montreal: Palm Publishers, 1967.

___. "Natural Right and Historical Mindedness." *A Third Collection : Papers by Bernard J.F. Lonergan, S.J.* Edited by Frederick F. Crowe. New York: Paulist Press, 1985.

___. *Insight: A Study of Human Understanding*. New York: Harper & Row, 1978

___. *Method in Theology*. Toronto: University of Toronto Press, 1990.

___. *Understanding and Being*. Edited by Elizabeth A. and Mark D. Morelli. Toronto: University of Toronto Press, 1990.

Long, Edward Leroy. *Conscience and Compromise: An Approach to Protestant Casuistry*. Philadelphia: Westminster Press, 1954.

Loomie, Abert J. "A Register of the Students at St. Gregory's College at Seville, 1591-1605." *Recusant History*. 9 no.3 (October, 1967): 163-169.

Loomis, Richard. "The Barrett Version of Robert Southwell's Short Rule of Good Life." *Recusant History*, 7 no.5 (April 1964): 239-248.

Lovelace, Richard C. "Puritan Spirituality: The Search for a Rightly Reformed Church." In *Christian Spirituality: Post Reformation and Modern*. Edited by Louis Dupré and Don E. Saliers. New York: Crossroad,1989.

Loyola, Ignacio de. *Autograph Directories*. Translated by Bernard Bush and Aloysius Owen. Program to Adapt the Spiritual Exercises.

___. *The Constitutions of the Society of Jesus*. Translated by George E. Ganss, S.J. St. Louis: The Institute of Jesuit Sources, 1970.

Lunn, David. *The English Benedictines 1540-1688: From Reformation to Revolution*. London: Burns & Oates and New York: Barnes and Noble, 1980.

___. "Augustine Baker and the English Mystical Tradition." *Journal of Ecclesiastical History*, XXVI (July 1975): 267-277.

Luria, Keith P. "The Counter-reformation and Popular Spirituality." In *Christian Spirituality: Post-Reformation and Modern*. Edited by Louis Dupré and Don E. Saliers. New York: Crossroad, 1989.

McCann, Timothy L., ed. *Recusants in the Exchequer Pipe Rolls, 1581-1592*, CRS (Record Series), Volume 71, London: 1986.

McCoog, Thomas M. *English and Welsh Jesuits 1555-1650*. CRS (Record Series) Volumes 74, 75. London: 1994, 1995.

McCormick, Richard A. *The Critical Calling*. Washington: Georgetown University Press, 1989.

___. "Moral Theology 1940-1989: An Overview." *Theological Studies* 50 (1989): 3-24

McGrath, Patrick. "The Bloody Questions Reconsidered." *Recusant History* 20 no. 3 (May 1991): 305-319.

McNally, Robert. "St. Ignatius, Prayer and the Early Society of Jesus." In *Jesuit Spirit in a Time of Change*. Edited by Raymond A. Schroth, S.J. Westminster, Md: Newman Press, 1968.

McNamara, Vincent. *The Truth in Love: Reflections on Christian Morality*. Dublin: Gill and Macmillan, Ltd., 1988.

Magee, Brian. *The English Recusants: A Study of the Post-Reformation Catholic Survival and the Operation of the Recusancy Laws*. London: Burns, Oates & Washbourne Ltd. 1938.

Mahoney, John. *The Making of Moral Theology: A Study of the Roman Catholic Tradition*. Oxford; Clarendon Press, 1990.

Malloch, A.E. "Father Henry Garnet's Treatise of Equivocation." *Recusant History*. 15 no. 6 (October 1981): 387-395.

Mandonnet, P. "Des Dangers du Probabilisme." *Revue Thomiste*. 10 année, 1902, n.5, 503-520

Manning, Roger B. *Religion and Society in Elizabethan Sussex: A Study of the Enforcement of the Religious Settlement 1558-1603*. Leicester University Press, 1969.

Margaret Mary, Sister. "Evolution of the Teaching on Commitment by Monastic Vow (Cluny to the End of the 19th Century)." *Cistercian Studies* 12 (1977): 40- 66.

Martindale, Joanna, ed. *English Humanism: Wyatt to Cowley*. Dover, New Hampshire: Croom Helm, 1985.

Matthew, David. *Catholicism in England 1535-1935: Portrait of a Minority: Its Culture and Tradition*. Toronto: Longmans, Green and Co., 1936.

Maurer, Armand A. *Medieval Philosophy*. New York: Random House,1962.

Meyer, Arnold O. *England and the Catholic Church under Queen Elizabeth*. Translated by the Rev. J. R. McMee, M.A. London: Kegan Paul, Trench, Trübner & Co., Ltd., 1916.

Michaud-Quantin, Pierre. *Sommes de Casuistique et Manuels de Confession au Moyen Age, (XII-XIV Siècles)*. Montreal: Dominican Library, 1962.

Molloy, J. "The Devotional Writings of Matthew J.Kellison." *Recusant History*. 9 no.3 (October, 1967): 159-163.

Monumenta Paedagogica Societatis Jesu. Nova editio penditus retractata edidit Laedislaus Lukács, S.J. IV, *1573-1580*; V, *Ratio Atque Institutio Studiorum Societatis Jesu (1586,1591,1599)*; VI, *Collectanea de Ratione Studiorum Societatis Jesu (1582-1587)*; VII, *Collectanea de Ratione Studiorum Societatis Jesu (1588-1616)*. *Monumentum Historica Societatis Jesu*, vols. 124, 129, 140, 141. Rome, 1981, 1986, 1992.

Morey, Adrian. *The Catholic Subjects of Elizabeth I*. London: George Allen & Unwin Ltd., 1978.

Morris, John, ed. *The Condition of Catholics Under James I: Father Gerard's Narrative of the Gunpowder Plot*. London: Longmans, Green, & Co., 1981.

___ed. *The Troubles of Our Catholic Fore-fathers - Related by Themselves*. First - Third Series. London: Burns and Oates, 1872, 1875, 1877.

Murphy, Martin. *St. Gregory's College, Seville, 1592-1767*. CRS, London: 1992.

Murray, John Courtney. *St. Robert Bellarmine on the Indirect Power*. *Theological Studies* 9 no. 4 (December 1948): 491-535.

New Catholic Encyclopedia. Toronto: McGraw Hill, 1967. s.v. "Conscience" by C. Wiliams; "Existential Ethics" by J.V. McGlynn; "Free Will" by P. Nolan; "Grace and Nature" by C. Regan; "History of Canon Law 4, Classical Period" by L.E. Boyle; "Lorenzo Scupoli" by P. Mulhern; "Spiritual Freedom," by Bernhard Häring.

The New Dictionary of Theology. Edited by Joseph A. Komonchak, Mary Collins and Dermot A. Lane. Wilmington, Delaware: Michael Glazier, 1989. s.v. "Anthropology, Christian: by Michael J. Scanlon, S.J.; "Conscience" by Seán Fagan; "Fundamental Option" and "Probabilism" by Brian V. Johnstone CSSR; "Mary Ward."by M.P. Trauth.

Norberg, Kathryn. "The Counter-Reformation and Women Religious and Lay." In *Catholicism in Early Modern History: A Guide to Research.* Volume 2. *Reformation Guides to Research.* Edited by John O'Malley, S.J. St. Louis, Missouri: Center for Reformation Research, 1988.

Norman, Marion, IBVM. "Seventeenth Century Devotional Prose." Paper delivered at Post-Reformation History Conference, St. Anne's College, Oxford, 1981. Photocopied.

O'Leary, Brian. "Third and Fourth Weeks: What the Directories Say." *The Way,* Supplement 58 (Spring 1987): 3-20.

O'Malley, John,ed. *Catholicism in Early Modern History: A Guide to Research.* Volume 2. *Reformation Guides to Research.* St. Louis, Missouri: Center for Reformation Research, 1988.

____. "Early Jesuit Spirituality: Spain and Italy." In *Christian Spirituality: Post-Reformation and Modern.* Edited by Louis Dupré and Don E. Saliers. New York: Crossroad, 1989.

Orsy, Ladislas. "Moral Theology and Canon Law: The Quest for a Sound Relationship." *Theological Studies* 50 no. 1 (March 1989).

Owen, Hywell Wyn. "Another Augustine Baker Manuscript." *Studien en Tekstuitgaven van ons geestelijk Erf,* vol. 16, (1964).

The Oxford Dictionary of the Christian Church. Edited by F.L. Cross. London, New York, Toronto: Oxford University Press, 1961. s.v. "Mary Ward"; "Moral Theology."

Pastor, Ludwig Freiherr von. *The History of the Popes.* Translated by Dom Ernest Graf. Volumes XXIV-XXIX. London: Routledge & Kegan Paul; St. Louis, Mo.: Herder Book Co., 1938-1952.

Petti, A.G. "Richard Verstegan and Catholic Martyrologies of the Later Elizabethan Period." *Recusant History.* 5 no. 2 (April 1959): 64-90.

Pinckaers, S. "La théologie morale au déclin du Moyen-Age: Le nominalisme." *Nova et Vetera* 52 no. 3 (July-September 1977): 209-221.

____. "Ockham and the Decline of Moral Theology." *Theology Digest.* 26 no. 3 (Fall, 1978): 239-241.

Pollen, John Hungerford. "A Relic in Times of Persecution." *The Month,* XCVI no. 433 (July 1900):46-51.

____ ed. *Bedingfield Papers, &c.* CRS, Miscellanea VI, Volume VII, London: 1909.

___ ed. *Memoirs of Father Robert Persons (continued); Tower Bills 1595-1681 with Gatehouse Certificates 1592-1603; The Nuns of the Institute of Mary at York from 1677-1825.* CRS, Miscellanea IV, Volume IV, London: 1907.

___ ed. *Memoirs of Father Robert Persons,* CRS, Miscellanea II, Volume II, London: 1906.

___. "Troubles of Jesuits and Benedictines at Valladolid in 1603." *The Month,* XCIV (July - December, 1899): 232-248.

___ ed. *Unpublished Documents Relating to the English Martyrs.* Volume I, 1584- 1603. CRS, Volume V, London: 1908.

Pourrat, Pierre. *Christian Spirituality.* Volume III, part 1. *From the Renaissance to Jansenism.* Translated by W. H. Mitchell. Westminster, Maryland: The Newman Press, 1953.

Principe, Walter H. "Mysticism: Its Meaning and Varieties." Paper given at Conference on Mysticism ("Mystics and Scholars") at the University of Calgary 1976. Photocopied.

___. "Toward Defining Spirituality." *Sciences Religieuses/ Studies in Religion,* 12/2, (Spring 1983): 127-141.

Pullen, G.F. *The Oscotian: Recusant Books at St. Mary's Oscott: Part 1: 1518-1687.* Sutton Coldfield, Warwickshire: St. Mary's Seminary, New Oscott, 1964.

Rahner, Karl. *The Dynamic Element in the Church.* Freiburg: Herder; Montreal: Palm Publishers, 1964.

___. "Following the Crucified." *Theological Investigations.* 18: 157-170.

___. "On the Question of a Formal Existential Ethics." *Theological Investigations.* 2: 217-234.

___. "The Concept of Mystery in Catholic Theology." *Theological Investigations* 4: 37-73.

Rapley, Elizabeth. *The Dévotes: Women and Church in Seventeenth Century France.* Montreal & Kingston, London, Buffalo: McGill–Queen's University Press, 1990.

Ravier, André. *Ignatius of Loyola and the Founding of the Society of Jesus.* Translated by Maura, Joan and Carson Daly). San Francisco: Ignatius Press, 1987.

Raymond Pennafort, O.P. "Index eorum quae hoc in *Summa* continetur." From the *Summa de Poenitentia.* Veronae: Ex Typographia Seminarii, apud Augustinum Carattonium, 1744.

Riedl, John. "Bellarmine and the Dignity of Man." In *Jesuit Thinkers of the Renaissance.* Edited by Gerard Smith, S.J. Milwaukee: Marquette University Press, 1939.

Roberts, John R. *A Critical Anthology of English Recusant Devotional Prose 1558-1603.* Duquesne Studies: Philological Series. Pittsburgh: Duquesne University Press, 1966.

Rodgers, J.F.T. *English Books Printed before 1700*. London: Robert Stockwell Ltd., 1971.

Rose, Elliot. *Cases of Conscience: Alternatives Open to Recusants and Puritans under Elizabeth I and James I*. New York: Cambridge University Press, 1975.

Sacramentum Mundi: An Encyclopedia of Theology. Edited by Karl Rahner, Cornelius Ernst and Kevin Smythe. Montreal: Palm Publishers, 1969. s.v. "Asceticism" by Friedrich Wulf; "Grace and Freedom" and "Man (Anthropology), III: Theological" by Karl Rahner; "Modern Church History" by Victor Conzemius; "Moral Theology" by Bernhard Häring; "Spirituality" by Josef Sudbrack.

Sanchez, Thomas, S.J. *Disputationum de Sancto Matrimonii Sacramento*, Tomus Secundus, Liber Septimus. 231-234. Venice: 1612.

Schrickx, Willem. "An Early Seventeenth Century Catalogue of Books from the English Jesuit Mission in Saint-Omer." *Archives et Bibliothèques de Belgique Brussels*. 45-46 (1974-5): 592-618.

Schuller, Bruno. "Autonomous Ethics Revisited." In *Personalist Morals*. Edited by Joseph A. Selling. Leuven: University Press, 1988.

Secker, Josephine Evetts. "Consolatory Literature of the English Recusants." *Renaissance and Reformation*, New Series 6; Old Series 18, (1982): 122-141.

Selling, Joseph A. "Evolution and Continuity in Conjugal Morality." In *Personalist Morals*. Louvain: University Press, 1988.

Somerville, Johann P. "The New Art of Lying," in *Conscience and Casuistry in Early Modern Europe*. Edited by Edmund Leites. Cambridge University Press, 1988.

Southern, A.C. *Elizabethan Recusant Prose 1559-1582: A Historical and Critical Account of the Books of the Catholic Refugees Printed and Published Abroad and at Secret Presses in England together with an Annotated Bibliography of the Same*. London: Sands & Co., Ltd., 1950.

Stanfield, Canon Raymund, contributor. "The Archpriest Controversy." Part 2 "Papers Relating to Dr. Richard Smith, Bishop of Chalcedon, and His Jurisdiction, 1625-1633." CRS, Miscellanea XII, Vol.XXII, London: 1921, 132-186.

Stierli, Josef. "Ignatian Prayer: Seeking God in all Things." In *Ignatius of Loyola: His Personality and Spiritual Heritage 1556-1856*. Edited by Friedrich Wulf. St. Louis: Institute of Jesuit Sources, 1977.

Suárez, Francisco, S.J. *De Legibus, ac Deo Legislatore*, 1612; *Defensio Fidei Catholicae, et Apostolicae adversus Anglicanae Sectae Errores*, 1613; *De Triplici Virtute Theologica, Fide, Spe, et Charitate*, 1621. Volume 1: Photographic reproductions of selections from original works. Volume 2: Translations by G.C. Williams. London: Humphrey Milford, 1944.

____. *The Religious State.* Selections translated by William Humphrey, S.J. Three Volumes. London: Burns and Oates, c. 1884.

Syon Abbey, Devon, England. Letter from Sister Mary Bridget, O.Ss.S. to Marion Norman I.B.V.M., October 13, 1980. Photocopied.

Talbot, Clare, ed. *Miscellanea: Recusant Records.* CRS, Volume LIII, London: 1961.

Tanqueray, Adolphe, S.S., D.D. *The Spiritual Life; A Treatise on Ascetical and Mystical Theology.* Translated by Hermann Branderis, S.S., A.M. Second Edition, Westminster, Maryland: The Newman Bookshop, 1948.

Tavard, G. *La Tradition au XVIIe Siecle en France et en Angleterre.* Paris: Les Editions du Cerf, 1969.

____. *The Seventeenth-Century Tradition: A Study in Recusant Thought.* Leiden: E.J. Brill, 1978.

Tentler, Thomas. *Sin and Confession on the Eve of the Reformation.* Princeton: Princeton University Press, 1977.

Theiner, Johann. *Die Entwicklung der Moraltheologie zur eigenständigen Disziplin.* Regensburg: Freidrich Pustet, 1970.

Thomas Aquinas. *Summa Theologiae.* Blackfriars. London: Eyre & Spottiswoode, 1974; Fathers of the English Dominican Province, New York: Benziger Brothers, Inc., 1947.

Thurston, H. "Catholic Writers and Elizabethan Readers. I. Father Parsons' *Christian Directory.*" *The Month,* LXXXII (September - December 1982): 457-477.

Tierney, Rev. M.A. *Dodd's Church History of England: from the Commencement of the Sixteenth Century to the Revolution in 1688 with Notes, Additions and a Continuation.* Vols. IV and V. London: Charles Dolman, 1841 -1843

Trappes-Lomax, T.B. "The Family of Poyntz and its Catholic Associations." *Recusant History* 6 no. 2 (April 1961): 68-79.

Trevor-Roper, H.R. *The Crisis of the Seventeenth Century: Religion, the Reformation and Social Change.* New York: Harper & Row, 1968.

Trimble, William Raleigh. *The Catholic Laity in Elizabethan England 1558-1603.* Cambridge, Mass.: The Belknap Press of Harvard University Press, 1964.

The Documents of Vatican II. Edited by Walter M. Abbott, S.J. New York: The America Press, 1966.

Vereecke, L. "La Concile de Trente et l'enseignment de la théologie morale." *Divinitas,* 5 (1961): 361-374.

____. "L'obligation morale selon Guillaume d'Ockham." *Vie Spirituelle,* II Supplement (1958): 123-143.

Veritatis Splendor. Encyclical Letter of John Paul II on Certain Fundamental Questions of the Church's Moral Teaching, 1993.

Villoslada, Riccardo G. *Storia del Collegio Romano dal suo inizio (1551) alla soppressione della Campagnia di Gesù (1773)*, Analecta Gregoriana. Volume LXVI, Series Facultatis Historiae Ecclesiasticae. Sectio A (n.2) (Rome: Gregorian University, 1954).

Wakefield, Gordon S. "Anglican Spirituality." In *Christian Spirituality: Post-Reformation and Modern*. Edited by Louis Dupré and Don E. Saliers. New York: Crossroad, 1989.

Walsh, Walter. *The Jesuits in Great Britain: An Historical Inquiry into Their Political Influence*. London: George Routledge & Sons, Ltd, New York: E.P. Dutton & Co. 1903.

Warnke, Olga. "The Contemplation to Obtain Love." *The Way* Supplement 58 (Spring 1987): 74-85.

Webster, Charles, ed. *The Intellectual Revolution of the Seventeenth Century*. London and Boston: Routledge & Kegan Paul, 1974.

Westminster Archives, London. Ms xxix (1637-1640).

Whelan, Dom Basil O.S.B. *Historic English Convents of Today: The Story of the English Cloisters in France and Flanders in Penal Times*. London: Burns Oates & Washbourne Ltd., 1936.

White, Helen C. *Social Criticism in Popular Religious Literature of the Sixteenth Century*. New York: The Macmillan Company, 1944.

___. *Tudor Books of Saints and Martyrs*. Wisconsin: University of Wisconsin Press, 1963.

Williams, Michael E. *St. Alban's College, Valladolid: Four Centuries of English Catholic Presence in Spain*, London: C. Hurst & Company, New York: St. Martin's Press, 1986.

___. *The Venerable English College Rome: A History 1579-1979*, London: Associated Catholic Publications Ltd., 1979.